UrbanRenewal.Biz
BERNARD LONZO

How to Flip a House Using Only a Laptop and Cell Phone as Your Tools

+ The Secrets and Rewards of Going Green ♲

2nd Edition

<u>CONTENTS</u>

INTRODUCTION

It is 1 o'clock on a Tuesday and I'm sitting in my truck parked at a truck stop on I-80 in Iowa. I just received an e-mail informing me that a house I had for sale in Houston, Texas just sold. The same house that I had purchased only a little over three months ago while sitting in a truck stop on I-95 in South Carolina! I found it on the internet, hired a home inspector on the internet, negotiated the price and purchased it on the internet, ordered "installed" home improvements on the internet, secured and monitored it on the internet, and finally flipped it on the internet. Never set foot in the place!

For thirty or so years I made my living as a carpenter flipping older homes after rehabilitating them, but have since retired my tools. Not truly ready for full retirement, my wife and I then purchased a Freightliner tractor-trailer with a condo sleeper and now we drive all over the country hauling freight. "Over the road" drivers they call it. It's a great life, seeing the country and getting paid as we watch the scenery change daily outside our windows. But I've never lost my love for building and I miss it so much more every time we haul lumber or building supplies to one of the big home improvement centers. So naturally, while browsing the web during our down time at the truck stops, I found myself gravitating to the websites that specialized in homes for sale and home improvements that you can now buy "installed" at places like Lowe's and Home Depot. Then it dawned on me. Everything I had to do in the past to flip a house in person is now available on the internet. You can do everything with the push of a button that I had to do in person just as effectively!

The rest is history. Limiting myself to a meager budget I found my first house to flip online and purchased it with a credit card. Then I set up security to control access and monitor it live online for a low monthly fee. Next I shopped for and purchased some key home improvements that included installation from the big home improvement stores online and paid for them with their own charge cards interest free! My total monthly payments were small enough so that I could carry the spec house for a while without much difficulty in case it didn't sell right away. I had virtually no cash tied up to get to this point. A local realtor handled the marketing and sale of the spec house, which much to my surprise took less than thirty days. After paying his commission I still walked away with a tidy profit. Not bad for just pushing a couple of buttons and making a few phone calls. The whole flip took less than 120 days, start to finish. I was hooked! Now, how about you?

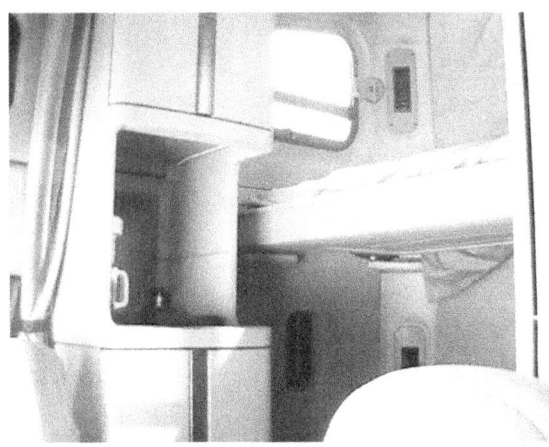

When I first mentioned to my wife my theory about flipping houses online using only my laptop and cell phone while we were parked at truck stops all over the U.S. she was a bit skeptical. It took some convincing I must say, and in convincing her it would work, I began to convince myself. The first and most obvious question I had to answer was of course, how? So I began by defining the steps I would need to take to accomplish this unusual task of flipping houses with only a laptop and cell phone and then addressing the probability that I could in fact perform each step successfully. An exhaustive search of the internet produced no real results for information of, or by anyone already actually flipping houses online, so I was on my own. Anything I would have to come up with would have to be from scratch, no outside help That being determined, I began to wonder, could this really be done?

It was a very unusual concept, to flip a house with only a laptop and cell phone. To accomplish this feat I would have to be able to find a spec house online, have the spec house inspected, research the local real estate market, purchase the spec house, insure the spec house, secure, monitor and control access to the spec house, shop for and purchase key home improvements that included installation, then maintain the spec house while on the market all online over the internet from my remote location. Then finally flip the spec house all in absentee! A daunting task to say the least, again I asked myself, could it really be done?

Determined to pursue the concept I then began to address each issue, one at a time. Much to my astonishment I began find that each step in the process was in fact possible to perform online. You can find thousands of houses online, virtually every house for sale in the US is listed somewhere online along with all its contact information. Numerous websites provide real estate market statistics for every city and town you can possibly want to know about. Home inspectors and security providers all over the country are numerous and available online, as well as insurance and real estate agents. Finally websites for home improvement centers like Lowe's and Home Depot offer everything from heating and cooling systems to kitchen and baths, even lawns and flowers installed at your property with just the push of a button and a few phone calls. The more I searched for answers online the more I began to realize, it can be done! Using today's technology I can flip houses online using only a laptop, cell phone and the internet. Now it was time to put my theory to the test.

"Laissez - Faire"

PART ONE

CHAPTER 1
ESTABLISH YOUR COMPANY, ITS WORTH & OBJECTIVE
"Setting up the books"

The first question I had to ask myself was how do I begin to flip a house online with only a laptop and a cell phone as my tools? What will I need to get started? How will I track my investment? How do I turn an idea into an actual functional, operating business? The answer was really quite simple. Everything begins with a chart of accounts. A chart of accounts is an accounting term for a list of accounts, linked together on a spreadsheet, which track the value of your assets, liabilities, income and expenses. In the beginning my assets were quite simple. They included an online checking account with a minimal cash balance, three credit cards, two in-house charge accounts, a laptop computer and a cell phone. I would later add a home equity line of credit and a savings account. There were no liabilities to add at that time because the credit card and charge accounts all had zero balances. I also didn't have to worry about tracking any income or paying any quarterly estimated income taxes either. I wasn't even anywhere near my first sale! For the cost accounts I simply used the Schedule C tax form from the IRS website irs.gov as a guide and copied the expense group's right from the form.

http://www.irs.gov/pub/irs-pdf/f1040sc.pdf

After conducting a thorough search of the internet I narrowed it down to two options for an accounting software program that would satisfy the need of being accessible to me anywhere and anytime I wanted to gather or input data from, or into it. The choices were simply, use an online accounting service such as QuickBooks quickbooks.com and pay a small monthly fee for access, or pay a few hundred dollars once to buy the same program and install it on my laptop myself. I chose the latter. Once installed it guided me step by step through the process of setting up my chart of accounts and in less than one hour, I had a practical company up and running.

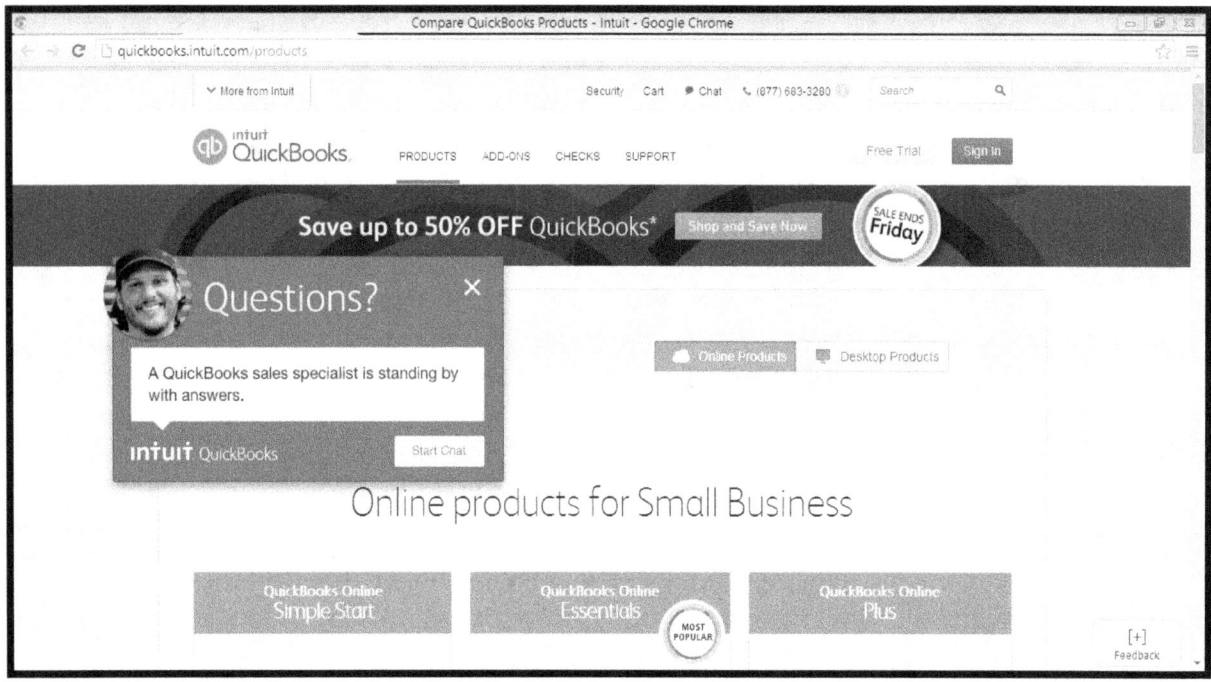

http://quickbooks.intuit.com/products

The QuickBooks quickbooks.com program is quite versatile and grows with your business. Every dollar in or out of the company are tracked in the chart of accounts that you set up in the beginning and new accounts can easily be added as the need occurs. With the push of a button, my favorite thing, you can generate reports and graphs that will give you the information you need to make sound business decisions and to give you an exact snapshot of the financial health of your organization. You can even link to your online bank and credit card accounts so the program will automatically record and itemize all their activity automatically! Finally, one more thing you will need is an e-mail address. If you don't already have one you can get a free one at Gmail gmail.com provided by Google google.com. It is easy to set up and use, and best of all its free!

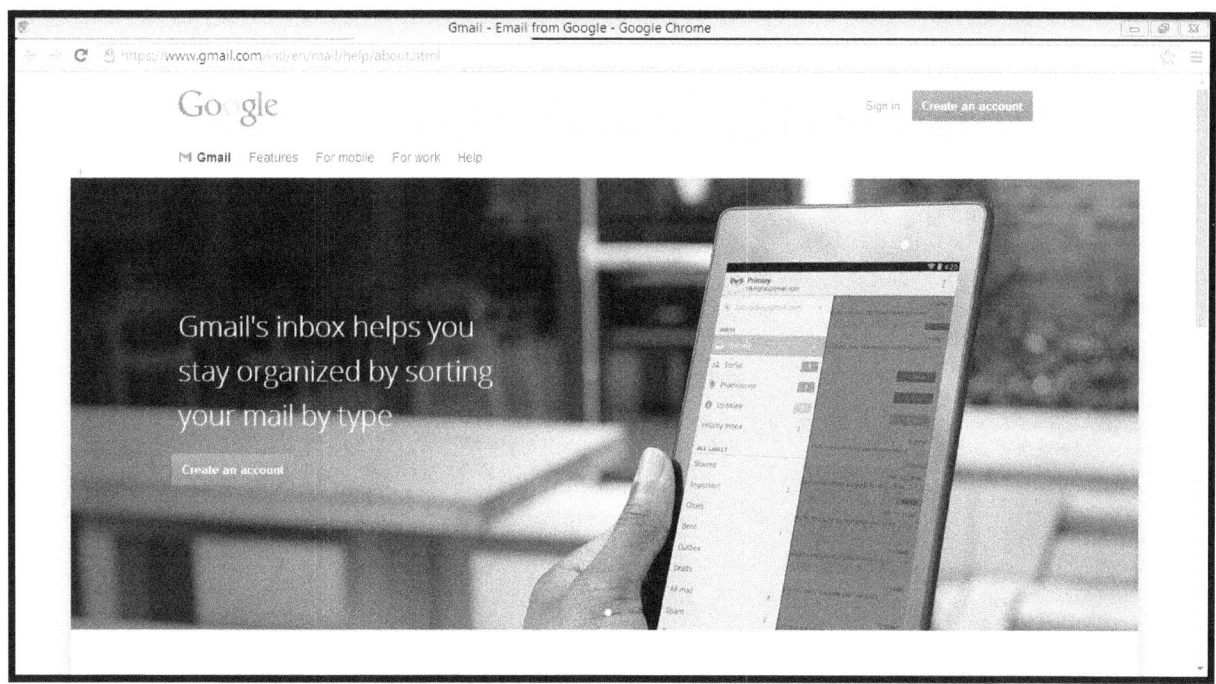

https://mail.google.com/intl/en/mail/help/about.html

CHAPTER 2
SET UP YOUR WEB SITE
"Set up shop"

The next step on my list was to "hang out my shingle", an idiomatic term meaning to open an office for business. Because my business was web-based it only made sense that my office would be web-based too. I needed a website! My own website that could tell the world that I was in the business of flipping houses. So once again I turned to the search engines for information on how to go about making this so. What I found out is that I would first need a domain. One that was available and not already in use by someone else. So I began by using a tool like the one at godaddy.com that allowed me to enter domain names of my choice and instantly check on their availability. When I found an available domain name that I liked I could buy it right there online. The package they offered also included an easy to use website builder that required no special or technical skills to run. It could easily add text or images and create awesome slide shows and galleries for my pictures.

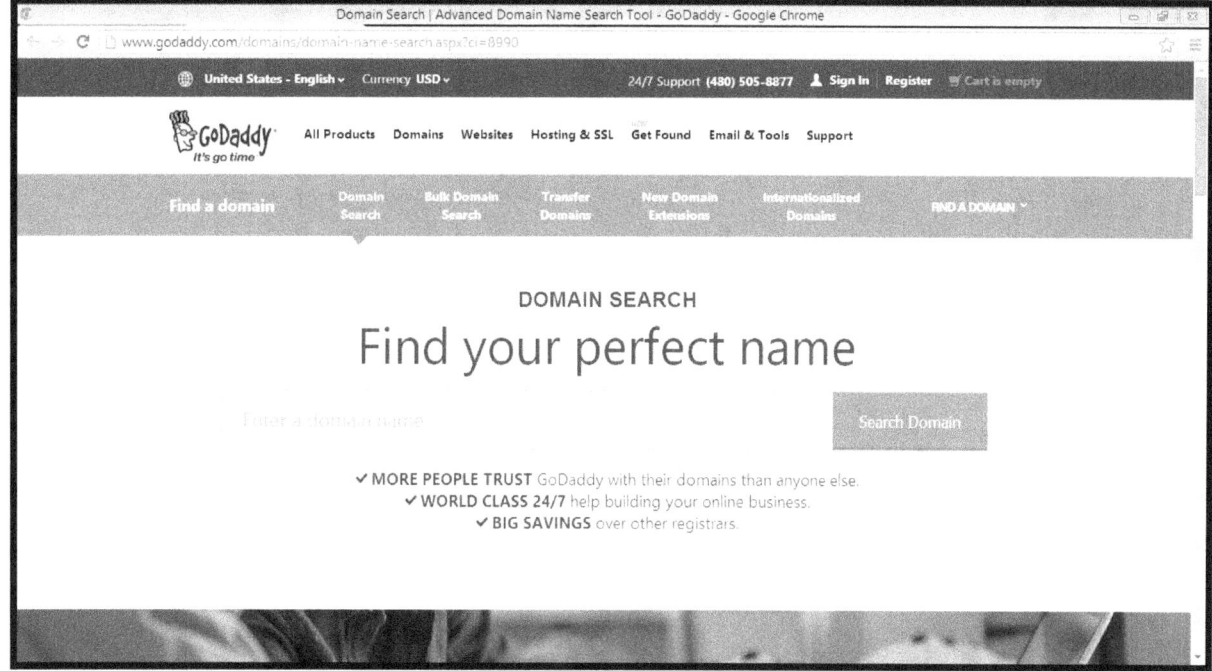

http://www.godaddy.com/domains/search-new.aspx?ci=8990

The first website I built was fairly simple. It consisted of only three pages. There was a main page, an about page and a contact page. The main page explained who I was and gave a brief background of my company and its mission. The about page went into a little more detail about what I did and highlighted with images and text some of the more typical home improvements I like to install. The contact page included two fill-in-the blank forms which both prospective buyers and sellers could complete and then send automatically to me. Also included in the offer were an online photo gallery and a blog along with the domain. I didn't use either in the beginning, but as the business grew I began to use the gallery to showcase past projects and the blog to boost my SEO.

For those of you that are not familiar with the term, SEO is short for search engine optimization, something you are going to want to learn more about later. Also, because my projects do need live on site security cameras like those available at adt.com

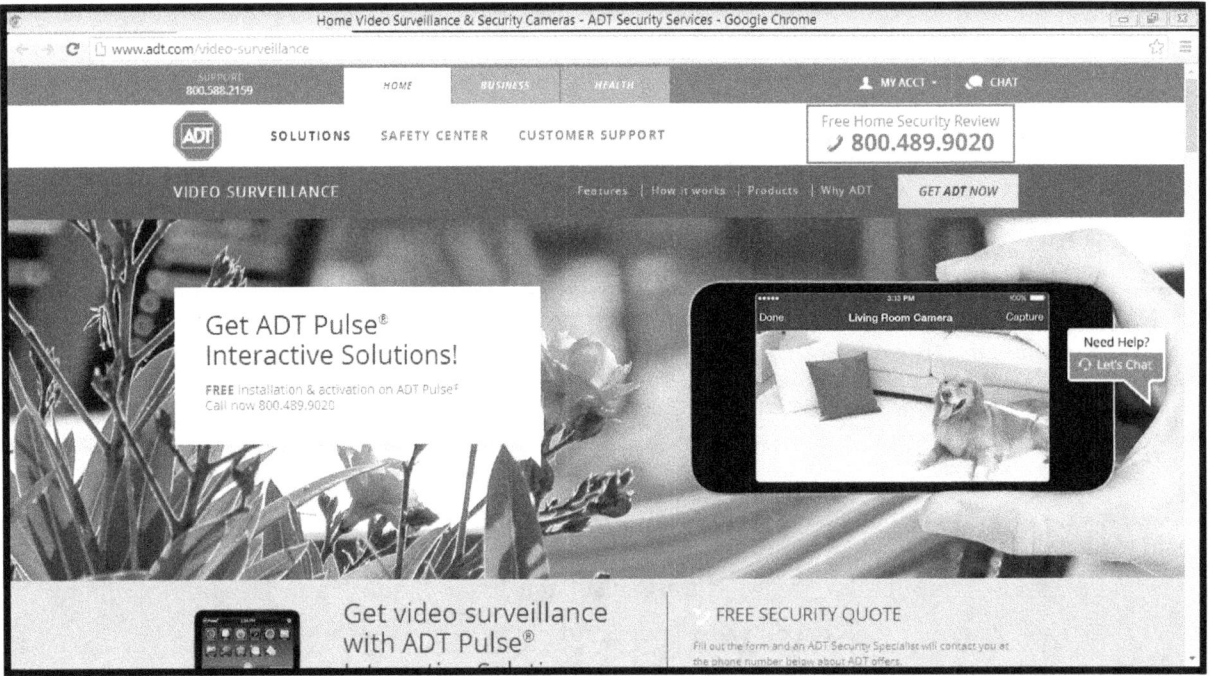

http://www.adt.com/video-surveillance

I soon learned how to link them to a new page I added to my website just for this purpose. From that page you can now view current and ongoing projects all over the country in real-time. Just one last note about building a website on your own, if you think the process is too complicated you can always go to websites like webstreet101.com and have a professional website built and maintained for you at a reasonable cost and in a short amount of time.

http://www.webstreet101.com/

CHAPTER 3
PROJECT PARAMETERS & SEARCH CRITERIA
"Set your goals"

When it was time to buy my first house to flip online I began by setting a few goals. The first was a budget. I arrived at this budget amount by totaling all of my available credit and cash to invest and holding back one-third in reserve to cover carrying costs. With this amount in mind I began my search on the internet. The search engines instantly produced pages of results for an inquiry for residential real estate for sale. A few of the larger national websites listed were Trulia.com, Zillow.com, Realtor.com and HUD.gov.

http://www.zillow.com/

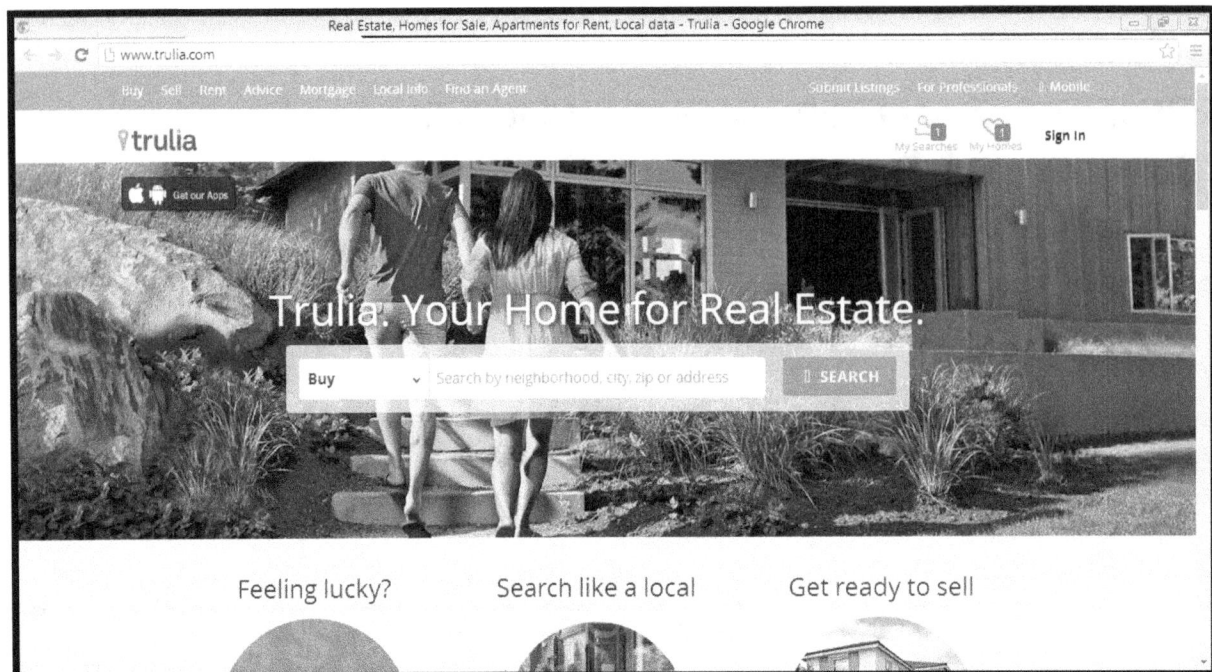

http://www.trulia.com/

http://www.realtor.com/

http://portal.hud.gov/hudportal/HUD?src=/topics/homes_for_sale

You will find hundreds of other websites in addition to these if you start a similar search yourself. When I began to explore each site I found an array of different tools and search options were available to further aid and refine my first inquiry which was simply for, residential real estate for sale.

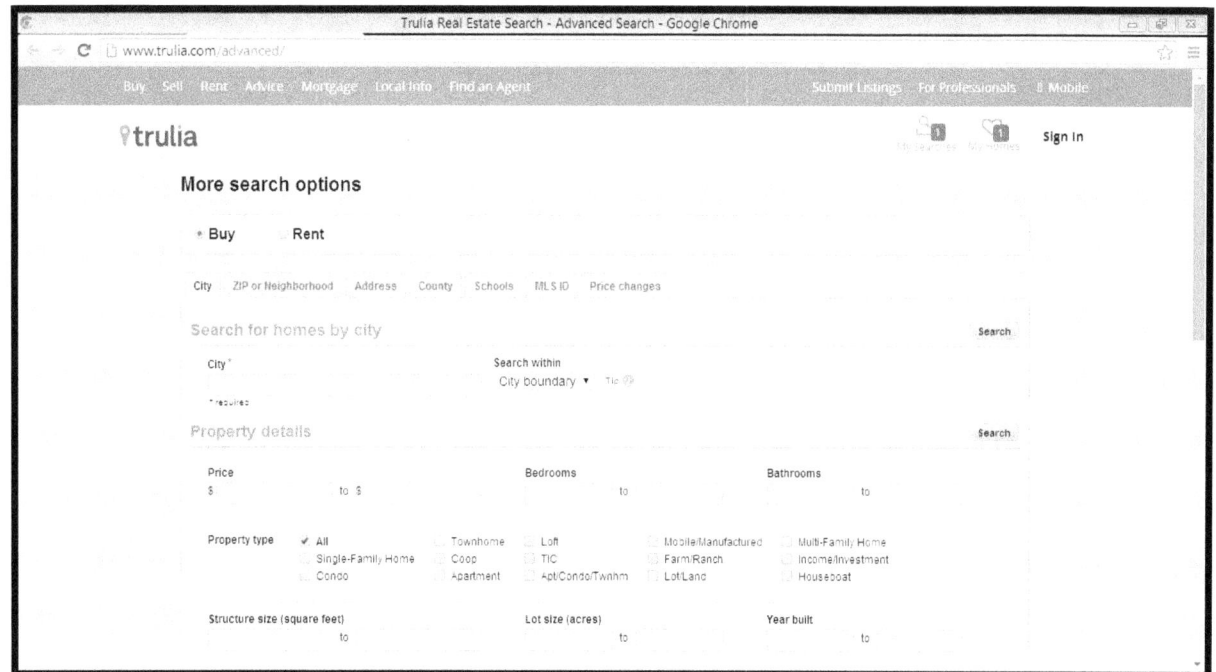

http://www.trulia.com/advanced/

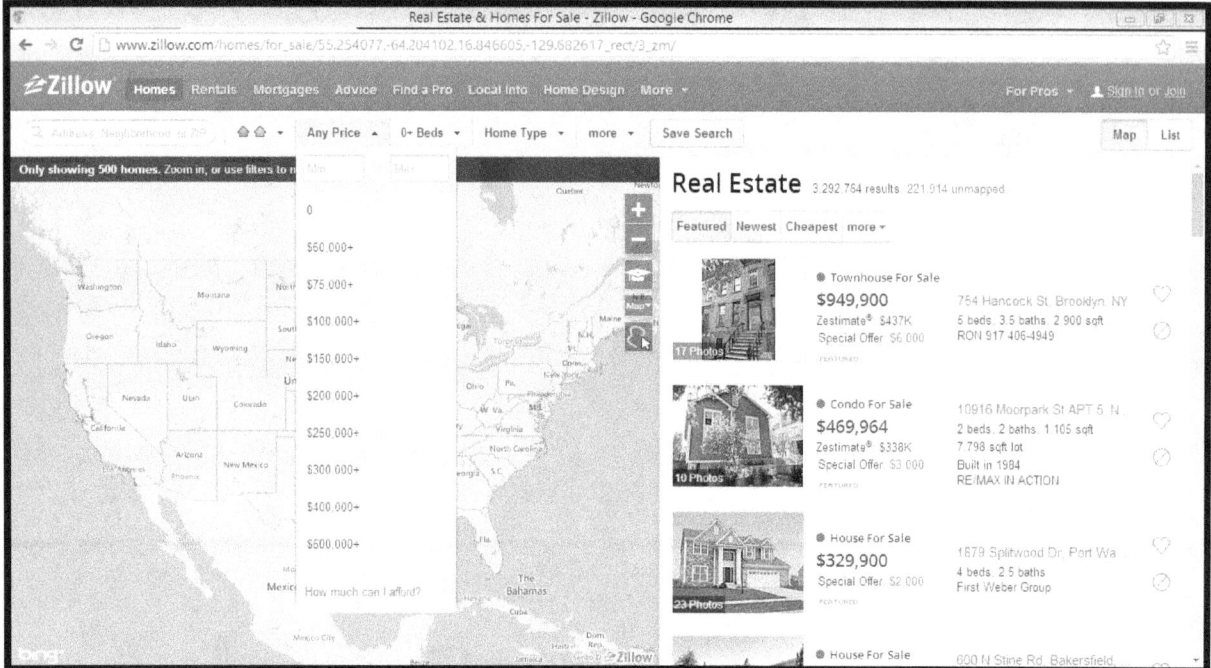

http://www.zillow.com/

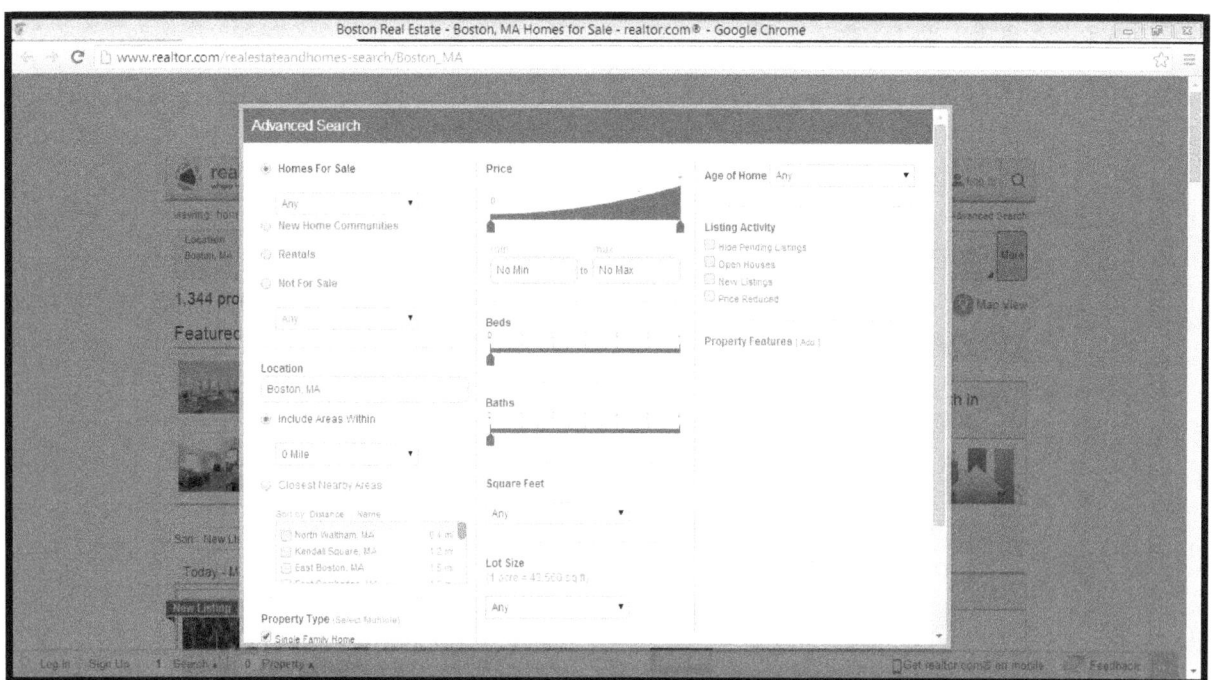

http://www.realtor.com/realestateandhomes-search/Boston_MA

Some, but by no means all the options available in a refined search at these websites are the price range, the type of property and the zip code of the property. A more advanced search could produce results for specific inquiries such as nearby schools and recent price drops.

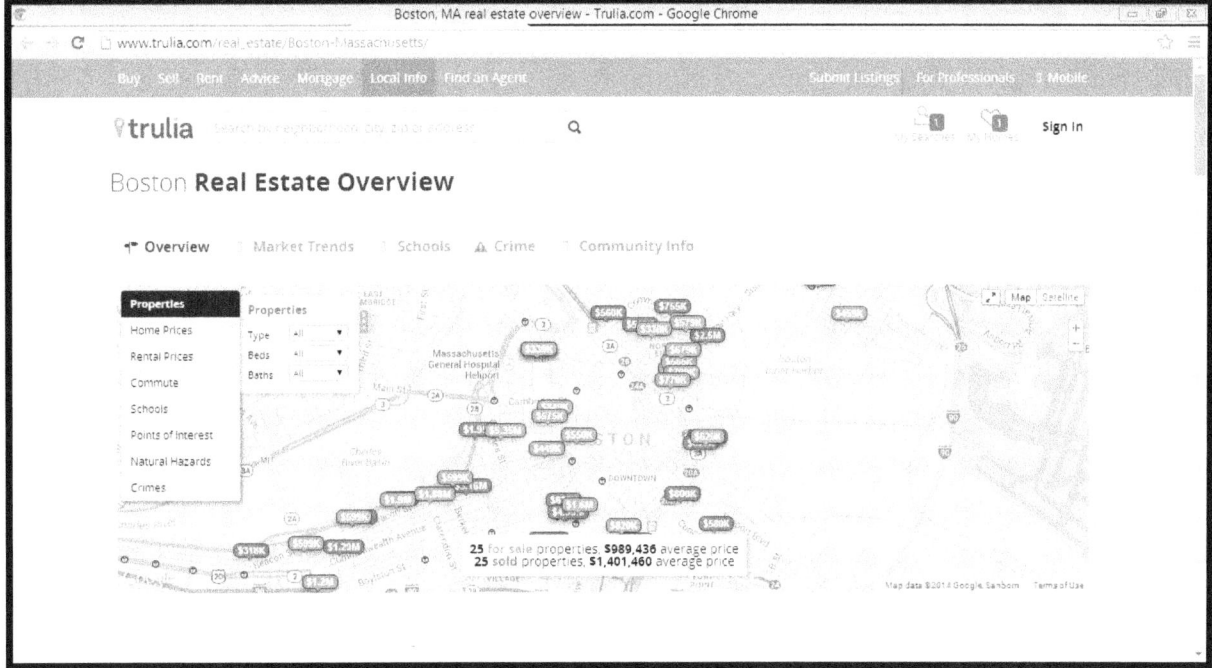

http://www.trulia.com/real_estate/Boston-Massachusetts/

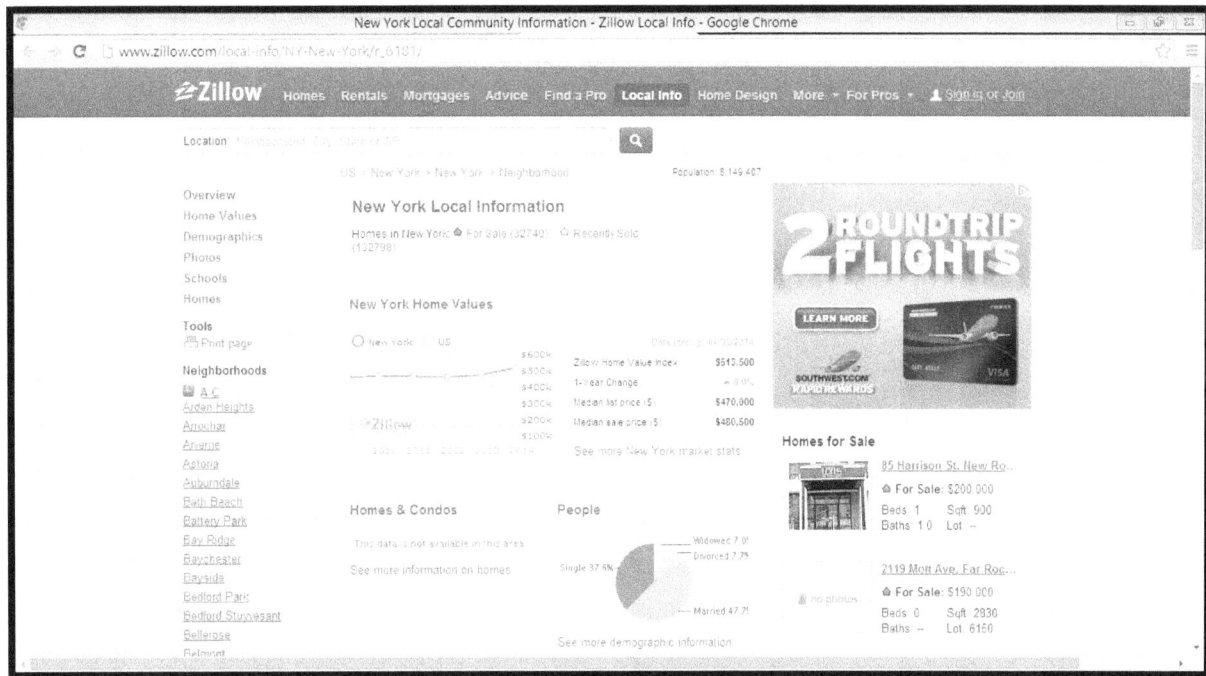

http://www.zillow.com/local-info/NY-New-York/r_6181/

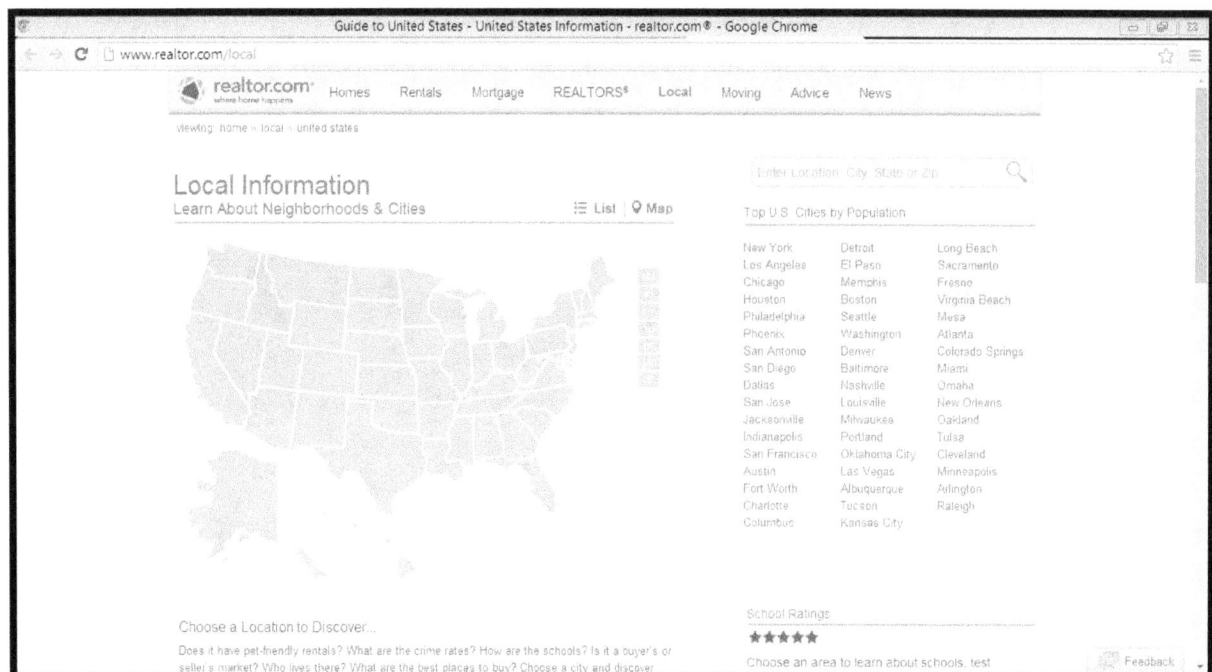

http://www.realtor.com/local

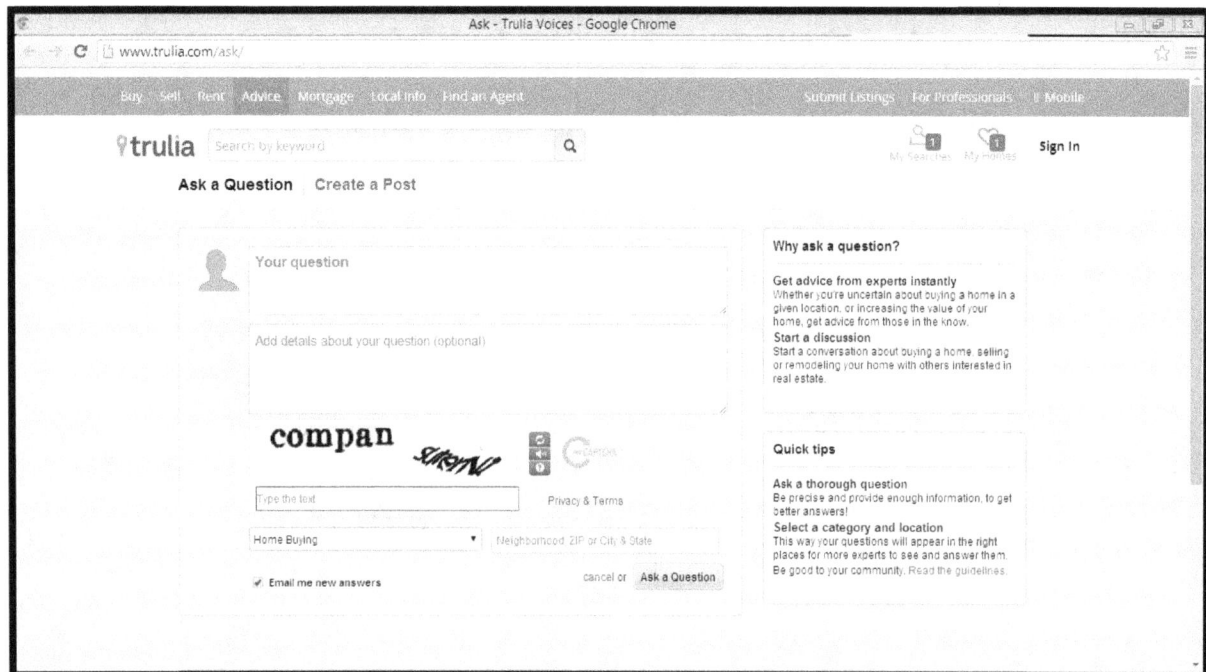

http://www.trulia.com/ask/

Average time on the market statistics for a particular type of property are also available for all the markets across the country. You can use this information to spot sales trends and which markets are hot and which are not. It became clear to me then that I could narrow down my search to produce results only for a particular type of house. One that was available for sale within my required price range, located near a specific university, that had recently reduced the original asking price, and the local average time on that areas market was less than 90 days to sell.

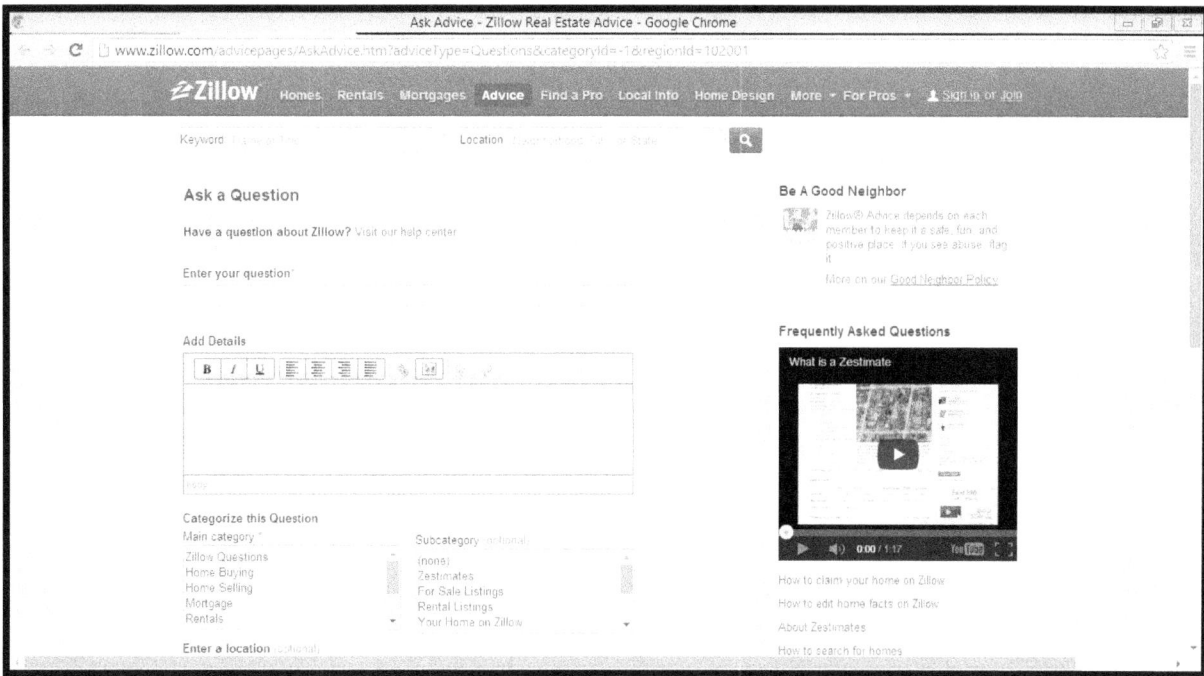

http://www.zillow.com/advicepages/AskAdvice.htm?adviceType=Questions&categoryId=-1&regionId=102001

Now that I had established these boundaries, or my goals, I only had to visit each website and enter my specific requirements to produce the search results that included only the properties that I was actually interested in. The more the results, the more rigid my requirements became until finally narrowing it down to only a few results. It was as simple as entering my responses to the questions on the search forms provided at each website and then submitting my answers. The results would then be returned and I would be offered an opportunity to even further refine my search. Also available at these websites are more tools and information like local market data and a live chat with a local agent. It's truly amazing how much you really can learn about a property using only online resources.

CHAPTER 4
HUMAN RESOURCES
"Build Your Team"

Once I had found the perfect house to flip it was time to buy, improve and sell it. But the house was in Houston and I, in Miami. I had to have a way to make things happen without me being there. Someone else would have to do the physical part of the flip. I needed human resources. I needed a team. So I set out to assemble a group of professionals and contractors that could help me to succeed in achieving my virtual goal. I began with a list of things I would need to do and then searched via the internet for the people who could get the job done in the Houston area. I initially determined that I would need, an appraiser to confirm the value of the property, a home inspector to report on the current condition of the property, a lawyer and a title company to handle the purchase of the property, an insurance agent to protect the investment, a home security agency to deploy surveillance and control access, maintenance contractors to clean and care for the property, home improvement contractors to produce and install the improvements, and a real estate broker to handle the marketing and sale of the property.

So once again I turned to the search engines and began to seek out those specialists in the Houston area. It wasn't long before I had compiled a list of many potential candidates for the jobs. I quickly located a number of qualified appraisers with websites in the Houston area at the AI website, appraisalinstitute.org.

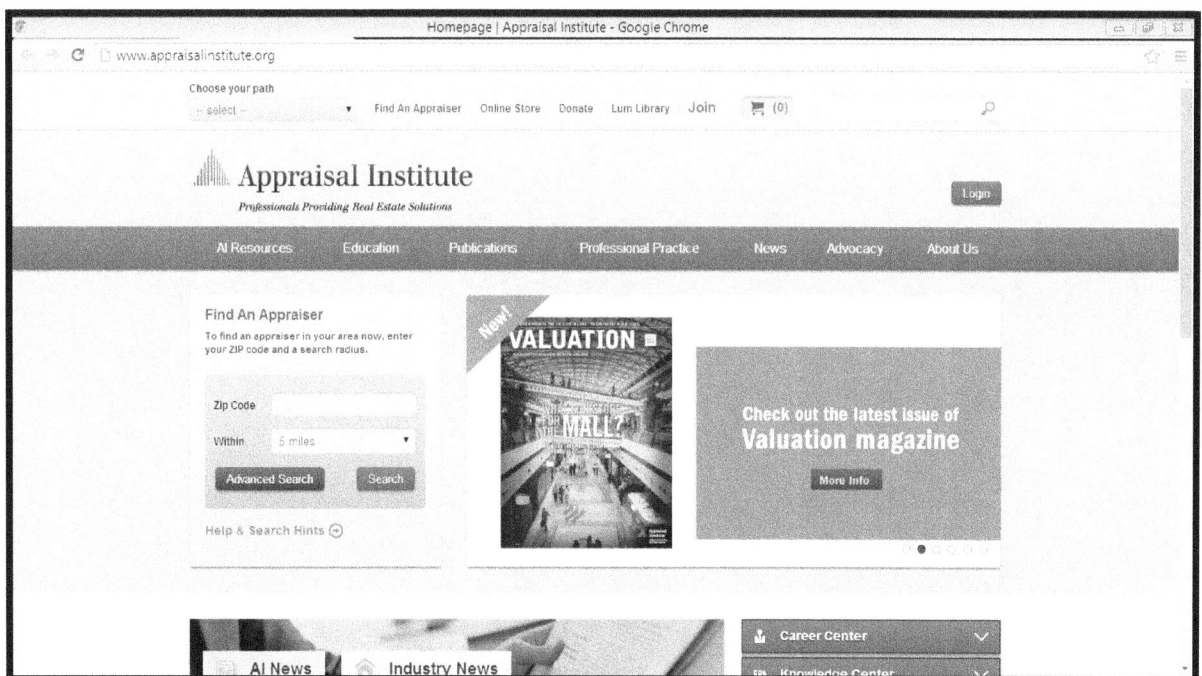

http://www.appraisalinstitute.org/

The National Association of Home Inspectors website, nahi.org, provided a list of home inspectors located within a 5 mile radius of the requested zip code and the links to their websites.

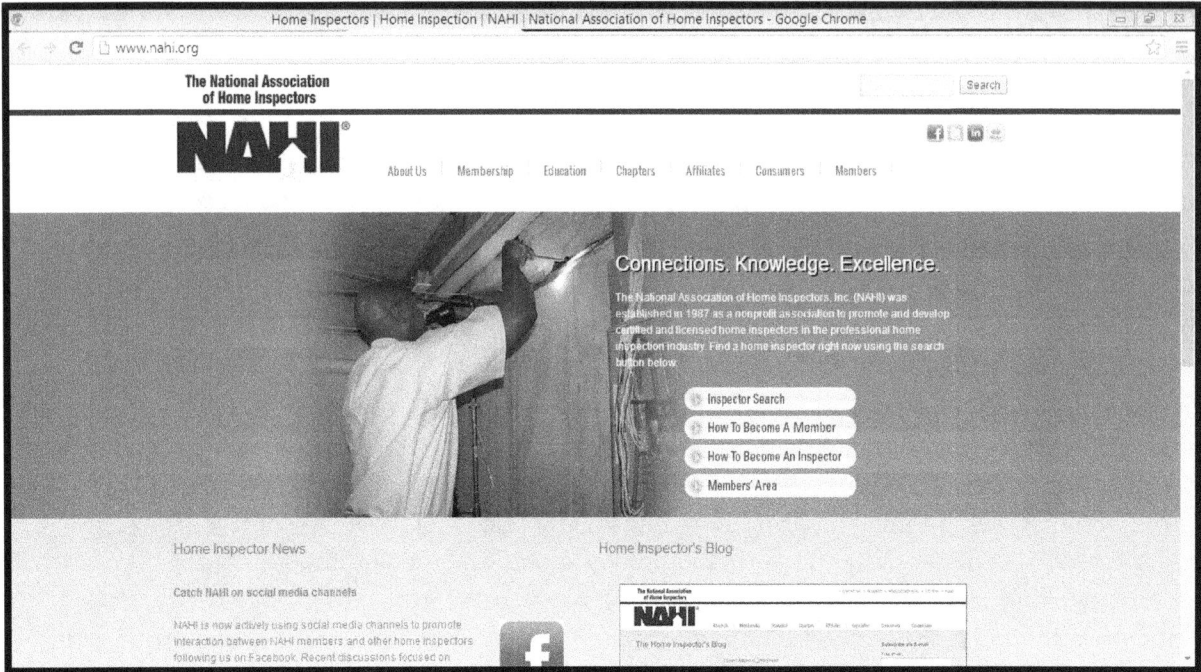

http://www.nahi.org/

I found a local real estate lawyer and a title company through the Houston Bar Association at hba.org.

http://www.hba.org/

StateFarm.com insured the house and adt.com provided security, live surveillance and controlled access.

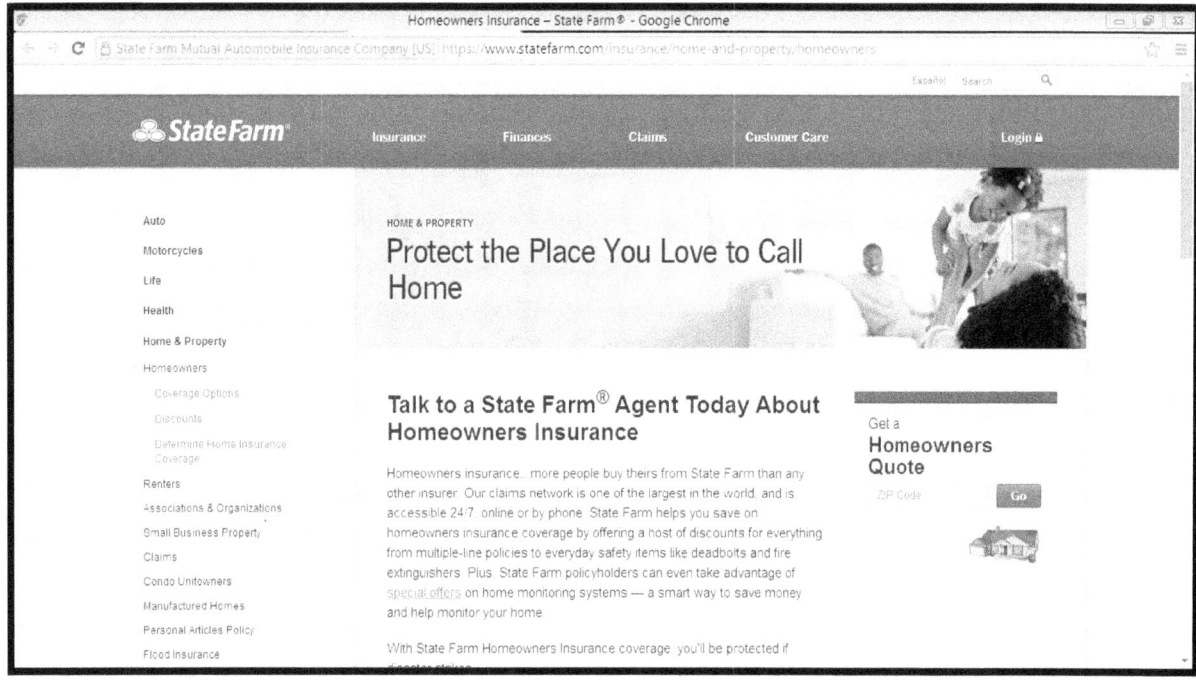

https://www.statefarm.com/insurance/home-and-property/homeowners

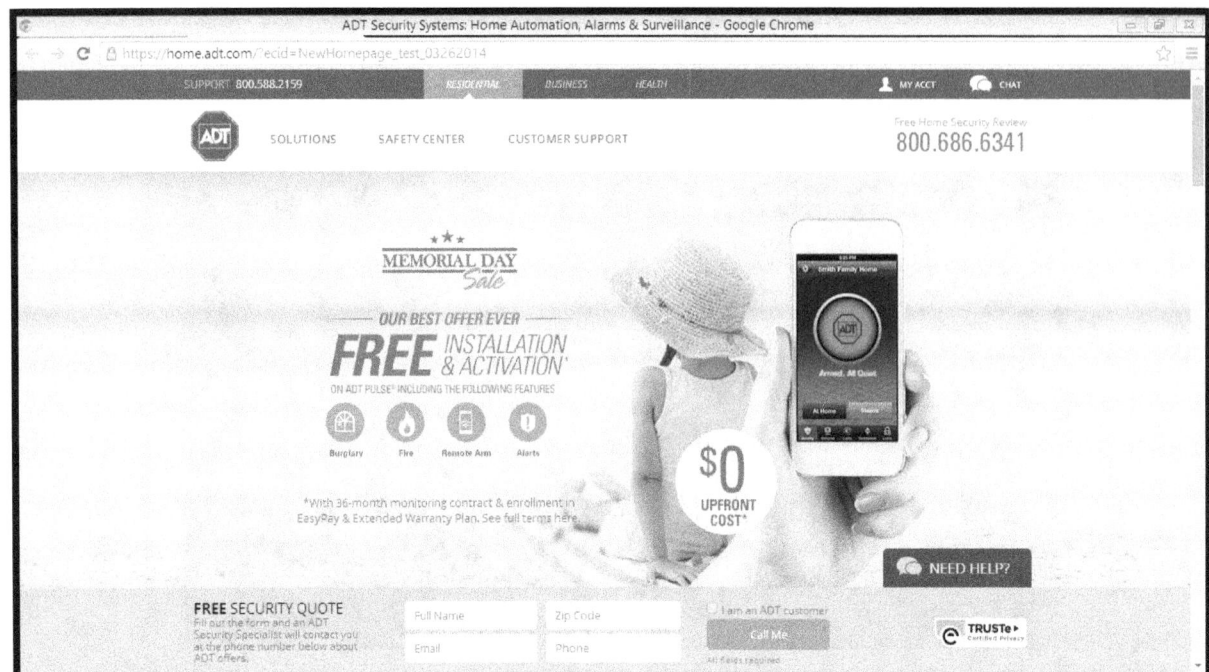

https://home.adt.com/?ecid=NewHomepage_test_03262014

Craigslist and Angie's List, both dot coms, supplied the online listings for local maintenance contractors and caretakers.

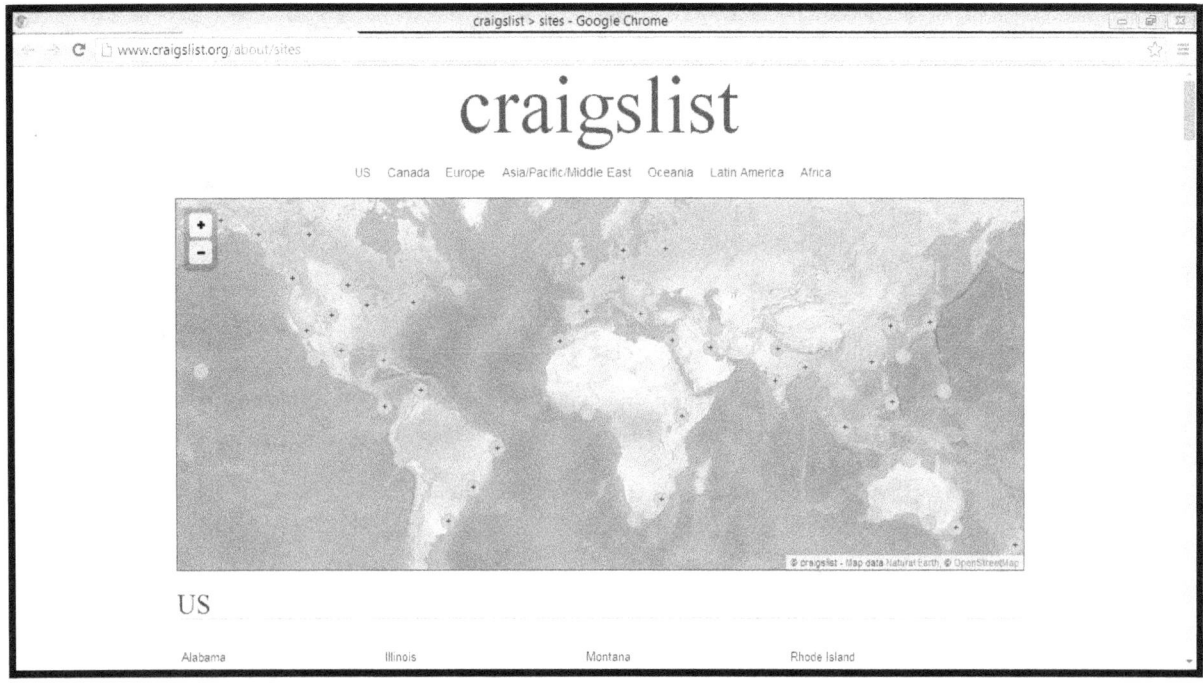

http://www.craigslist.org/about/sites

http://www.angieslist.com/

HomeDepot.com and Lowes.com both sold and installed the improvements I wanted and Century21.com handled the marketing and sale of the property.

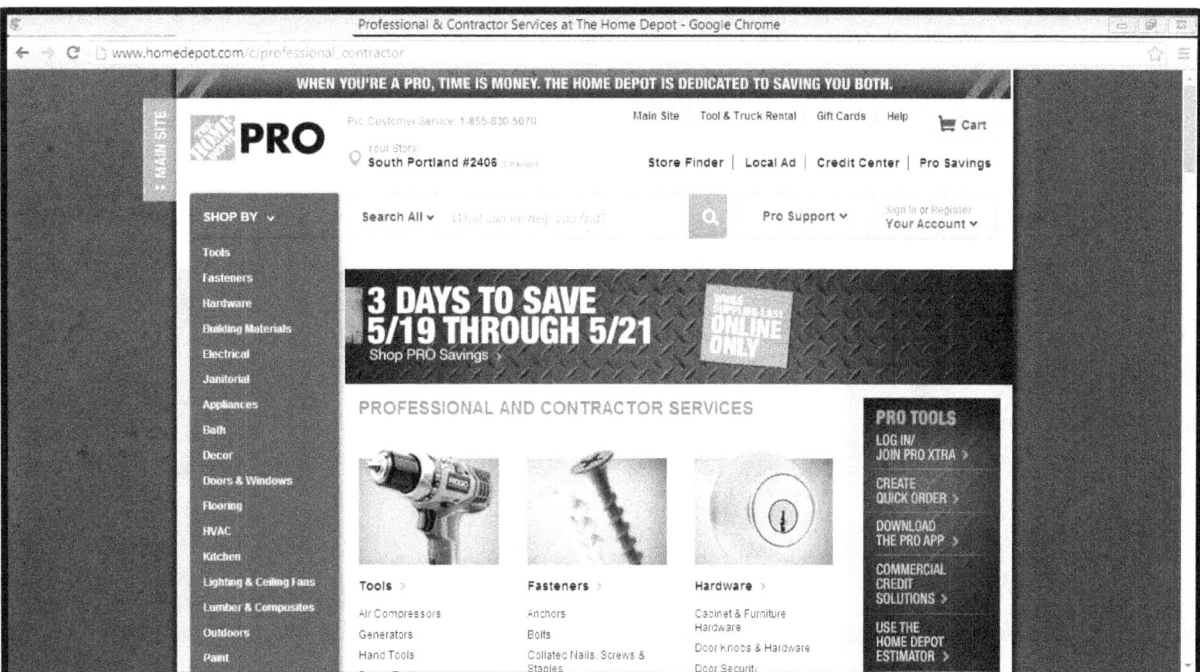

http://www.homedepot.com/c/professional_contractor

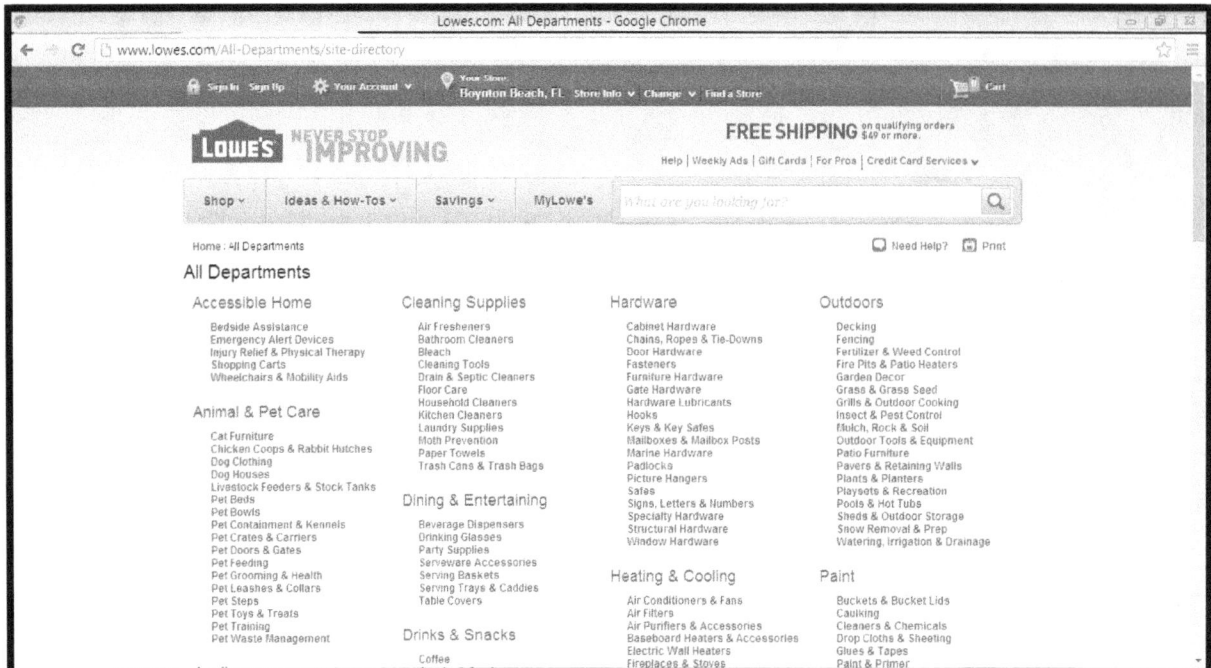

http://www.lowes.com/

http://www.century21.com/

In fact it wasn't very difficult at all to assemble my first team in the Houston area with only the internet as my resource. It wasn't long after that I had teams assembled and in place in all the major cities and markets throughout the country. It didn't matter where I was anymore, I could make things happen all over the United States now with just the push of a button or a short conversation on my cell phone, and my team would do the rest.

CHAPTER 5
PROJECT EVALUATION AND SELECTION
"Do the Math / Start Making Offers"

I knew how much money I could spend to buy a house to flip, the question was how much money I should spend to buy a house to flip. To answer this question I had to develop a formula. A formula that would take all the expenditures involved in a flip into account, then would arrive at the price I would actually have to buy the house for to make a profit when it sold. The real dollar amounts would vary with the acquisition price range of the investment but the formula would not. Every flip had the same four basic elements that would decide my target purchase price. They are the current fair market value of the property based on the recent sales of comparable properties in excellent condition in the area, the improvements needed to bring the subject property to excellent condition, how long the project should take acquisition to sale, and what return on the investment I expected.

The first part of the formula is to decide the fair market value of the house if it was in excellent condition. Excellent condition in my opinion means that it needs no repairs or improvements and the expected life of the existing building and improvements is at least twenty years. You can find this value by searching for the recent sales data of comparable properties in the area and paying particular attention to those properties in excellent shape at the time of sale and the length of time they took to sell.

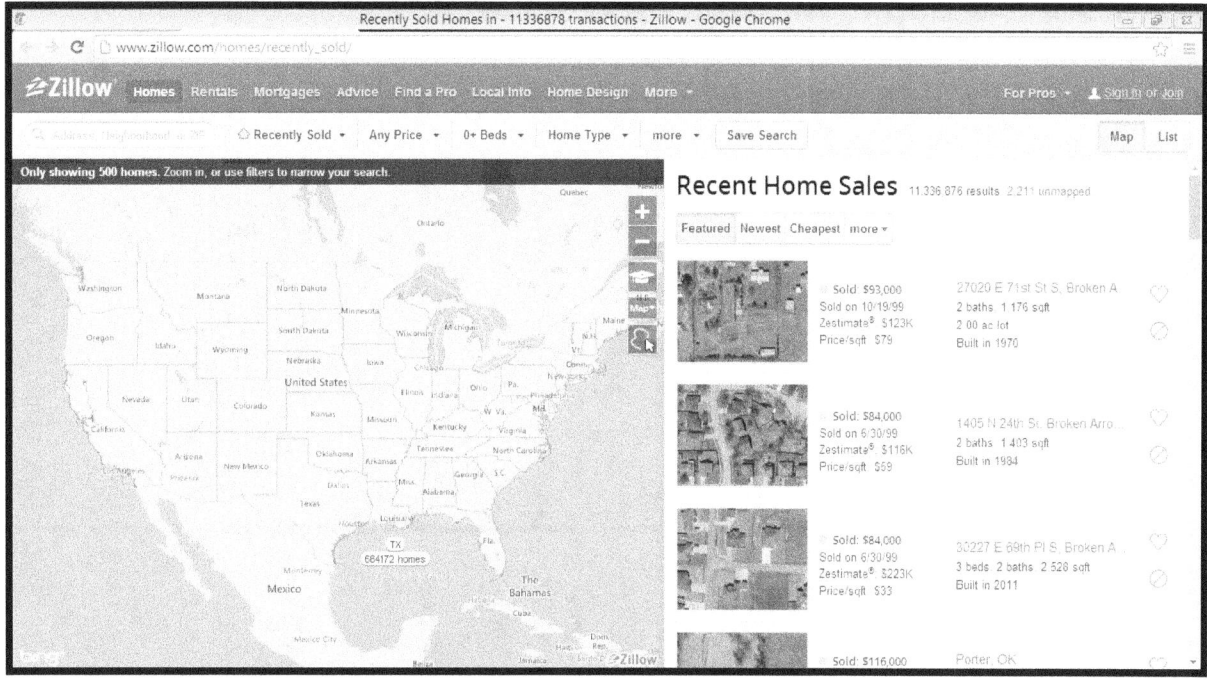

http://www.zillow.com/homes/recently_sold/

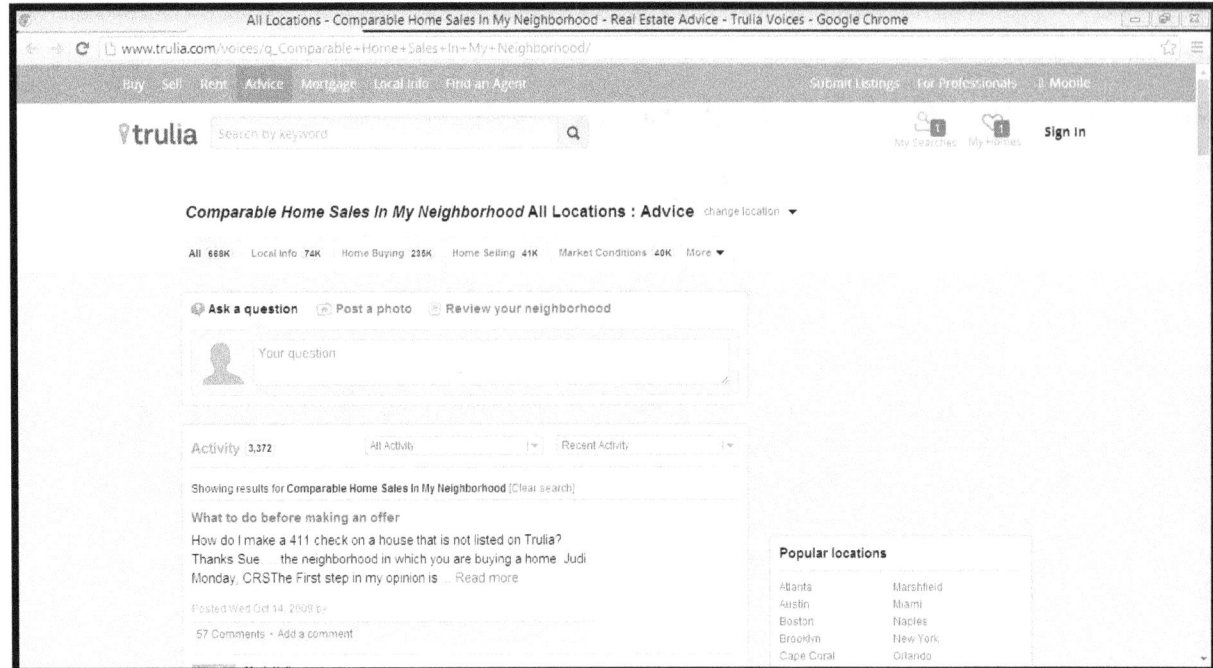

http://www.trulia.com/voices/q_Comparable+Home+Sales+In+My+Neighborhood/

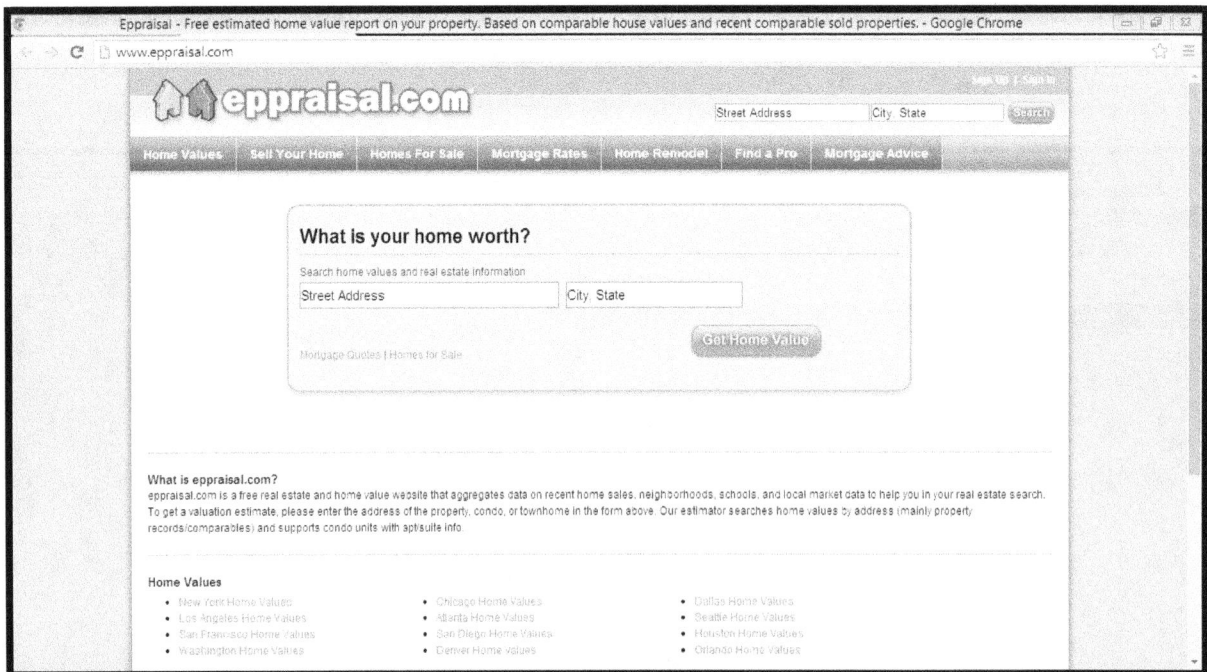

http://www.eppraisal.com/

Once you decide upon the fair market value of a house in excellent condition you need to make a list of the total cost of all the improvements you will have to do to get your house to that point.

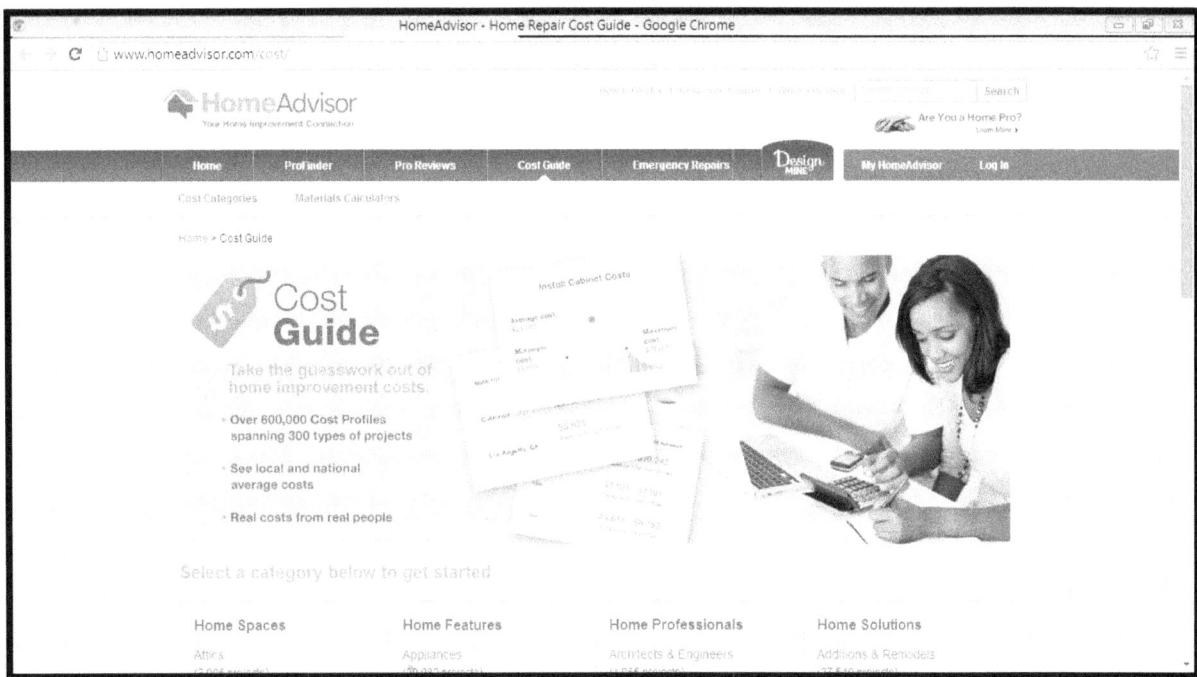

http://www.homeadvisor.com/cost/

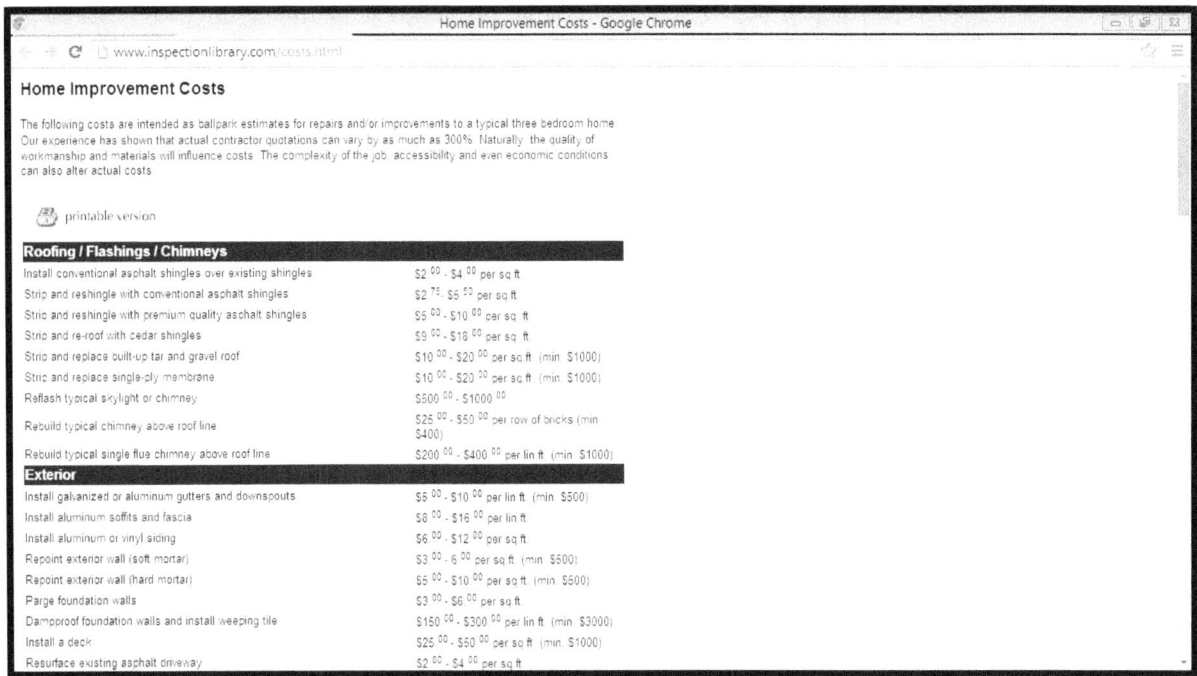

http://www.inspectionlibrary.com/costs.html

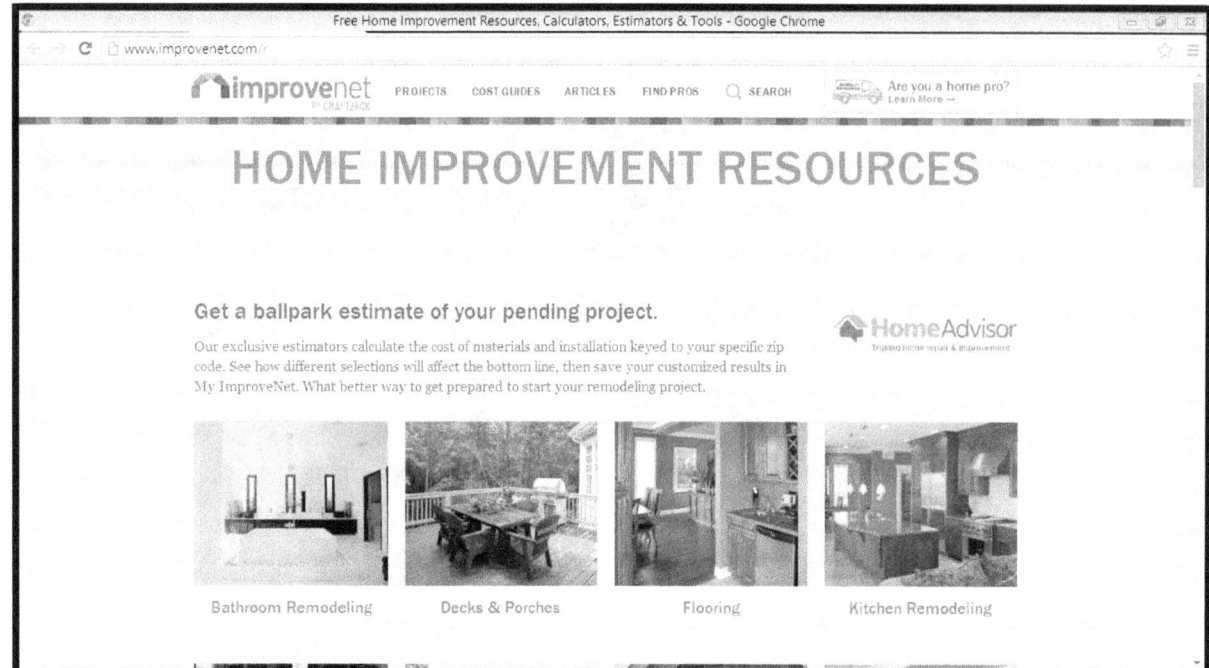

http://www.improvenet.com/r

You then subtract this amount plus twenty percent from that fair market value price.

You are not finished yet. Next you will have some carrying costs and a profit to figure. A simple rule of thumb would be to subtract an extra twenty percent from the first result leaving you with your target purchase price for the property. What this all looks like in numerical form goes something like this. Let's say that you have a fair market value of $100,000.00 and you decide that it needs $30,000.00 in improvements. You subtract $30,000.00 plus 20% or $36,000.00 from this amount leaving $64,000.00. Next subtract your margin of 20% or $12,800 leaving $51,200.00 as your target purchase price. This is the most you should pay for this house regardless of what the seller is asking. Begin negotiating by offering 50% of your target purchase price along with a lengthy explanation of the improvements you will have to make to bring the property to its full potential.

http://new.realtor.com/basics/buy/chooseoffer/makeoffer.asp

http://www.lawdepot.com/contracts/real-estate-purchase-offer/

SAMPLE

AGREEMENT TO PURCHASE REAL ESTATE

The undersigned (herein "Purchaser") hereby offers to purchase from the owner (herein "Seller") the real estate located at _____ in the city of_____, County of_____, State of_____, the legal description of which is:_____
_____
_____

upon the following terms and conditions:

1. Purchase Price and Conditions of Payment

The purchase price shall be _____Dollars ($_____) to be paid in accordance with subparagraph_____, below:

A: <u>Cash.</u> The purchase price shall be paid in its entirety in cash at the time of closing the sale.

B: <u>Cash Subject to New Mortgage.</u> The purchase price shall be paid in cash at the time of closing the sale subject, however, to Purchaser's ability to obtain a first mortgage loan within _____days after the acceptance of this offer by Seller in the amount of $_____, payable in not less than _____monthly installments, including interest at a rate not to exceed _____% financing. If such financing cannot be obtained within the time specified above then either Purchaser or Seller may terminate this agreement and any earnest money deposited by Purchaser will be promptly refunded.

C: <u>Cash Subject to Existing Mortgage.</u> The purchase price shall be paid in cash at the time of closing the sale after deducting from the purchase price the then outstanding balance due and owing under the existing mortgage in favor of _____, dated_____, 20___, in the original amount of $_____; of such mortgage debt is approximately $_____ as of _____, 20___.

D: <u>Cash With Assumption of Existing Mortgage.</u> The purchase price shall be paid in cash at the time of the closing of the sale after deducting from the purchase price the then outstanding balance due and owing under the existing mortgage in favor of _____, dated_____, 20___,having a present balance of

https://www.cmich.edu/fas/fsr/cps/PropertyAcquisition/Documents/Sample-AgreementToPurchaseRealEstate.pdf

CHAPTER 6
ACQUISITION
"Make the Deal"

When it becomes time to pull the trigger I always begin negotiations by offering 50% of my target purchase price along with a narrative account of all the work I will need to do in order for the property to sell at its full potential. I figure that you can always go up with a counter offer but never down. Don't be discouraged if the first offer is not accepted because it inevitably will be. Your goal is to spur a counter offer by the Seller and open the door for further negotiations. You need to learn a few things about the Seller like their reason for selling and their expectations from the sale. In turn they should learn things about you like the value you have placed upon their house is real and substantiated, not just predatory and profit mongering.

http://www.realtor.com/Basics/Buy/InspNegot/Yes.asp

You have based your offer upon the real condition of their house and current market versus the ideal condition of their house and wishful thinking. You have taken into account the work and cost involved to repair and improve the house in its current state and what houses in comparable shape versus ideal shape are for sale for and have recently sold for in the area. Of course if they want top dollar they can invest in the work and improvements that the house needs themselves. So why don't they? Who knows their reason? But the fact is they haven't and that is why you are here. You are willing to step in where they are ready to step out. You and your team will get them out and pay them the real value of their house in cash. You and your team will speculate on their house and put the time, money and work into it that it needs to sell at top dollar.

http://www.realtor.com/Basics/Buy/InspNegot/Bidding.asp

Be clear to yourself and think with your head and not your heart. To fall in love with a house or the vision or idea you see for it usually spells financial suicide. Do your homework and study the market. If the numbers don't jive, move on. Not every house you go after will result in deal. If you stick to your original plan and stay within the confines of your formula it will take many offers before you consummate your first deal. How many offers is unknown. Just stick to your plan. Search, find and offer. When the right one comes along it will all fall into place.

www.zillow.com/home-buying-guide/negotiating-home-price/

Zillow Homes Rentals Mortgages **Advice** Find a Pro Local Info Home Design More ▾ For Pros ▾ 👤 Sign In or Join

Advice › Buyer's Guide › Home Negotiation Strategies

BUYER'S GUIDE: BUY THE HOME

Buying a Home: Negotiation Strategies

Negotiation strategy is different from negotiation style. From pit bull to diplomat, each of us has a personal style. But the strategy for negotiating the purchase of a home is based on facts: the real estate market at the moment of your attempt to purchase, the seller's requirements and the property itself (condition, amenities and comparative value in relation to other sold or listed properties).

The best real estate agents have tremendous expertise when it comes to market value in particular areas. In many instances, the most experienced agents have seen just about all the homes that have come on the market over the years. They also work with other agents and speak the same language. For buyers, that is the primary reason to work with an agent. They have the information and background to engage knowledgeably in what can be a very intense, fast process.

Now, does that mean you can't undertake your own negotiation? Absolutely not. In fact, many buyers do. It means

- Doing intensive research about the market, the property you want to buy and the seller's situation
- Figuring out an appropriate negotiating strategy and style based on that information

Tips for staying sane with or without an agent
- Do your homework

Zillow Buyer's Guide

First Steps ›
Get Financing ›
Find a Home ›
Buy the Home ›
Close the Deal ›

SeaWorld Busch Gardens
AQUATICA
Save over 20%
Length of Stay Ticket

http://www.zillow.com/home-buying-guide/negotiating-home-price/

CHAPTER 7
PROJECT PLAN AND MANAGEMENT
"Set Up a Schedule"

We have all heard the saying that "time is money" and it couldn't be truer than when it comes to flipping houses. If you based your budget on a 90 day turnover then every day over that cuts into your margin of profit. Go too long over 90 days and you can actually begin to lose money! My general rule is to always double your expectations then add 10%. Be ready for the worse. You just can't imagine the things that can go wrong that will turn days into weeks and weeks into months. The most simple of flips that should only take 90 days on the outside will inevitably take 180 days. Experience taught me this valuable lesson. There are always those things that are just out of your control that will always turn up. You must expect and prepare for them if you want to successfully schedule a flip.

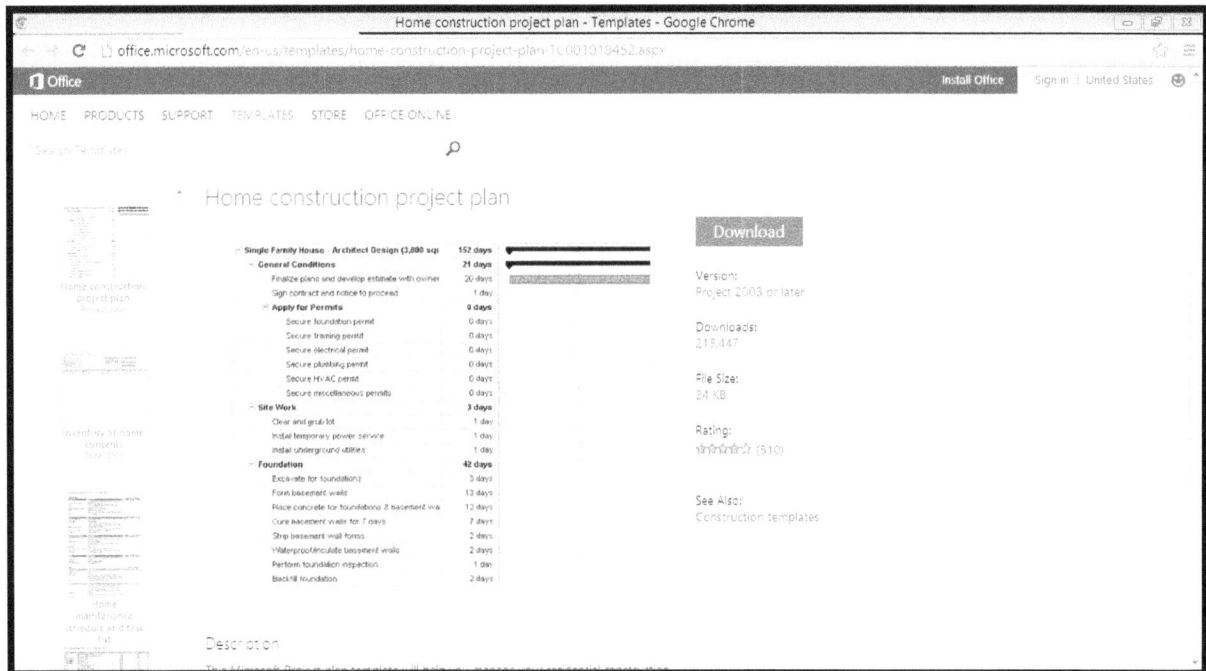

http://office.microsoft.com/en-us/templates/home-construction-project-plan-TC001018452.aspx

You can break down any residential construction project into twenty main areas of work. You must define each task in this scope of work down to the minutest detail. Be very thorough. Having to stop progress and wait while you go back and finish something that should have already been done at the proper time is usually both costly and time-consuming. The main areas of a residential project are as follows;

1. Legal and Permits

2. Site

3. Utilities, Water and Septic

4. Foundation and Masonry

5. Framing

6. Roofing

7. Exterior Doors and Windows

8. Siding

9. Rough Plumbing

10. Rough Electric

11. Insulation

12. Interior Walls and Ceilings

13. Interior Doors

14. Interior Mill-work and Trim

15. Cabinets and Countertops

16. Plumbing Finish and Fixtures

17. Electric Finish and Fixtures

18. Paint, Stain and Decorating

19. Finish Floors

20. Landscaping

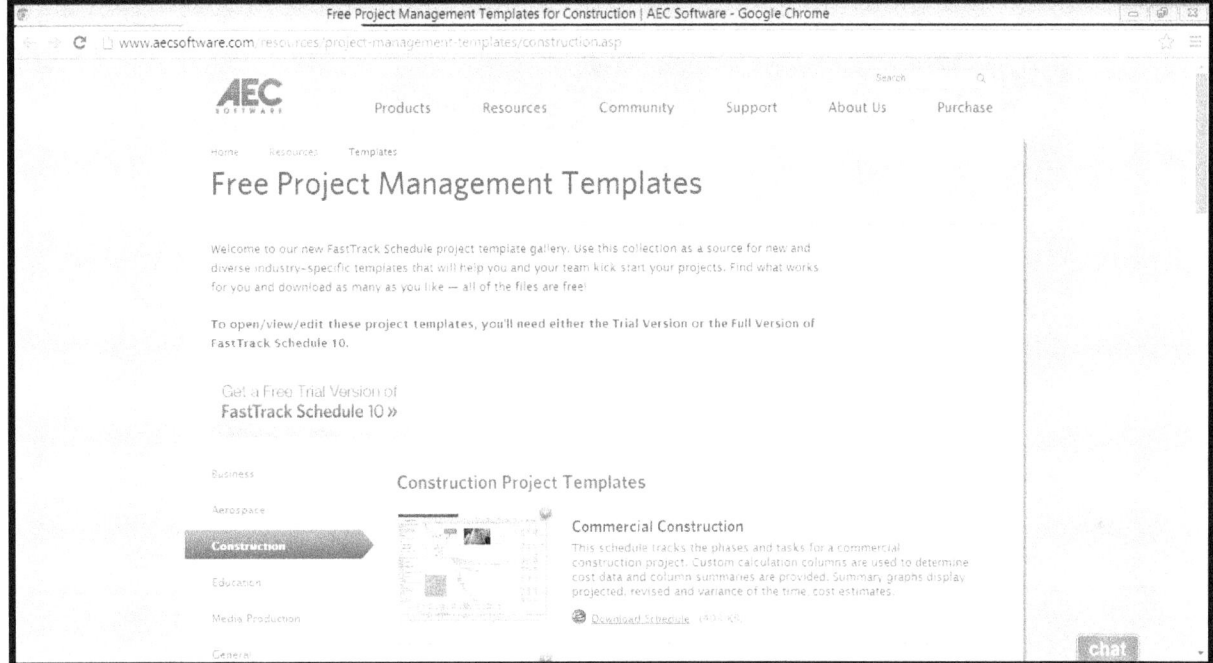

http://www.aecsoftware.com/resources/project-management-templates/construction.asp

By thoroughly studying each area and listing the tasks in each area you will begin to assemble a time line of things you will have to do to complete your project. You can complete some tasks simultaneously but most will have a prerequisite. For an example building permits first, installing your exterior windows and doors second and your cabinets and countertops before your plumbing finish and fixtures. Can you imagine a plumber showing up to install your kitchen sink before the kitchen cabinets are in? This won't happen if you schedule properly and closely monitor its progress and update it daily. Unfortunately just because it is on the schedule it doesn't mean it is going to always get done, welcome to the world of residential construction.

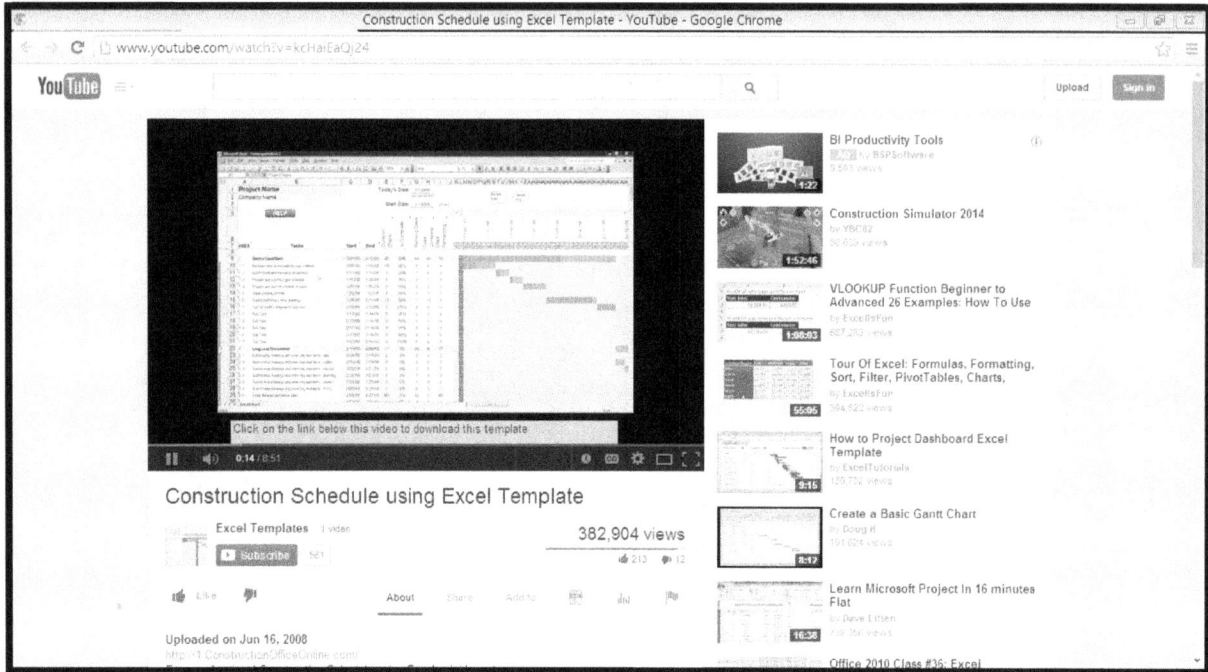

http://www.youtube.com/watch?v=kcHaiEaQj24

http://planningtemplate.com/

PART TWO

CHAPTER 8
MARKETING AND SALE
"Grandpa's Sure Fire Five Day Way"

This method is also known as a round robin sale. The procedure to follow has five steps that you complete over a five to seven-day period. This process will decide the highest price an active qualified buyer is willing to pay for your house on the specific day you offered it for sale. This process will not decide the highest price you can actually sell the house for given unlimited time and effective marketing. But the fact remains, if the property is average in an average market you will usually get average results. If the property is below average in a below average market then it would make sense that you get below average results. However, if you have done your homework and produced an above average house in a high demand market you will inevitably reap the rewards. Every property is what it is and the results can vary from little or no interest to an all-out bidding war. As the saying goes "when you plant roses you get roses".

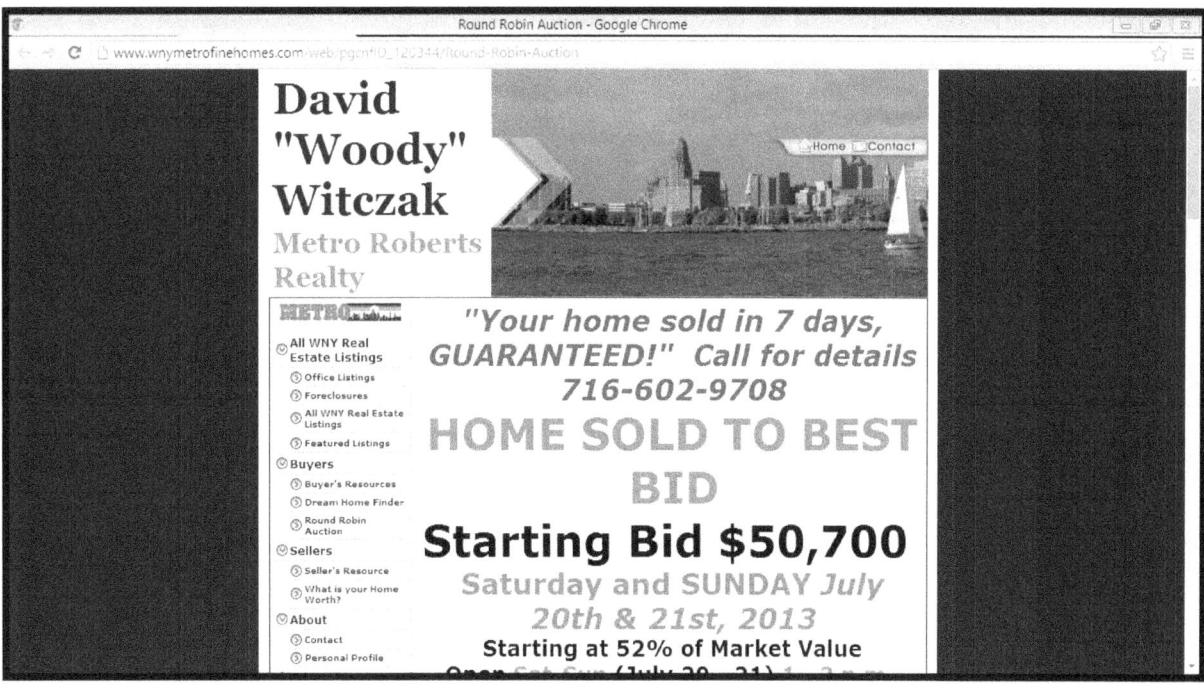

http://www.wnymetrofinehomes.com/web/pgcnfID_120344/Round-Robin-Auction

Day one of the program is simple. Take out a small classified ad in the local newspaper and advertise your property for sale at 50% of what you think it is actually worth. If you think your three bedroom and two bath ranch on Easy Street is worth $100,000.00 then start the bidding at $50,000.00. Be sure to state the house will sell to the highest bidder at the close of the sale in five or seven days. This is very important. The next few days will decide your next step. If you do not have at least 10 responses by the end of the third day cancel your ad. Your price is probably too high, start over. On day 4 and 5 of the program have an open house and begin showing the property. At this time take written offers only. It will help if you have standard blank purchase offers available possibly tailored to this specific auction. Make the offers contingent and non-binding so that either party can withdraw under certain conditions. Some conditions might be time, financing or inspection results.

On day five of the program show the house until noon and continue to accept written offers only. At 1 o'clock start calling all the bidders and decide what will be the most an active qualified buyer is willing to pay for your property. Give each bidder the opportunity to outbid the highest bidder by going round and round until you are left with only one bidder. Thus the name round robin. You can either accept or decline that offer. You are under no legal obligation. The whole process takes only five to seven days of your time and costs only the amount of a small classified ad.

http://money.cnn.com/2006/02/24/real_estate/quick_home_sales/

CHAPTER 9
THE TRADES
"Who Does What"

Throughout the course of your project to flip a house you are going to come in contact with a variety of people who offer their own specialized skills that enable you to complete all the different tasks involved in the complete construction process. The skills are commonly referred to as the trades and the people as tradesmen.

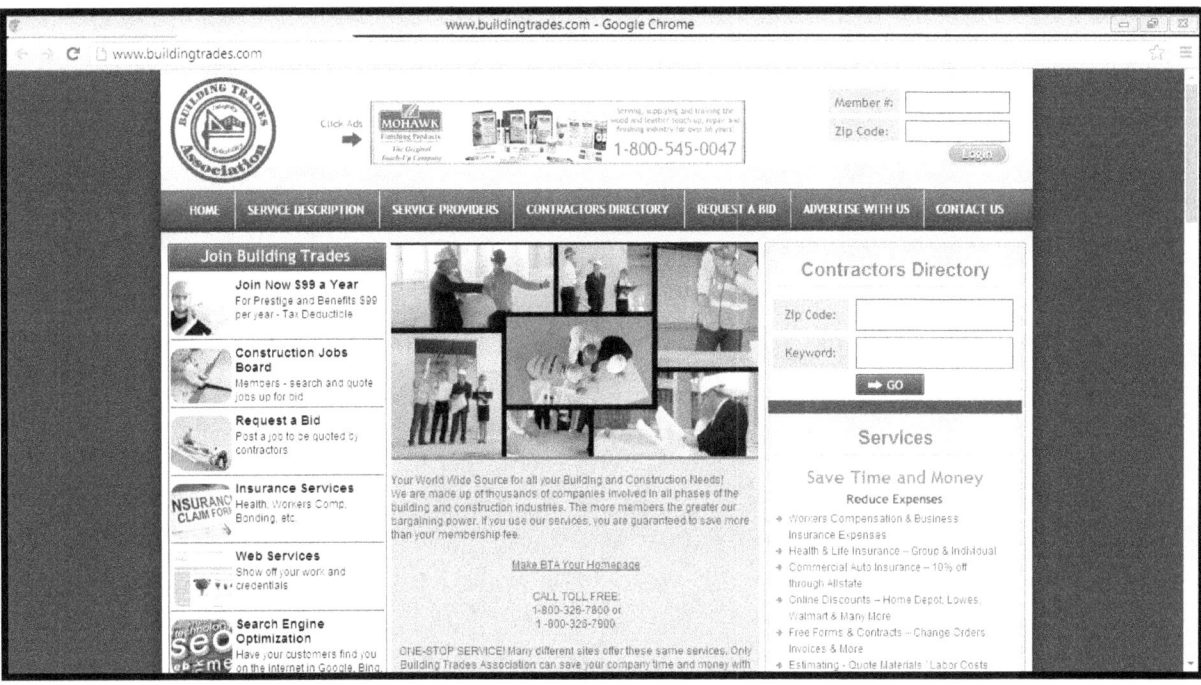

http://www.buildingtrades.com/

 Just as you arrange your project into sequential tasks so is the order in which you come into contact with the various tradesmen. The trades are constantly changing along with developing technology as new ones develop and old ones disappear. Some do a multitude of services while others simply specialize in one. Different parts of the country even have their own unique trades found only there. But for the most part there are a few basic trades that are the most common you will come in contact with. That list and what they do is;

1. Building Inspector - Issues building permits and performs inspections

2. Electrical Inspector - Performs electrical inspections

3. Plumbing Inspector - Performs plumbing inspections

4. Health Inspector - Performs health inspections

5. Surveyor - Does plot plans and stakes out lot lines and foundations

6. Excavator - Prepares ground work and installs septic

7. Mason - Installs foundations, brick, stone and chimneys

8. Carpenter - Woodworker frame to finish

9. Lead Carpenter - Coordinates all trades on project

10. Side Waller - Specializes in installing exterior siding

11. Roofer - Specializes in installing roofing

12. Electrician - Installs electric service and fixtures

13. Plumber - Installs plumbing and gas service and fixtures

14. Dry Waller - Installs interior sheet rock

15. Plasterers - Installs plaster on interior walls and ceilings

16. Tile Installer - Installs ceramic tile

17. Kitchen Installer - Specializes in installing kitchen cabinets and countertops

18. Painter - Installs paint and stain on the interior and exterior

19. Paper Hanger - Installs wallpaper

20. Floor Installer - Installs carpet, vinyl and laminate flooring

21. Landscapers - Installs and finishes grounds, walkways and driveways

These are by no means all the trades but rather the most common ones you will come in contact with during a renovation project.

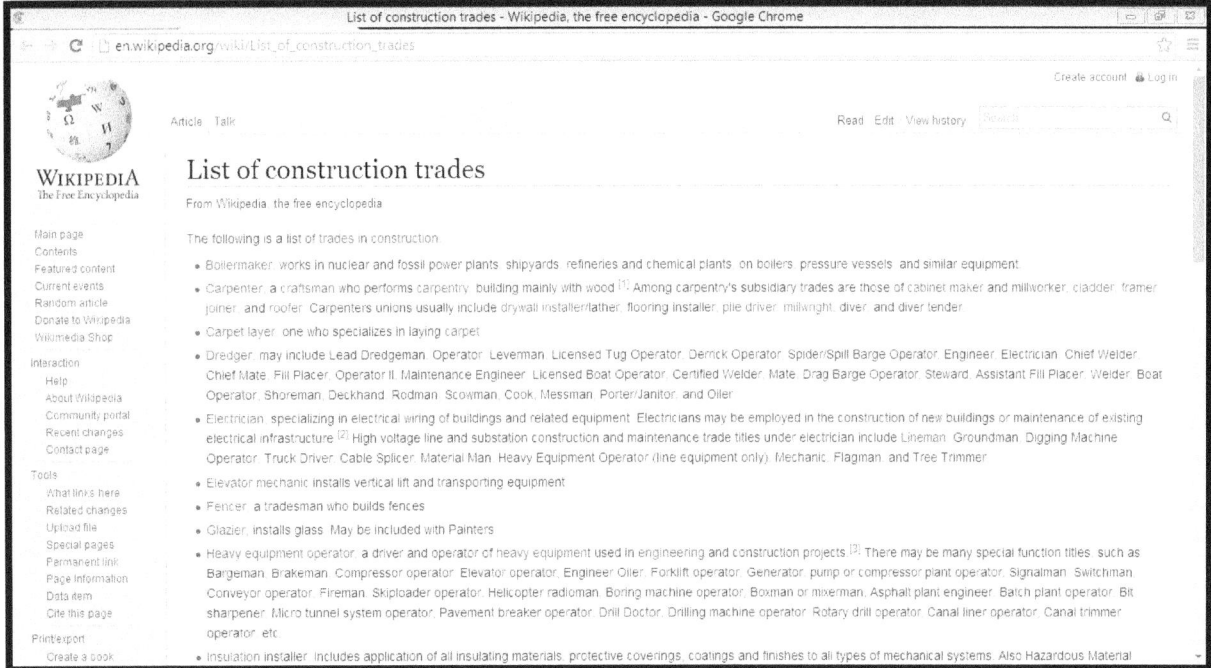

http://en.wikipedia.org/wiki/List_of_construction_trades

Some of the other less common trades deal with specialties like lead abatement, security and home entertainment systems and window treatments. If there is a product out there for today's home improvement consumer you can rest assured that someone has specialized themselves in its application or installation. A simple search of the internet will produce many results for both the product you want and the local tradesman to install it.

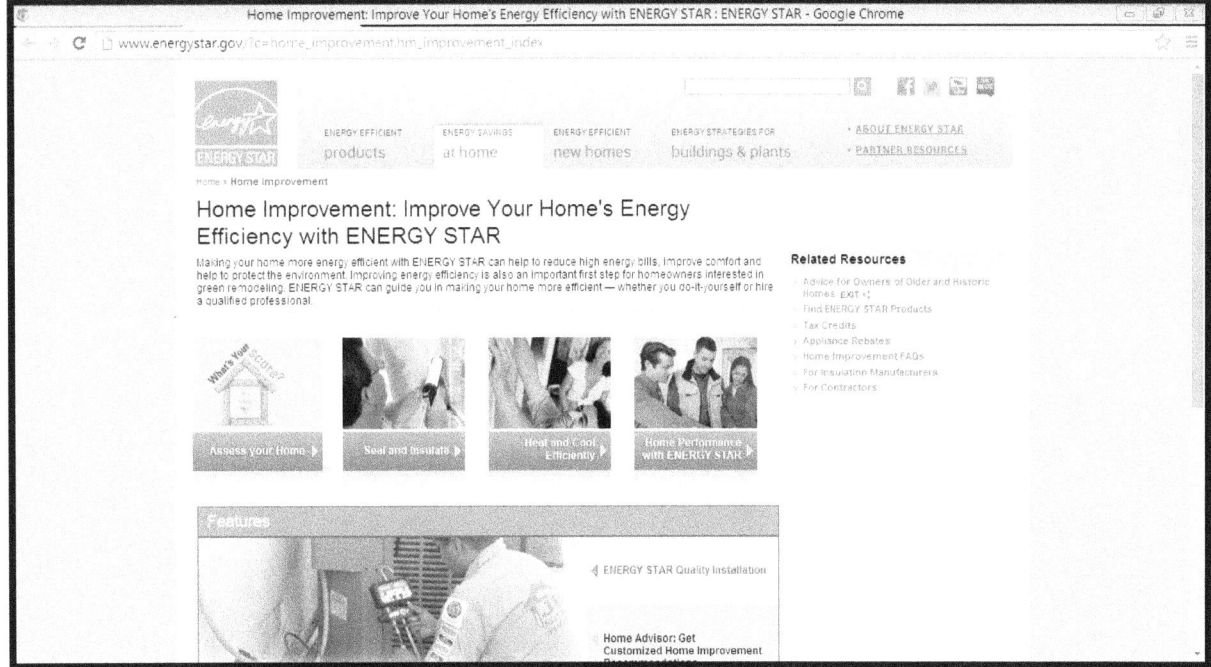

http://www.energystar.gov/?c=home_improvement.hm_improvement_index

CHAPTER 10
BEST IMPROVEMENTS
"The Secrets and Rewards of Going Green"

Try to imagine a house that is total electric. It has electric heat and air conditioning. The hot water heated by electricity and the stove top and oven powered by electricity. The refrigerator and all the appliances are electric. The TV, your computer, and the lights are all-electric. The house is total electric. The meter spins so fast it could double as a ceiling fan. Well it's true. These houses do in fact exist. Mostly because of a promise the electric companies made back in the 70's and 80's then promptly reneged on. They proclaimed electricity is the energy source of the future and the best choice for all. So they offered to anyone that would build or convert their house to total electric a special reduced rate, lower than the standard rate as an incentive. It worked and millions took their offer. I still come across house after house with the tell-tale double meters. The meters are still there but the reduced rate is long gone.

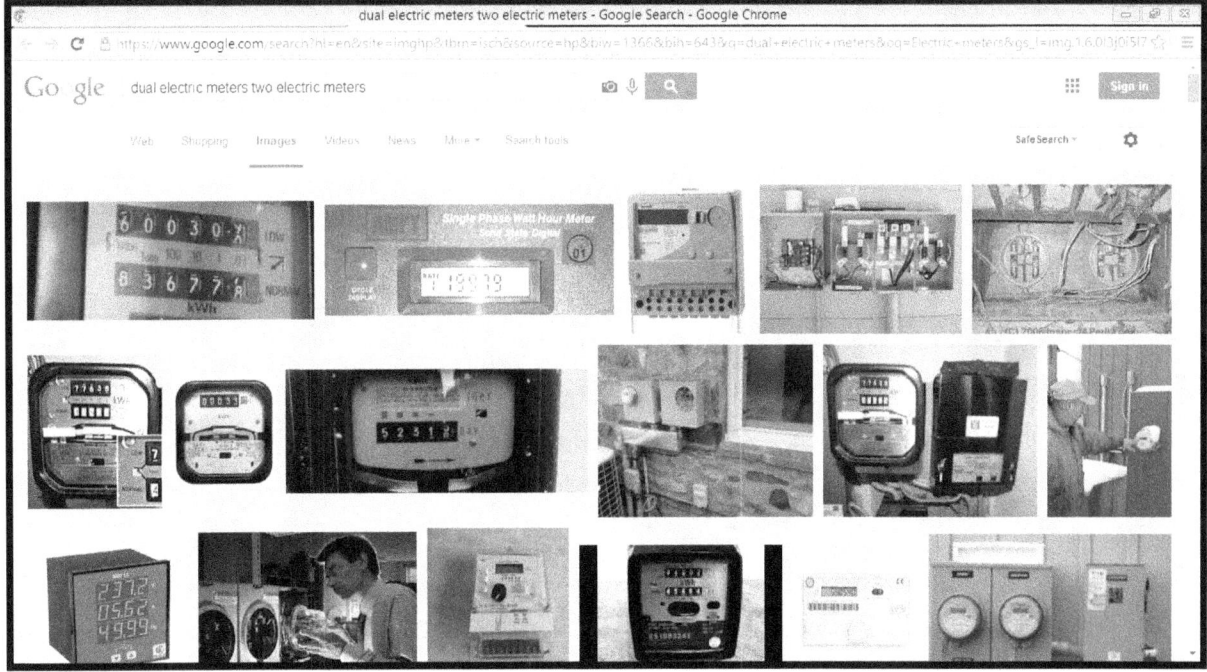

https://www.google.com/search?hl=en&site=imghp&tbm=isch&source=hp&biw=1366&bih=643&q=dual+electric+meters&oq=Electric+meters&gs_l=img.1.6.0l3j0i5l7.2431.8955.0.14055.15.11.0.4.4.0.226.1347.0j10j1.11.0....0...1ac.1.43.img..0.15.1382.PmKkeDYJAFM#hl=en&q=two+electric+meters&tbm=isch

So what is a total electric house like that worth in your mind? Do you envision electric bills that exceed your mortgage payments choking every last dollar out of your housing budget and even tapping into your food budget during those cold winter months and hot summer ones? What does the nostalgic time stamp you clearly see surrounding you do to your perception of the value of the property. Does it lower the value even more? Imagine a three bedroom two bath ranch that is totally dependent on electricity then place a value on it. And pause awhile.

Now what if I told you from now on your electricity is free. That's right. You will never receive a bill from your local electric company, in fact, there will be months when they actually send you money! Your heat, air conditioning, hot water, cooking, lights and all your other appliances will not cost you one dime for electricity! Has your perceived value of the same house we were talking about before changed? Did it increase in value or decline? I would be willing to guess that it increased because the property without an electric bill is obviously worth more. How much more? Start with the amount of an average monthly electric bill for an all-inclusive house and convert that to mortgage terms. Just as an example you could say that $500.00 per month equals $50.000.00. Did your perceived value of this house increase by $50,000.00 or more from the original amount you felt it was worth? This increase in value came about by installing a photovoltaic system.

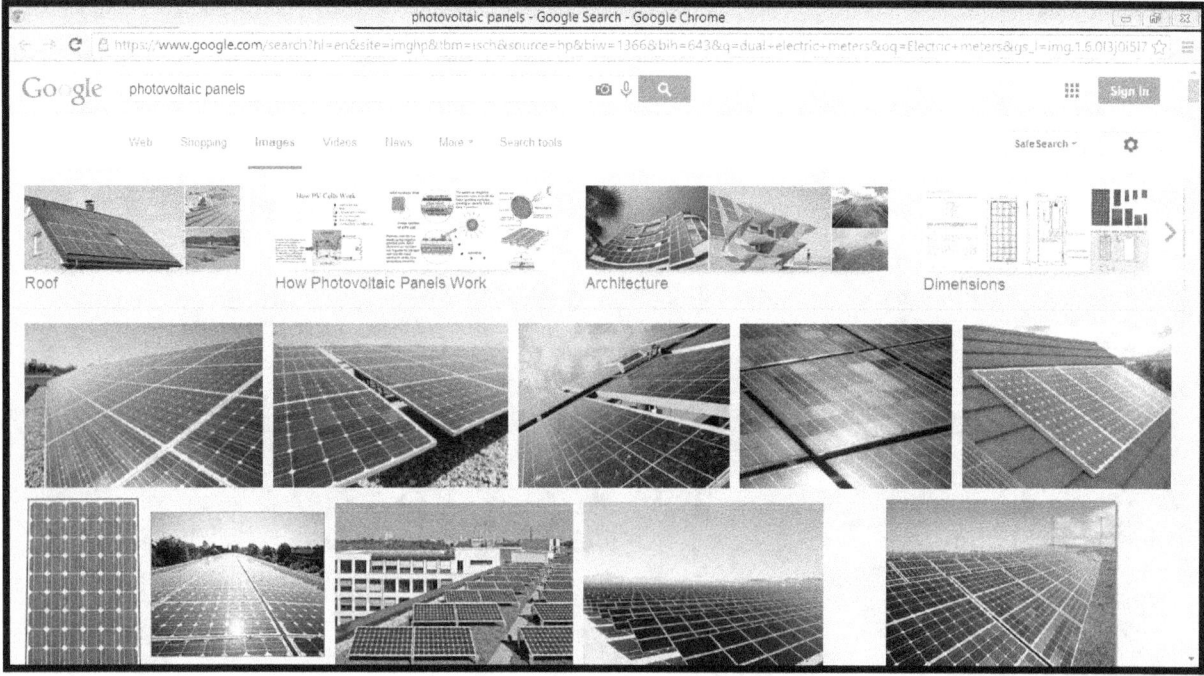

https://www.google.com/search?hl=en&site=imghp&tbm=isch&source=hp&biw=1366&bih=643&q=dual+electric+meters&oq=Electric+meters&gs_l=img.1.6.0l3j0i5l7.2431.8955.0.14055.15.11.0.4.4.0.226.1347.0j10j1.11.0....0...1ac.1.43.img..0.15.1382.PmKkeDYJAFM#hl=en&q=photovoltaic+panels&tbm=isch

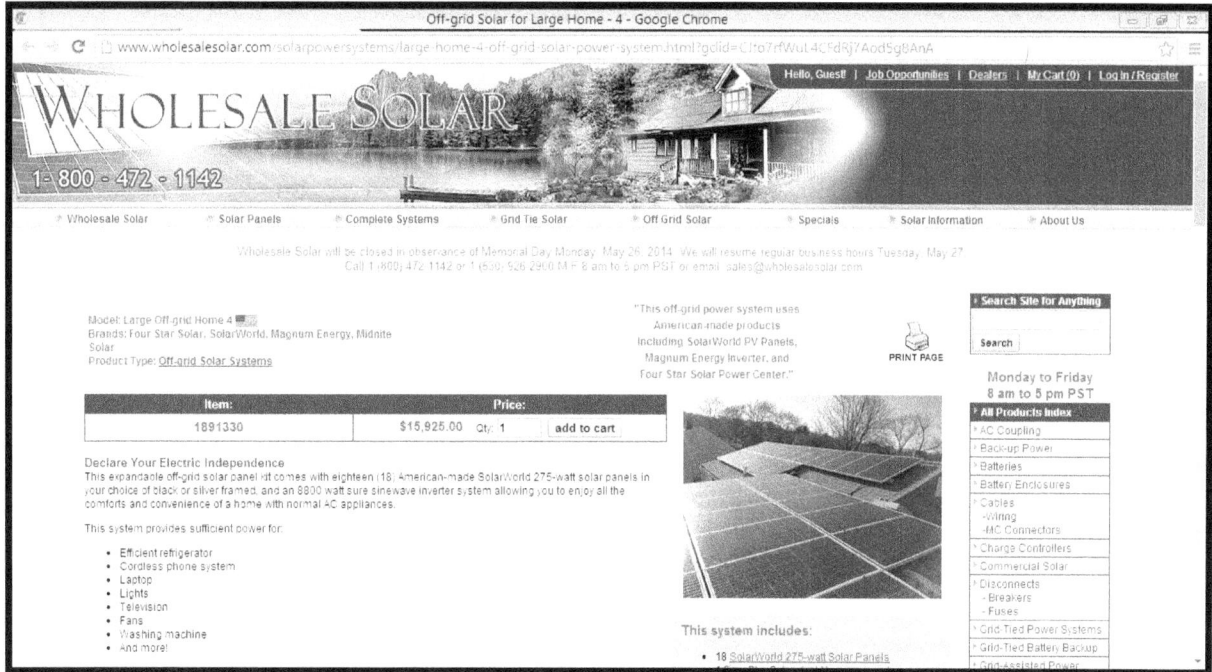

http://www.wholesalesolar.com/solarpowersystems/large-home-4-off-grid-solar-power-system.html?gclid=CJfo7rfWuL4CFdRj7Aod5g8AnA

Powered by the sun it's just one of the hundreds of green technologies that are available today. Technologies that reduce our energy consumption and produce energy itself without the use of fossil fuel. The secret is out, it's a magic way to increase the value of your property, now it's up to you to reap the rewards.

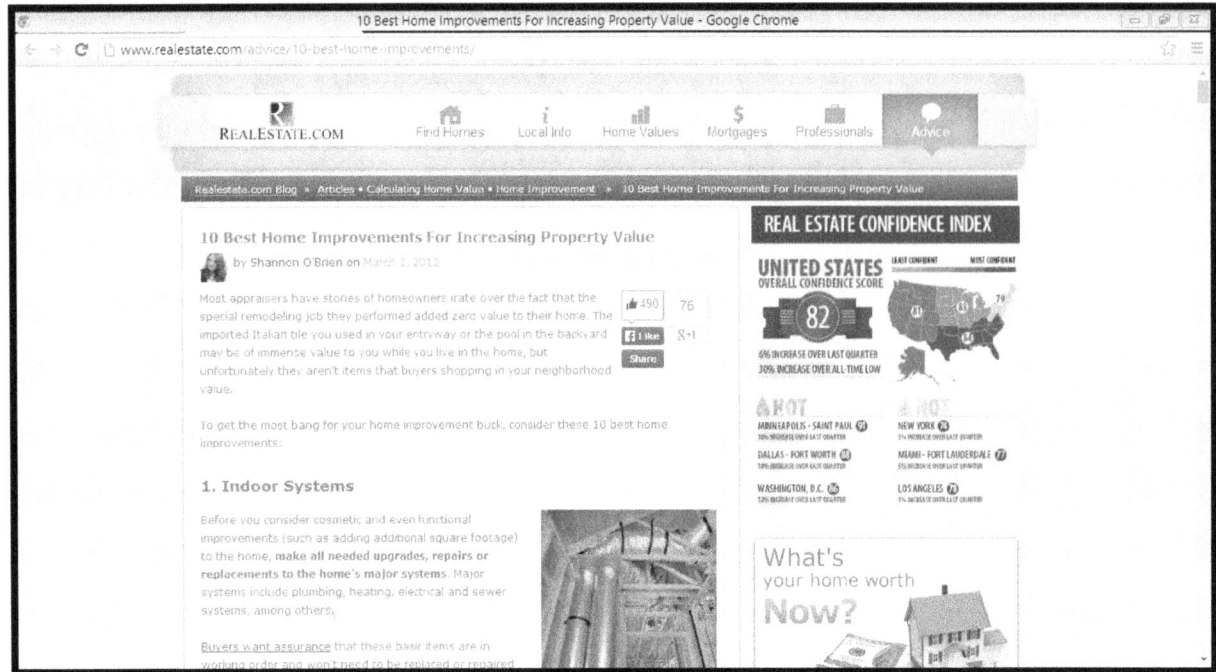

http://www.realestate.com/advice/10-best-home-improvements/

CHAPTER 11

COMPONENTS OF A HOUSE
"Shop Talk"

The National Association of Home Builders estimates there are over 3,000 components used in constructing a house. I have put together the following list to single out and describe some of the most common structural components of a home. I have broken down those components into seven categories. They are the roof, the walls, the floors and ceilings, the windows and doors, the foundation and basement, and the stairs.

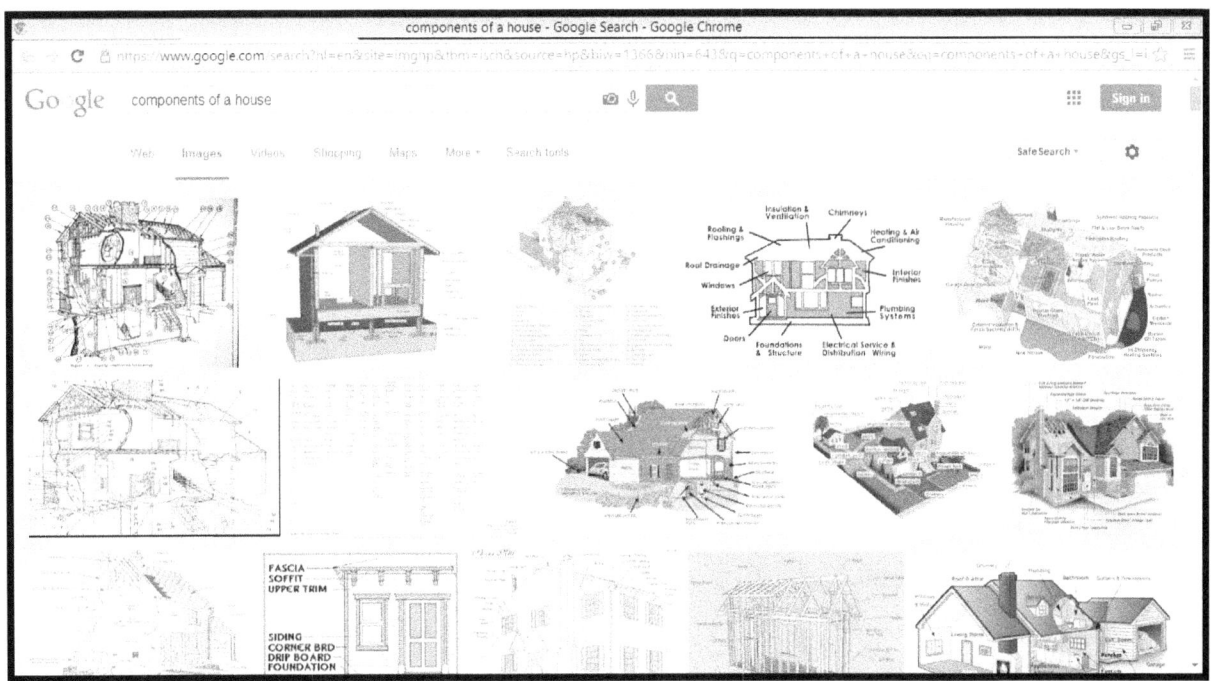

https://www.google.com/search?hl=en&site=imghp&tbm=isch&source=hp&biw=1366&bih=643&q=components+of+a+house&oq=components+of+a+house&gs_l=img.12..0j0i5j0i24l6.2600.11545.0.14571.21.15.0.6.6.0.137.1710.0j15.15.0....0...1ac.1.43.img..0.21.1762.EaavKtBnhK0

The Roof

Ridge - The top edge of the roof where two adjoining roof surfaces meet.

Ridge Board - Board under the ridge used to support rafters.

Rafters - Structural members used to frame and support a roof.

Collar Beam - (Sometimes referred to as a Rafter Tie) Horizontal wooden tie strung between rafters on opposite sides of the roof to prevent rafters from spreading.

Roof Sheathing - Structural covering of boards or plywood placed over roof rafters to give a structural base for the finish roof.

Roofing - The asphalt, fiberglass, wood shingle, tile, slate or metal covering that provides protection against the weather.

Gutter - Trough attached to the eave line of the roof for gathering and carrying water away from the structure.

Downspout - A vertical pipe used to carry water from the gutter to ground level.

Gable - The triangular end of a building where two sloping roofs meet.

Gable Vent - A metal or wooden insert with slanted openings arranged to allow entry of ventilation air but keep out rain.

Soffit Vent - A metal or wooden insert with openings arranged to allow entry of ventilation air on the underside of the rafter rail.

The Walls

Studs - The vertical framing members supporting the walls of the house.

Sill - A horizontal wooden member that rests on the foundation wall supporting the house framing and structure.

Corner Post - Vertical wooden member at the corner of the structure designed to support inner and outer covering materials.

Corner Bracing - Diagonal braces placed at the corners of a frame structure to strengthen the walls and keep the frame square.

Plate - Flat horizontal framing member connected to the top and the bottom of the studs to keep them square, rigid and evenly spaced.

Sheathing - Structural covering boards or plywood placed over exterior wall studs.

Building Paper - A heavy waterproof paper placed on the exterior side of the wall sheathing to prevent the passage of air and water into the home.

Clapboard - Wedge shaped boards with a thick lower butt and a thin upper edge overlapped to give an exterior covering which will shed water.

Floors and Ceilings

Girder - A main support beam in the floor framing system.

Joist - A horizontal structural member that supports floors and ceilings.

Bridging - Framing members placed between joists to brace them and to prevent the joists from twisting or deflecting.

Sub-floor - Rough boards or plywood sheets laid over the joists providing a base for the finish floor.

Finish Flooring - Visible floor covering often vinyl, carpet or tongue and grooved hardwood strips.

Windows and Doors

Window Sash - The inner frame or movable part of the window that holds the glass.

Header - (Also called a Lintel) A structural beam across the top of the window or door opening supporting the weight of the wall above the opening.

Casing - The decorative strips surrounding and finishing the interior and exterior sides of the window or door opening.

Foundation and Basement

Finish Grade Line - The slope of the ground away from the foundation.

Footing - An enlargement at the base of the foundation wall that spreads and transmits the weight of the house to the ground.

Footing Drain Tile - A pipe with small perforated holes along its length to collect and move ground water away from the foundation.

Stairs

Tread - The step or horizontal board of a stair.

Riser - The vertical board in a stairway connecting two treads.

Stringer - The sloping notched board that supports the stair treads and risers.

Newel - The post supporting the handrail at the top and the bottom of the stairs.

Balusters - Thin columns or spindles supporting the stair railing.

So now when a carpenter tells you that someone has removed the collar ties to make that extra bedroom in the attic and that you will have to open up the wall to install a new header for that larger window you want you will have a little more insight into what they are trying to tell you. As for the other 2,500 or so components not mentioned here, remember, if it was easy, everyone would be doing it!

PART THREE

PERSONAL FINANCIAL STATEMENT

MORTGAGE LOAN APPLICATION

CHART OF ACCOUNTS

RESIDENTIAL APPRAISAL CRITERIA

PURCHASE AND SALE AGREEMENT

HOME INSPECTION FORM

SPECIFICATIONS AND ESTIMATE

LISTING AGREEMENT

SCHEDULE C

SCHEDULE E

SCHEDULE E

WEB SITE LINKS

PERSONAL FINANCIAL STATEMENT

http://www.sba.gov/sites/default/files/tools_sbf_finasst413 0.pdf

Address			
Date Purchased			
Original Cost			
Present Market Value			
Name & Address of Mortgage Holder			
Mortgage Account Number			
Mortgage Balance			
Amount of Payment per Month/Year			
Status of Mortgage			

Section 5. Other Personal Property and Other Assets. (Describe, and if any is pledged as security, state name and address of lien holder, amount of lien, terms of payment and if delinquent, describe delinquency)

Section 6.   Unpaid Taxes.   (Describe in detail, as to type, to whom payable, when due, amount, and to what property, if any, a tax lien attaches.)

Section 7.   Other Liabilities.   (Describe in detail.)

Section 8.   Life Insurance Held.   (Give face amount and cash surrender value of policies - name of insurance company and beneficiaries)

I authorize SBA/Lender to make inquiries as necessary to verify the accuracy of the statements made and to determine my creditworthiness. I certify the above and the statements contained in the attachments are true and accurate as of the stated date(s). These statements are made for the purpose of either obtaining a loan or guaranteeing a loan. I understand FALSE statements may result in forfeiture of benefits and possible prosecution by the U.S. Attorney General (Reference 18 U.S.C. 1001).

Signature: Date: Social Security Number.

RESIDENTIAL MORTGAGE APPLICATION

http://www.freddiemac.com/uniform/unifurla.html

Uniform Residential Loan Application

This application is designed to be completed by the applicant(s) with the Lender's assistance. Applicants should complete this form as "Borrower" or "Co-Borrower," as applicable. Co-Borrower information must also be provided (and the appropriate box checked) when ☐ the income or assets of a person other than the Borrower (including the Borrower's spouse) will be used as a basis for loan qualification or ☐ the income or assets of the Borrower's spouse or other person who has community property or similar rights pursuant to applicable state law will not be used as a basis for loan qualification, but his or her liabilities must be considered because the spouse or other person who has community property or similar rights and the Borrower resides in a community property state, the security property is located in a community property state, or the Borrower is relying on other property located in a community property state as a basis for repayment of the loan.

If this is an application for joint credit, Borrower and Co-Borrower each agree that we intend to apply for joint credit (sign below):

Borrower _____   Co-Borrower _____

I. TYPE OF MORTGAGE AND TERMS OF LOAN			
Mortgage Applied for:	☐ VA ☐ USDA/Rural Housing Service ☐ FHA ☐ Conventional ☐ Other (explain):	Agency Case Number	Lender Case Number
Amount $	Interest Rate %	No. of Months	Amortization Type: ☐ Fixed Rate ☐ Other (explain) ☐ GPM ☐ ARM (type):

II. PROPERTY INFORMATION AND PURPOSE OF LOAN	
Subject Property Address (street, city, state & ZIP)	No. of Units
Legal Description of Subject Property (attach description if necessary)	Year Built
Purpose of Loan ☐ Purchase ☐ Refinance ☐ Construction ☐ Construction-Permanent ☐ Other (explain):	Property will be: ☐ Primary Residence ☐ Secondary Residence ☐ Investment

Complete this line if construction or construction-permanent loan.

Complete this line if construction or construction-permanent loan.

Year Lot Acquired	Original Cost	Amount Existing Liens	(a) Present Value of Lot	(b) Cost of Improvements	Total (a + b)
	$	$	$	$	$

Complete this line if this is a refinance loan.

Year Acquired	Original Cost	Amount Existing Liens	Purpose of Refinance	Describe Improvements	☐ made ☐ to be made
	$	$			

Title will be held in what Name(s)	Manner in which Title will be held	Estate will be held in: ☐ Fee Simple ☐ Leasehold (show expiration date)

Source of Down Payment, Settlement Charges, and/or Subordinate Financing (explain)

Uniform Residential Loan Application   Page 1 of 11
Freddie Mac Form 65   7/05 (rev.6/09)   Fannie Mae Form 1003   7/05 (rev.6/09)

Borrower	III. BORROWER INFORMATION		Co-Borrower	
Borrower's Name (include Jr. or Sr. if applicable)			Co-Borrower's Name (include Jr. or Sr. if applicable)	

Social Security Number	Home Phone (incl. Area code)	DOB (mm/dd/yyyy)	Yrs. School	Social Security Number	Home Phone (incl. Area code)	DOB (mm/dd/yyyy)	Yrs. School
			Dependents				Dependents

☐ Married ☐ Separated ☐ Unmarried (include single, divorced, widowed)	Dependents (not listed by Co-Borrower) no. ages	☐ Married ☐ Separated ☐ Unmarried (include single, divorced, widowed)	Dependents (not listed by Borrower) no. ages
Present Address ☐ Own ☐ Rent __No. Yrs. (street, city, state, ZIP)		Present Address ☐ Own ☐ Rent __No. Yrs. (street, city, state, ZIP)	
Mailing Address, if different from Present Address		Mailing Address, if different from Present Address	

If residing at present address for less than two years, complete the following:

Former Address ☐ Own ☐ Rent __No. Yrs. (street, city, state, ZIP)		Former Address ☐ Own ☐ Rent __No. Yrs. (street, city, state, ZIP)	

Borrower		IV. EMPLOYMENT INFORMATION	Co-Borrower	
Name & Address of Employer	☐ Self Employed	Yrs. on this job	Name & Address of Employer ☐ Self Employed	Yrs. on this job
		Yrs. employed in this line of work/profession		Yrs. employed in this line of work/profession
Position/Title/Type of Business		Business Phone (incl. area code)	Position/Title/Type of Business	Business Phone (incl. area code)

If employed in current position for less than two years or if currently employed in more than one position, complete the following:

Name & Address of Employer	☐ Self Employed	Dates (from - to)	Name & Address of Employer ☐ Self Employed	Dates (from - to)
		Monthly Income $		Monthly Income $
Position/Title/Type of Business		Business Phone	Position/Title/Type of Business	Business Phone

---

	$		$
Position/Title/Type of Business	Business Phone (incl. area code)	Position/Title/Type of Business	Business Phone (incl. area code)
Name & Address of Employer ☐ Self Employed	Dates (from - to)	Name & Address of Employer ☐ Self Employed	Dates (from - to)

Uniform Residential Loan Application
Freddie Mac Form 65   7/05 (rev.3/09)

Page 1 of 11

Fannie Mae Form 1003   7/05 (rev.6/09)

	Monthly Income		Monthly Income
	$		$
Position/Title/Type of Business	Business Phone (incl. area code)	Position/Title/Type of Business	Business Phone (incl. area code)

V. MONTHLY INCOME AND COMBINED HOUSING EXPENSE INFORMATION

Gross Monthly Income	Borrower	Co-Borrower	Total	Combined Monthly Housing Expense	Present	Proposed
Base Empl. Income*	$	$	$	Rent	$	
Overtime				First Mortgage (P&I)		$
Bonuses				Other Financing (P&I)		
Commissions				Hazard Insurance		
Dividends/ Interest				Real Estate Taxes		
Net Rental Income				Mortgage Insurance		
Other (before completing, see the notice in "describe other income," below)				Homeowner Assn Dues		
				Other:		
Total	$	$	$	Total	$	$

* Self Employed Borrower(s) may be required to provide additional documentation such as tax returns and financial statements.

Describe Other Income	*Notice:* Alimony, child support, or separate maintenance income need not be revealed if the Borrower (B) or Co-Borrower (C) does not choose to have it considered for repaying this loan.

B/C		Monthly Amount
		$

VI. ASSETS AND LIABILITIES

This Statement and any applicable supporting schedules may be completed jointly by both married and unmarried Co-Borrowers if their assets and liabilities are sufficiently joined so that the Statement can be meaningfully and fairly presented on a combined basis; otherwise, separate Statements and Schedules are required. If the Co-Borrower section was completed about a non-applicant spouse or other person, this Statement and supporting schedules

---

ASSETS Description	Cash or Market Value	Liabilities and Pledged Assets. List the creditor's name, address, and account number for all outstanding debts, including automobile loans, revolving charge accounts, real estate loans, alimony, child support, stock pledges, etc. Use continuation sheet, if necessary. Indicate by (*) those liabilities, which will be satisfied upon sale of real estate owned or upon refinancing of the subject property.		
Cash deposit toward purchase held by:	$	LIABILITIES	Monthly Payment & Months Left to Pay	Unpaid Balance
List checking and savings accounts below		Name and address of Company	$ Payment/Months	$

Uniform Residential Loan Application
Freddie Mac Form 65   7/05 (rev 6/09)

Page 4 of 11

Fannie Mae Form 1003   7/05 (rev 6/09)

Name and address of Bank, S&L, or Credit Union				
		Acct. no.		
Acct. no.	$	Name and address of Company	$ Payment/Months	$

VI. ASSETS AND LIABILITIES (cont'd)				
Name and address of Bank, S&L, or Credit Union		Acct. no.		
Acct. no.	$	Name and address of Company	$ Payment/Months	$
Name and address of Bank, S&L, or Credit Union				
		Acct. no.		
Acct. no.	$	Name and address of Company	$ Payment/Months	$
Name and address of Bank, S&L, or Credit Union				
		Acct. no.		
Acct. no.	$	Name and address of Company	$ Payment/Months	$
Stocks & Bonds (Company name/ number & description)	$			
		Acct. no.		
Life insurance net cash value	$	Name and address of Company	$ Payment/Months	$
Face amount: $				
Subtotal Liquid Assets	$	Acct. no.		
Real estate owned (enter market value from schedule of real estate owned)	$	Alimony/Child Support/Separate Maintenance Payments Owned to:	$	$
Vested interest in retirement fund	$			
Net worth of business(es) owned (attach financial statement)	$	Job-Related Expense (child care, union dues, etc.)	$	

(attach financial statement)				
Automobiles owned (make and year)	$			
Other Assets (itemize)	$			
		Total Monthly Payments	$	
Total Assets a.	$	Net Worth (a minus b) $	Total Liabilities b.	$

Uniform Residential Loan Application
Freddie Mac Form 65   7/06 (rev 6 09)   Page 6 of 11   Fannie Mae Form 1003   7/06 (rev 6 09)

Schedule of Real Estate Owned (If additional properties are owned, use continuation sheet.)

Property Address (enter S if sold, PS if pending sale or R if rental being held for income)		Type of Property	Present Market Value	Amount of Mortgages & Liens	Gross Rental Income	Mortgage Payments	Insurance, Maintenance, Taxes & Misc.	Net Rental Income
			$	$	$	$	$	$

| | | | g. | Are you obligated to pay alimony, child support, or separate maintenance? | ☐ | ☐ | ☐ | ☐ |
| i. | Total costs (add items a through h) | | | | | | | |

Uniform Residential Loan Application
Freddie Mac Form 65 7/05 (rev.6/09)   Page 7 of 11   Fannie Mae Form 1003 7/05 (rev.6/09)

| | | | h. | Is any part of the down payment borrowed? | ☐ | ☐ | ☐ | ☐ |
| j. | Subordinate financing | | | | | | | |

VII. DETAILS OF TRANSACTION (cont'd)			VIII. DECLARATIONS (cont'd)					
k.	Borrower's closing costs paid by Seller		i.	Are you a co-maker or endorser on a note?	☐	☐	☐	☐
l.	Other Credits (explain)							
			j.	Are you a U.S. citizen?	☐	☐	☐	☐
			k.	Are you a permanent resident alien?	☐	☐	☐	☐
m.	Loan amount (exclude PMI, MIP, Funding Fee financed)		l.	**Do you intend to occupy the property as your primary residence?** If "Yes," complete question m below.	☐	☐	☐	☐
n.	PMI, MIP, Funding Fee financed		m.	Have you had an ownership interest in a property in the last three years?	☐	☐	☐	☐
o.	Loan amount (add m & n)			(1) What type of property did you own—principal residence (PR), second home (SH), or investment property (IP)?	—	—	—	—
p.	Cash from/to Borrower (subtract j, k, l & o from i)			(2) How did you hold title to the home— by yourself (S), jointly with your spouse or jointly with another person (O)?	—	—	—	—

---

another person (O)?

ACKNOWLEDGMENT AND AGREEMENT

Each of the undersigned specifically represents to Lender and to Lender's actual or potential agents, brokers, processors, attorneys, insurers, servicers, successors and assigns and agrees and acknowledges that: (1) the information provided in this application is true and correct as of the date set forth opposite my signature and that any intentional or negligent misrepresentation of this information contained in this application may result in civil liability, including monetary damages, to any person who may suffer any loss due to reliance upon any misrepresentation that I have made on this application, and/or in criminal penalties including, but not limited to, fine or imprisonment or both under the provisions of Title 18, United States Code, Sec. 1001, et seq.; (2) the loan requested pursuant to this application (the "Loan") will be secured by a mortgage or deed of trust on the property described in this application; (3) the property will not be used for any illegal or prohibited purpose or use; (4) all statements made in this application are made for the purpose of obtaining a residential mortgage loan; (5) the property will be occupied as indicated in this application; (6) the Lender, its servicers, successors or assigns may retain the original and/or an electronic record of this application, whether or not the Loan is approved; (7) the Lender and its agents, brokers, insurers, servicers, successors, and assigns may continuously rely on the information contained in the application, and I am obligated to amend and/or supplement the information provided in this application if any of the material facts that I have represented should change prior to closing of the Loan; (8) in the event that my payments on the Loan become delinquent, the Lender, its servicers, successors or assigns may, in addition to any other rights and remedies that it may have relating to such delinquency, report my name and account information to one or more consumer reporting agencies; (9) ownership of the Loan and/or administration of the Loan account may be transferred with such notice as may be required by law; (10) neither Lender nor its agents, brokers, insurers, servicers, successors or assigns has made any representation or warranty, express or implied, to me regarding the property or the condition or value of the property; and (11) my transmission of this application as an "electronic record" containing my "electronic signature," as those terms are defined in applicable federal and/or state laws (excluding audio and video recordings), or my facsimile transmission of this application containing a facsimile of my signature, shall be as effective, enforceable and valid as if a paper version of this application were delivered containing my original written signature.

Acknowledgement. Each of the undersigned hereby acknowledges that any owner of the Loan, its servicers, successors and assigns, may verify or reverify any information contained in this application or obtain any information or data relating to the Loan, for any legitimate business purpose through any source, including a source named in this

Uniform Residential Loan Application
Freddie Mac Form 65 7/05 (rev.6/09)   Page 8 of 11   Fannie Mae Form 1003 7/05 (rev.6/09)

application or a consumer reporting agency.

Borrower's Signature	Date	Co-Borrower's Signature	Date
X		X	

X. INFORMATION FOR GOVERNMENT MONITORING PURPOSES

The following information is requested by the Federal Government for certain types of loans related to a dwelling in order to monitor the lender's compliance with equal credit opportunity, fair housing and home mortgage disclosure laws. You are not required to furnish this information, but are encouraged to do so. The law provides that a lender may not discriminate either on the basis of this information, or on whether you choose to furnish it. If you furnish the information, please provide both ethnicity and race. For race, you may check more than one designation. If you do not furnish ethnicity, race, or sex, under Federal regulations, this lender is required to note the information on the basis of visual observation and surname if you have made this application in person. If you do not wish to furnish the information, please check the box below. (Lender must review the above material to assure that the disclosures satisfy all requirements to which the lender is subject under applicable state law for the particular type of loan applied for.)

BORROWER	CO-BORROWER
☐ I do not wish to furnish this information	☐ I do not wish to furnish this information
Ethnicity: ☐ Hispanic or Latino ☐ Not Hispanic or Latino	**Ethnicity:** ☐ Hispanic or Latino ☐ Not Hispanic or Latino
Race: ☐ American Indian or Alaska Native ☐ Asian ☐ Black or African American ☐ Native Hawaiian or Other Pacific Islander ☐ White	**Race:** ☐ American Indian or Alaska Native ☐ Asian ☐ Black or African American ☐ Native Hawaiian or Other Pacific Islander ☐ White
Sex: ☐ Female ☐ Male	**Sex:** ☐ Female ☐ Male

To be Completed by Loan Originator

This information was provided:
☐ In a face-to-face interview
☐ In a telephone interview
☐ By the applicant and submitted by fax or mail
☐ By the applicant and submitted via e-mail or the Internet

Loan Originator's Signature		Date

Loan Originator's Name (print or type)	Loan Originator Identifier	Loan Originator's Phone Number (including area code)

Loan Origination Company's Name	Loan Origination Company Identifier	Loan Origination Company's Address

Uniform Residential Loan Application
Freddie Mac Form 65 (rev 6/09)

Page 9 of 11

Fannie Mae Form 1003 7/05 (rev 6/09)

CONTINUATION SHEET/RESIDENTIAL LOAN APPLICATION

Use this continuation sheet if you need more space to complete the Residential Loan Application. Mark **B** for Borrower or **C** for Co-Borrower.	Borrower:	Agency Case Number:
	Co-Borrower:	Lender Case Number:

I/We fully understand that it is a Federal crime punishable by fine or imprisonment, or both, to knowingly make any false statements concerning any of the above facts as applicable under the provisions of Title 18, United States Code, Section 1001, et seq.

Borrower's Signature	Date	Co-Borrower's Signature	Date

Uniform Residential Loan Application   Page 10 of 11   Fannie Mae Form 1003   7/05 (rev 6/09)
Freddie Mac Form 65 7/05 (rev 6/09)

X		X	

CHART OF ACCOUNTS

http://www.simplesolutionsconsulting.com/wp-content/uploads/Sample+Construction+Business+Chart+of+Accounts.pdf

Construction Business
Construction Business Chart of Accounts
December 15, 2017

4:58 PM
12/15/17

Account	Type	Balance Total	Description	Accnt #	Tax Line
1110 · Company Checking Account	Bank	99,761.86		1110	<Unassigned>
1111 · Adjustment Register	Bank	0.00		1111	<Unassigned>
1120 · Company Savings Account	Bank	167,550.00		1120	<Unassigned>
1130 · Payroll Checking Account	Bank	58.06		1130	<Unassigned>
1140 · Petty Cash Account	Bank	131.10		1140	<Unassigned>
1210 · Accounts Receivable	Accounts Receivable	43,680.00		1210	<Unassigned>
1310 · Employee Advances	Other Current Asset	0.00		1310	<Unassigned>
1320 · Retentions Receivable	Other Current Asset	3,350.00		1320	<Unassigned>
1330 · Security Deposit	Other Current Asset	1,200.00		1330	<Unassigned>
1340 · Vendor Deposits	Other Current Asset	0.00		1340	<Unassigned>
1390 · Undeposited Funds	Other Current Asset	0.00		1390	<Unassigned>
1400 · Refundable Workers Comp Deposit	Other Current Asset	0.00		1400	<Unassigned>
1560 · Escrow Deposit	Other Current Asset	0.00		1560	<Unassigned>
1570 · Land Purchase	Other Current Asset	0.00	Land Purchase	1570	<Unassigned>
1571 · Land Interest/Closing Costs	Other Current Asset	0.00		1571	<Unassigned>
1580 · WIP - Land Development	Other Current Asset	0.00		1580	<Unassigned>
1590 · WIP - Construction	Other Current Asset	0.00		1590	<Unassigned>
1510 · Automobiles & Trucks	Fixed Asset	32,952.00		1510	<Unassigned>
1520 · Computer & Office Equipment	Fixed Asset	19,662.00		1520	<Unassigned>
1530 · Machinery & Equipment	Fixed Asset	25,643.00		1530	<Unassigned>
1540 · Accumulated Depreciation	Fixed Asset	-6,600.00		1540	<Unassigned>
2010 · Accounts Payable	Accounts Payable	43,489.84		2010	<Unassigned>
2050 · Mastercard Payable	Credit Card	211.83		2050	<Unassigned>
2060 · Visa Card Payable	Credit Card	0.00		2060	<Unassigned>
2100 · Payroll Liabilities	Other Current Liability	1,942.33		2100	<Unassigned>
2200 · Customer Deposits	Other Current Liability	27,500.00	Customer Deposits	2200	<Unassigned>
2240 · Worker's Comp Payable	Other Current Liability	621.96		2240	<Unassigned>
2300 · Loans Payable	Other Current Liability	0.00		2300	<Unassigned>
2310 · Loan - Dale Olsen	Other Current Liability	0.00		2310	<Unassigned>
2400 · Land Aquisition Loan	Other Current Liability	0.00		2400	<Unassigned>
2405 · Land Development Loan	Other Current Liability	0.00		2405	<Unassigned>
2410 · Construction Loan	Long Term Liability	0.00		2410	<Unassigned>
2460 · Truck Loan	Long Term Liability	13,985.00		2460	<Unassigned>
3000 · Opening Balance Equity	Equity	0.00		3000	<Unassigned>
3100 · Common Stock	Equity	0.00		3100	<Unassigned>
3910 · Retained Earnings	Equity		Retained Earnings	3910	<Unassigned>
4110 · Construction Income	Income		Sales	4110	Schedule C: Gross receipts or sales
4810 · Vendor Refunds	Income			4810	<Unassigned>
4910 · Workers' Comp Dividend	Income			4910	<Unassigned>
5110 · Job Related Costs	Cost of Goods Sold			5110	<Unassigned>
5200 · Job Labor Costs	Cost of Goods Sold			5200	Schedule C: Wages paid
5210 · Job Labor (Gross Wages)	Cost of Goods Sold			5210	Schedule C: Wages paid
5220 · Worker's Compensation Costs	Cost of Goods Sold			5220	Schedule C: Insurance, other than health
5230 · Direct Payroll Taxes	Cost of Goods Sold			5230	Schedule C: Taxes and licenses
5240 · Direct Employee Benefits	Cost of Goods Sold			5240	Schedule C: Employee benefit programs
6020 · Advertising	Expense			6020	<Unassigned>
6040 · Amortization Expense	Expense		Amortization Expense	6040	<Unassigned>
6050 · Bad Debt	Expense			6050	<Unassigned>

4:58 PM

12/15/17

Construction Business
Construction Business Chart of Accounts
December 15, 2017

Account	Type	Balance Total	Description	Acnt. #	Tax Line
6107 · Insurance-Auto	Expense			6107	<Unassigned>
6130 · Cleaning/Janitorial	Expense		Cleaning Expense	6130	Schedule C: Office expenses
6135 · Computer Supplies/Equipment	Expense			6135	<Unassigned>
6140 · Contributions	Expense		Contributions	6140	<Unassigned>
6150 · Depreciation Expense	Expense		Depreciation Expense	6150	<Unassigned>
6160 · Dues and Subscriptions	Expense		Dues and Subscriptions	6160	Schedule C: Other business expenses
6180 · Insurance	Expense		Insurance	6180	Schedule C: Insurance, other than health
6181 · Disability Insurance	Expense		Disability Insurance	6181	Schedule C: Insurance, other than health
6182 · Liability Insurance	Expense		Liability Insurance	6182	Schedule C: Insurance, other than health
6185 · Worker's Comp	Expense		Workman's Compensation	6185	Schedule C: Insurance, other than health
6200 · Interest Expense	Expense		Interest Expense	6200	Schedule C: Interest expense, other
6201 · Finance Charge	Expense		Finance Charge	6201	Schedule C: Interest expense, other
6202 · Loan Interest	Expense		Loan Interest Expense	6202	Schedule C: Interest expense, other
6203 · Credit Card Interest	Expense		Mortgage Interest	6203	Schedule C: Interest expense, mortgage
6230 · Licenses and Permits	Expense		Licenses	6230	Schedule C: Taxes and licenses
6240 · Miscellaneous	Expense		Miscellaneous	6240	Schedule C: Other business expenses
6490 · Office Supplies	Expense			6490	<Unassigned>
6500 · Payroll Expenses (office)	Expense			6500	<Unassigned>
6501 · Payroll (office staff)	Expense			6501	Schedule C: Wages paid
6502 · Payroll tax expense	Expense			6502	Schedule C: Taxes and licenses
6503 · Officer's Labor	Expense			6503	<Unassigned>
6504 · Designer's Wages	Expense			6504	<Unassigned>
6508 · Vac/Holiday/Sick Pay	Expense			6508	<Unassigned>
6509 · Employee Bonus	Expense			6509	<Unassigned>
6510 · Employee Benefits	Expense			6510	<Unassigned>
6570 · Professional Fees	Expense		Professional Fees	6570	Schedule C: Legal and professional fees
6571 · Accounting	Expense		Accounting Fees	6571	Schedule C: Legal and professional fees
6572 · Legal Fees	Expense		Legal Fees	6572	Schedule C: Legal and professional fees
6573 · Computer Consultants	Expense			6573	<Unassigned>
6610 · Postage and Delivery	Expense		Postage and Delivery	6610	Schedule C: Other business expenses
6650 · Rent	Expense		Rent	6650	Schedule C: Rent/lease other bus. prop.
6670 · Repairs	Expense		Repairs and Maintenance	6670	Schedule C: Repairs and maintenance
6671 · Building Repairs	Expense		Building Repairs	6671	Schedule C: Repairs and maintenance
6672 · Computer Repairs	Expense		Computer Repairs	6672	Schedule C: Repairs and maintenance
6673 · Equipment Repairs	Expense		Equipment Repairs	6673	Schedule C: Repairs and maintenance
6800 · Telephone	Expense		Telephone	6800	Schedule C: Utilities
6820 · Taxes	Expense		Taxes	6820	Schedule C: Taxes and licenses
6830 · Training and Conferences	Expense			6830	<Unassigned>
6900 · Meals and Entertainment	Expense		Meals and Entertainment	6900	Schedule C: Meals and entertainment
6910 · Travel	Expense		Travel	6910	Schedule C: Travel
6920 · Tools & Machinery (under $500)	Expense		Tools and Machinery	6920	Schedule C: Other business expenses
6970 · Utilities	Expense		Utilities	6970	Schedule C: Utilities
7010 · Interest Income	Other Income		Interest Income	7010	Schedule C: Other business income
7030 · Other Income	Other Income		Other Income	7030	Schedule C: Other business income
7800 · Trade Discount	Other Income			7800	<Unassigned>
8010 · Other Expenses	Other Expense		Other Expenses	8010	Schedule C: Other business expenses
2 · Purchase Orders	Non-Posting			2	<Unassigned>
4 · Estimates	Non-Posting			4	<Unassigned>

RESIDENTIAL APPRAISAL FORM

https://www.fanniemae.com/content/guide_form/1004.pdf

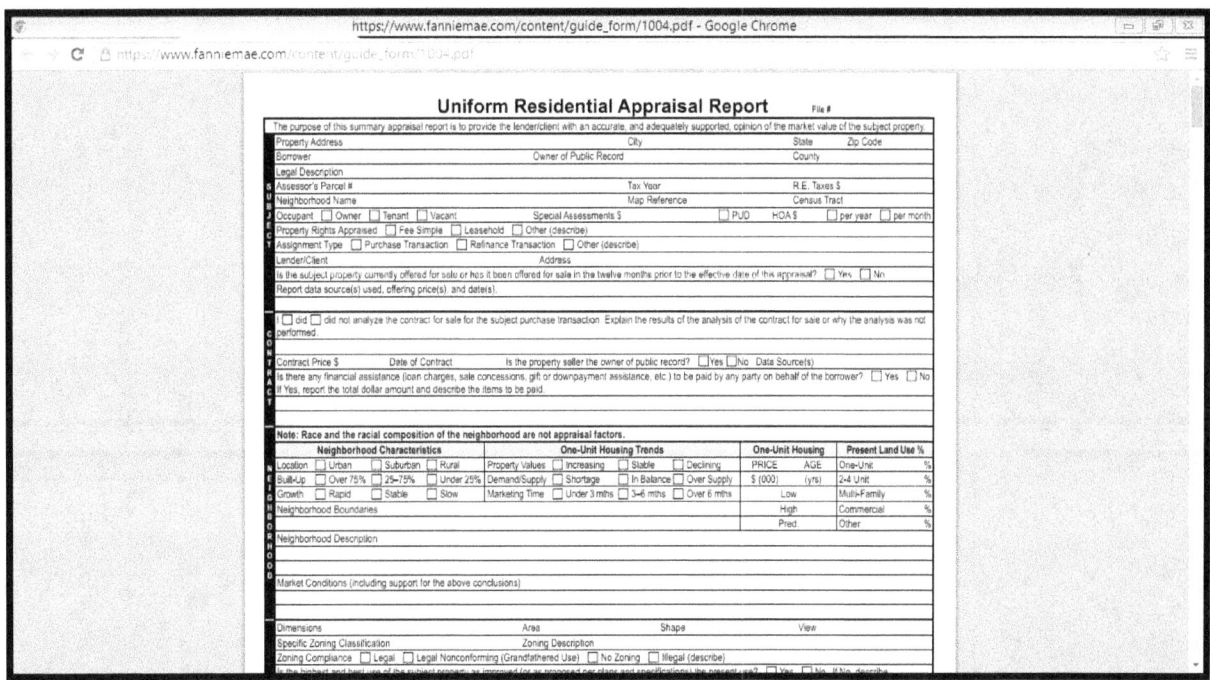

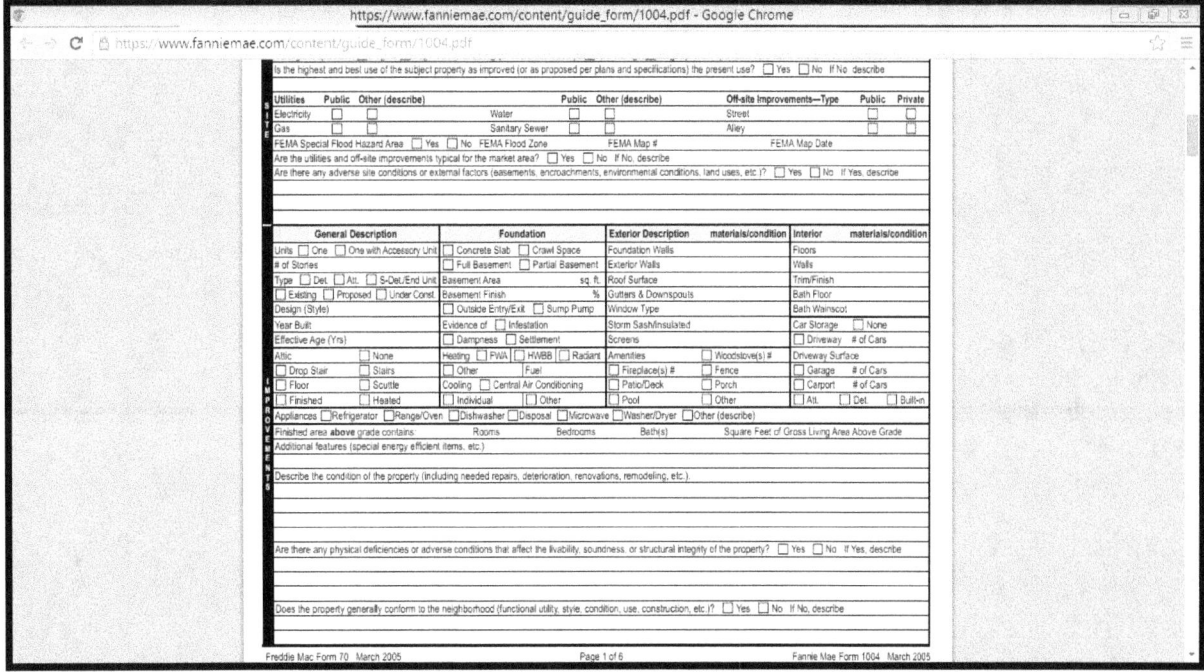

Uniform Residential Appraisal Report

File #

There are _____ comparable properties currently offered for sale in the subject neighborhood ranging in price from $ _____ to $ _____

There are _____ comparable sales in the subject neighborhood within the past twelve months ranging in sale price from $ _____ to $ _____

FEATURE	SUBJECT	COMPARABLE SALE # 1		COMPARABLE SALE # 2		COMPARABLE SALE # 3	
Address							
Proximity to Subject							
Sale Price	$		$		$		$
Sale Price/Gross Liv. Area	$ sq. ft.	$ sq. ft.		$ sq. ft.		$ sq. ft.	
Data Source(s)							
Verification Source(s)							
VALUE ADJUSTMENTS	DESCRIPTION	DESCRIPTION	+(-) $ Adjustment	DESCRIPTION	+(-) $ Adjustment	DESCRIPTION	+(-) $ Adjustment
Sale or Financing Concessions							
Date of Sale/Time							
Location							
Leasehold/Fee Simple							
Site							
View							
Design (Style)							
Quality of Construction							
Actual Age							
Condition							
Above Grade	Total Bdrms. Baths	Total Bdrms. Baths		Total Bdrms. Baths		Total Bdrms. Baths	
Room Count							
Gross Living Area	sq. ft.	sq. ft.		sq. ft.		sq. ft.	
Basement & Finished Rooms Below Grade							
Functional Utility							
Heating/Cooling							
Energy Efficient Items							
Garage/Carport							
Porch/Patio/Deck							
Net Adjustment (Total)		☐ + ☐ -	$	☐ + ☐ -	$	☐ + ☐ -	$
Adjusted Sale Price of Comparables		Net Adj. % Gross Adj. %	$	Net Adj. % Gross Adj. %	$	Net Adj. % Gross Adj. %	$

☐ I did ☐ did not research the sale or transfer history of the subject property and comparable sales. If not, explain

---

My research ☐ did ☐ did not reveal any prior sales or transfers of the subject property for the three years prior to the effective date of this appraisal.

Data source(s) _____

My research ☐ did ☐ did not reveal any prior sales or transfers of the comparable sales for the year prior to the date of sale of the comparable sale.

Data source(s) _____

Report the results of the research and analysis of the prior sale or transfer history of the subject property and comparable sales (report additional prior sales on page 3).

ITEM	SUBJECT	COMPARABLE SALE # 1	COMPARABLE SALE # 2	COMPARABLE SALE # 3
Date of Prior Sale/Transfer				
Price of Prior Sale/Transfer				
Data Source(s)				
Effective Date of Data Source(s)				

Analysis of prior sale or transfer history of the subject property and comparable sales

Summary of Sales Comparison Approach

Indicated Value by Sales Comparison Approach $ _____

Indicated Value by: Sales Comparison Approach $ _____   Cost Approach (if developed) $ _____   Income Approach (if developed) $ _____

This appraisal is made ☐ "as is", ☐ subject to completion per plans and specifications on the basis of a hypothetical condition that the improvements have been completed, ☐ subject to the following repairs or alterations on the basis of a hypothetical condition that the repairs or alterations have been completed, or ☐ subject to the following required inspection based on the extraordinary assumption that the condition or deficiency does not require alteration or repair:

Based on a complete visual inspection of the interior and exterior areas of the subject property, defined scope of work, statement of assumptions and limiting conditions, and appraiser's certification, my (our) opinion of the market value, as defined, of the real property that is the subject of this report is $ _____ , as of _____ , which is the date of inspection and the effective date of this appraisal.

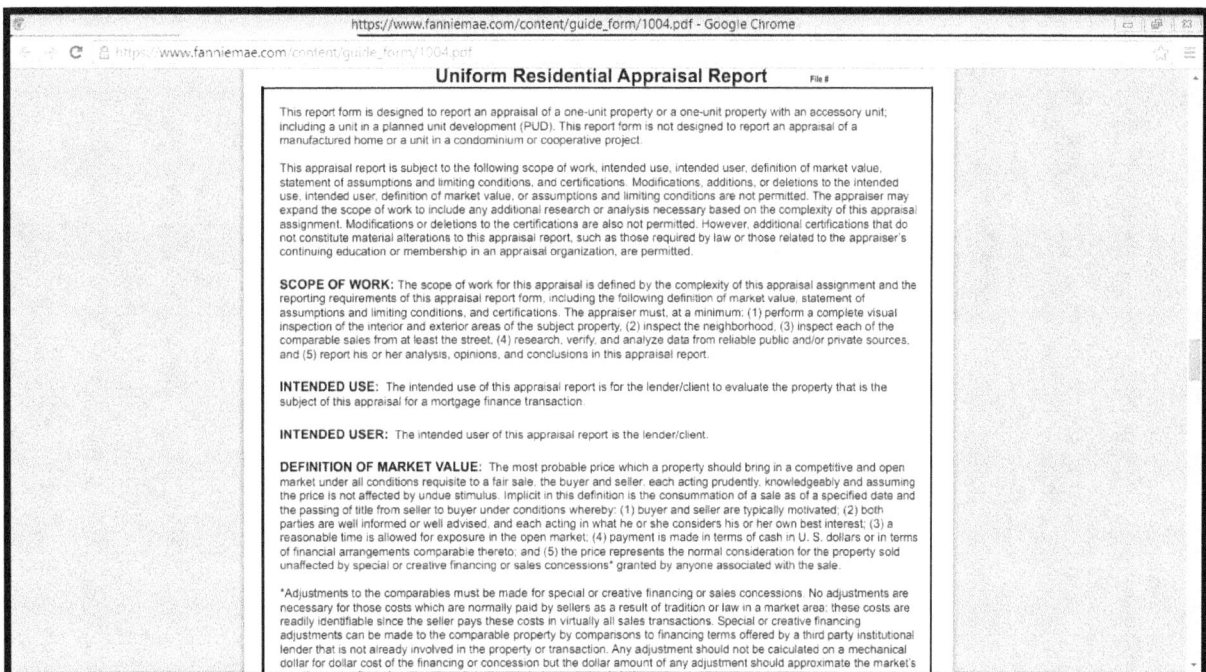

COST APPROACH TO VALUE (not required by Fannie Mae)

Provide adequate information for the lender/client to replicate the below cost figures and calculations.

Support for the opinion of site value (summary of comparable land sales or other methods for estimating site value)

ESTIMATED ☐ REPRODUCTION OR ☐ REPLACEMENT COST NEW	OPINION OF SITE VALUE .... = $	
Source of cost data	Dwelling Sq. Ft. @ $ .... = $	
Quality rating from cost service Effective date of cost data	Sq. Ft. @ $ .... = $	
Comments on Cost Approach (gross living area calculations, depreciation, etc.)	Garage/Carport Sq. Ft. @ $ .... = $	
	Total Estimate of Cost-New .... = $	
	Less Physical Functional External	
	Depreciation = $( )	
	Depreciated Cost of Improvements .... = $	
	"As-is" Value of Site Improvements .... = $	
Estimated Remaining Economic Life (HUD and VA only) Years	Indicated Value By Cost Approach .... = $	

INCOME APPROACH TO VALUE (not required by Fannie Mae)

Estimated Monthly Market Rent $ X Gross Rent Multiplier   = $ Indicated Value by Income Approach

Summary of Income Approach (including support for market rent and GRM)

PROJECT INFORMATION FOR PUDs (if applicable)

Is the developer/builder in control of the Homeowners' Association (HOA)? ☐ Yes ☐ No Unit type(s) ☐ Detached ☐ Attached

Provide the following information for PUDs ONLY if the developer/builder is in control of the HOA and the subject property is an attached dwelling unit.

Legal name of project

Total number of phases	Total number of units	Total number of units sold
Total number of units rented	Total number of units for sale	Data source(s)

Was the project created by the conversion of an existing building(s) into a PUD? ☐ Yes ☐ No If Yes, date of conversion

Does the project contain any multi-dwelling units? ☐ Yes ☐ No Data source(s)

Are the units, common elements, and recreation facilities complete? ☐ Yes ☐ No If No, describe the status of completion.

Are the common elements leased to or by the Homeowners' Association? ☐ Yes ☐ No If Yes, describe the rental terms and options.

Describe common elements and recreational facilities.

Freddie Mac Form 70 March 2005   Page 3 of 6   Fannie Mae Form 1004 March 2005

Uniform Residential Appraisal Report   File

This report form is designed to report an appraisal of a one-unit property or a one-unit property with an accessory unit; including a unit in a planned unit development (PUD). This report form is not designed to report an appraisal of a manufactured home or a unit in a condominium or cooperative project.

This appraisal report is subject to the following scope of work, intended use, intended user, definition of market value, statement of assumptions and limiting conditions, and certifications. Modifications, additions, or deletions to the intended use, intended user, definition of market value, or assumptions and limiting conditions are not permitted. The appraiser may expand the scope of work to include any additional research or analysis necessary based on the complexity of this appraisal assignment. Modifications or deletions to the certifications are also not permitted. However, additional certifications that do not constitute material alterations to this appraisal report, such as those required by law or those related to the appraiser's continuing education or membership in an appraisal organization, are permitted.

SCOPE OF WORK: The scope of work for this appraisal is defined by the complexity of this appraisal assignment and the reporting requirements of this appraisal report form, including the following definition of market value, statement of assumptions and limiting conditions, and certifications. The appraiser must, at a minimum: (1) perform a complete visual inspection of the interior and exterior areas of the subject property, (2) inspect the neighborhood, (3) inspect each of the comparable sales from at least the street, (4) research, verify, and analyze data from reliable public and/or private sources, and (5) report his or her analysis, opinions, and conclusions in this appraisal report.

INTENDED USE: The intended use of this appraisal report is for the lender/client to evaluate the property that is the subject of this appraisal for a mortgage finance transaction.

INTENDED USER: The intended user of this appraisal report is the lender/client.

DEFINITION OF MARKET VALUE: The most probable price which a property should bring in a competitive and open market under all conditions requisite to a fair sale, the buyer and seller, each acting prudently, knowledgeably and assuming the price is not affected by undue stimulus. Implicit in this definition is the consummation of a sale as of a specified date and the passing of title from seller to buyer under conditions whereby: (1) buyer and seller are typically motivated; (2) both parties are well informed or well advised, and each acting in what he or she considers his or her own best interest; (3) a reasonable time is allowed for exposure in the open market; (4) payment is made in terms of cash in U. S. dollars or in terms of financial arrangements comparable thereto; and (5) the price represents the normal consideration for the property sold unaffected by special or creative financing or sales concessions* granted by anyone associated with the sale.

*Adjustments to the comparables must be made for special or creative financing or sales concessions. No adjustments are necessary for those costs which are normally paid by sellers as a result of tradition or law in a market area; these costs are readily identifiable since the seller pays these costs in virtually all sales transactions. Special or creative financing adjustments can be made to the comparable property by comparisons to financing terms offered by a third party institutional lender that is not already involved in the property or transaction. Any adjustment should not be calculated on a mechanical dollar for dollar cost of the financing or concession but the dollar amount of any adjustment should approximate the market's

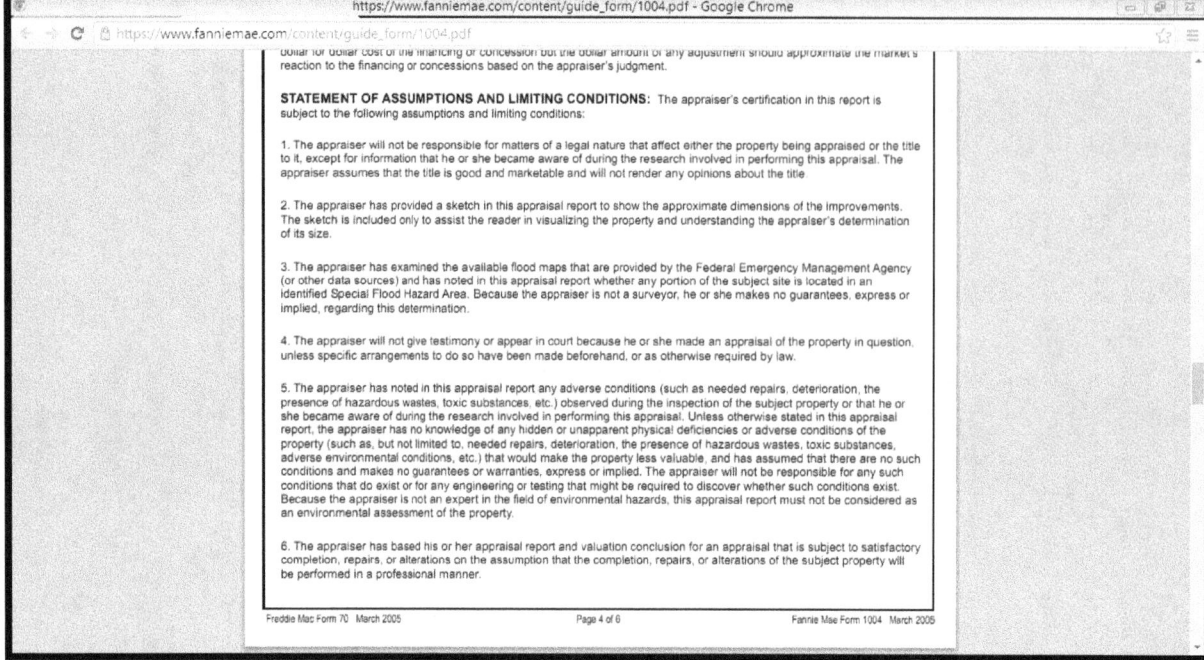

dollar for dollar cost of the financing or concession but the dollar amount of any adjustment should approximate the market's reaction to the financing or concessions based on the appraiser's judgment.

STATEMENT OF ASSUMPTIONS AND LIMITING CONDITIONS: The appraiser's certification in this report is subject to the following assumptions and limiting conditions:

1. The appraiser will not be responsible for matters of a legal nature that affect either the property being appraised or the title to it, except for information that he or she became aware of during the research involved in performing this appraisal. The appraiser assumes that the title is good and marketable and will not render any opinions about the title

2. The appraiser has provided a sketch in this appraisal report to show the approximate dimensions of the improvements. The sketch is included only to assist the reader in visualizing the property and understanding the appraiser's determination of its size.

3. The appraiser has examined the available flood maps that are provided by the Federal Emergency Management Agency (or other data sources) and has noted in this appraisal report whether any portion of the subject site is located in an identified Special Flood Hazard Area. Because the appraiser is not a surveyor, he or she makes no guarantees, express or implied, regarding this determination.

4. The appraiser will not give testimony or appear in court because he or she made an appraisal of the property in question, unless specific arrangements to do so have been made beforehand, or as otherwise required by law.

5. The appraiser has noted in this appraisal report any adverse conditions (such as needed repairs, deterioration, the presence of hazardous wastes, toxic substances, etc.) observed during the inspection of the subject property or that he or she became aware of during the research involved in performing this appraisal. Unless otherwise stated in this appraisal report, the appraiser has no knowledge of any hidden or unapparent physical deficiencies or adverse conditions of the property (such as, but not limited to, needed repairs, deterioration, the presence of hazardous wastes, toxic substances, adverse environmental conditions, etc.) that would make the property less valuable, and has assumed that there are no such conditions and makes no guarantees or warranties, express or implied. The appraiser will not be responsible for any such conditions that do exist or for any engineering or testing that might be required to discover whether such conditions exist. Because the appraiser is not an expert in the field of environmental hazards, this appraisal report must not be considered as an environmental assessment of the property.

6. The appraiser has based his or her appraisal report and valuation conclusion for an appraisal that is subject to satisfactory completion, repairs, or alterations on the assumption that the completion, repairs, or alterations of the subject property will be performed in a professional manner.

Freddie Mac Form 70   March 2005   Page 4 of 6   Fannie Mae Form 1004   March 2005

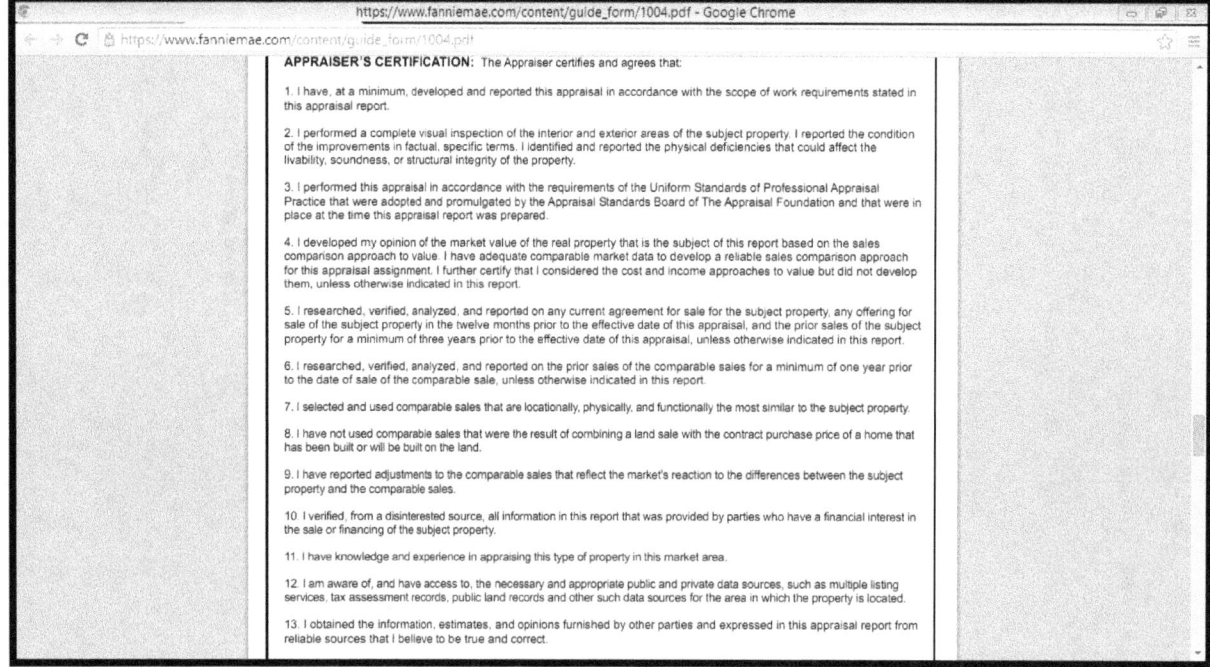

APPRAISER'S CERTIFICATION: The Appraiser certifies and agrees that:

1. I have, at a minimum, developed and reported this appraisal in accordance with the scope of work requirements stated in this appraisal report.

2. I performed a complete visual inspection of the interior and exterior areas of the subject property. I reported the condition of the improvements in factual, specific terms. I identified and reported the physical deficiencies that could affect the livability, soundness, or structural integrity of the property.

3. I performed this appraisal in accordance with the requirements of the Uniform Standards of Professional Appraisal Practice that were adopted and promulgated by the Appraisal Standards Board of The Appraisal Foundation and that were in place at the time this appraisal report was prepared.

4. I developed my opinion of the market value of the real property that is the subject of this report based on the sales comparison approach to value. I have adequate comparable market data to develop a reliable sales comparison approach for this appraisal assignment. I further certify that I considered the cost and income approaches to value but did not develop them, unless otherwise indicated in this report.

5. I researched, verified, analyzed, and reported on any current agreement for sale for the subject property, any offering for sale of the subject property in the twelve months prior to the effective date of this appraisal, and the prior sales of the subject property for a minimum of three years prior to the effective date of this appraisal, unless otherwise indicated in this report.

6. I researched, verified, analyzed, and reported on the prior sales of the comparable sales for a minimum of one year prior to the date of sale of the comparable sale, unless otherwise indicated in this report.

7. I selected and used comparable sales that are locationally, physically, and functionally the most similar to the subject property.

8. I have not used comparable sales that were the result of combining a land sale with the contract purchase price of a home that has been built or will be built on the land.

9. I have reported adjustments to the comparable sales that reflect the market's reaction to the differences between the subject property and the comparable sales.

10. I verified, from a disinterested source, all information in this report that was provided by parties who have a financial interest in the sale or financing of the subject property.

11. I have knowledge and experience in appraising this type of property in this market area.

12. I am aware of, and have access to, the necessary and appropriate public and private data sources, such as multiple listing services, tax assessment records, public land records and other such data sources for the area in which the property is located.

13. I obtained the information, estimates, and opinions furnished by other parties and expressed in this appraisal report from reliable sources that I believe to be true and correct.

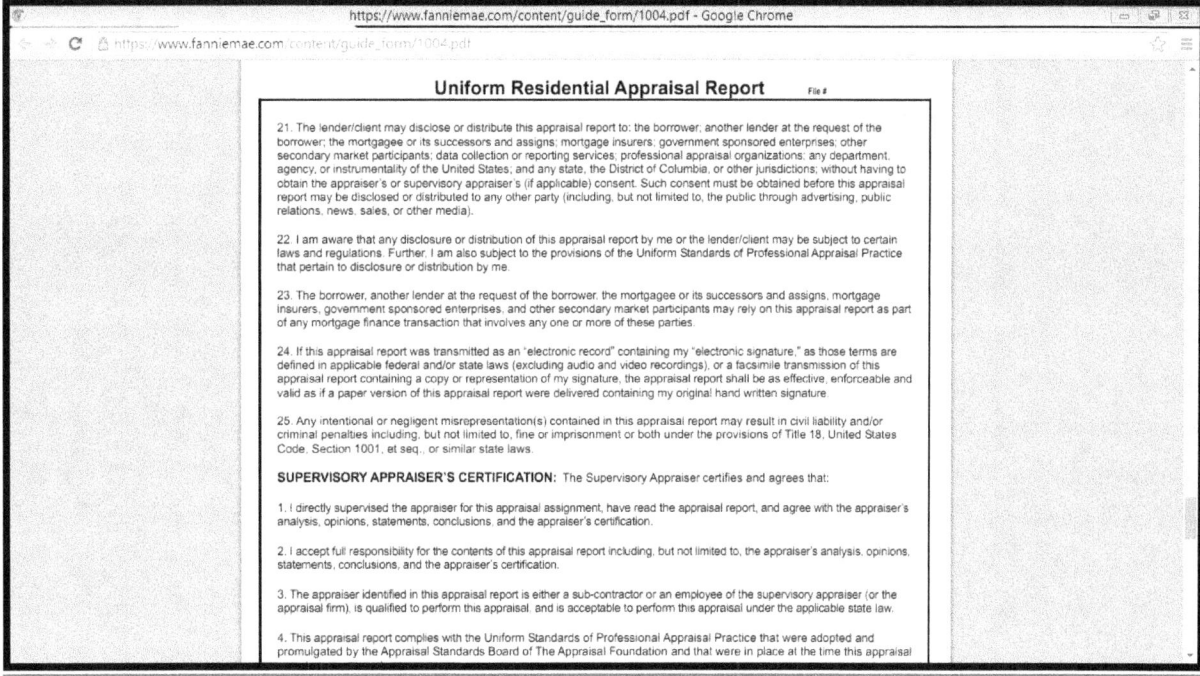

14. I have taken into consideration the factors that have an impact on value with respect to the subject neighborhood, subject property, and the proximity of the subject property to adverse influences in the development of my opinion of market value. I have noted in this appraisal report any adverse conditions (such as, but not limited to, needed repairs, deterioration, the presence of hazardous wastes, toxic substances, adverse environmental conditions, etc.) observed during the inspection of the subject property or that I became aware of during the research involved in performing this appraisal. I have considered these adverse conditions in my analysis of the property value, and have reported on the effect of the conditions on the value and marketability of the subject property.

15. I have not knowingly withheld any significant information from this appraisal report and, to the best of my knowledge, all statements and information in this appraisal report are true and correct.

16. I stated in this appraisal report my own personal, unbiased, and professional analysis, opinions, and conclusions, which are subject only to the assumptions and limiting conditions in this appraisal report.

17. I have no present or prospective interest in the property that is the subject of this report, and I have no present or prospective personal interest or bias with respect to the participants in the transaction. I did not base, either partially or completely, my analysis and/or opinion of market value in this appraisal report on the race, color, religion, sex, age, marital status, handicap, familial status, or national origin of either the prospective owners or occupants of the subject property or of the present owners or occupants of the properties in the vicinity of the subject property or on any other basis prohibited by law.

18. My employment and/or compensation for performing this appraisal or any future or anticipated appraisals was not conditioned on any agreement or understanding, written or otherwise, that I would report (or present analysis supporting) a predetermined specific value, a predetermined minimum value, a range or direction in value, a value that favors the cause of any party, or the attainment of a specific result or occurrence of a specific subsequent event (such as approval of a pending mortgage loan application).

19. I personally prepared all conclusions and opinions about the real estate that were set forth in this appraisal report. If I relied on significant real property appraisal assistance from any individual or individuals in the performance of this appraisal or the preparation of this appraisal report, I have named such individual(s) and disclosed the specific tasks performed in this appraisal report. I certify that any individual so named is qualified to perform the tasks. I have not authorized anyone to make a change to any item in this appraisal report; therefore, any change made to this appraisal is unauthorized and I will take no responsibility for it.

20. I identified the lender/client in this appraisal report who is the individual, organization, or agent for the organization that ordered and will receive this appraisal report.

Uniform Residential Appraisal Report
File #

21. The lender/client may disclose or distribute this appraisal report to: the borrower; another lender at the request of the borrower; the mortgagee or its successors and assigns; mortgage insurers; government sponsored enterprises; other secondary market participants; data collection or reporting services; professional appraisal organizations; any department, agency, or instrumentality of the United States; and any state, the District of Columbia, or other jurisdictions; without having to obtain the appraiser's or supervisory appraiser's (if applicable) consent. Such consent must be obtained before this appraisal report may be disclosed or distributed to any other party (including, but not limited to, the public through advertising, public relations, news, sales, or other media).

22. I am aware that any disclosure or distribution of this appraisal report by me or the lender/client may be subject to certain laws and regulations. Further, I am also subject to the provisions of the Uniform Standards of Professional Appraisal Practice that pertain to disclosure or distribution by me.

23. The borrower, another lender at the request of the borrower, the mortgagee or its successors and assigns, mortgage insurers, government sponsored enterprises, and other secondary market participants may rely on this appraisal report as part of any mortgage finance transaction that involves any one or more of these parties.

24. If this appraisal report was transmitted as an "electronic record" containing my "electronic signature," as those terms are defined in applicable federal and/or state laws (excluding audio and video recordings), or a facsimile transmission of this appraisal report containing a copy or representation of my signature, the appraisal report shall be as effective, enforceable and valid as if a paper version of this appraisal report were delivered containing my original hand written signature.

25. Any intentional or negligent misrepresentation(s) contained in this appraisal report may result in civil liability and/or criminal penalties including, but not limited to, fine or imprisonment or both under the provisions of Title 18, United States Code, Section 1001, et seq., or similar state laws.

SUPERVISORY APPRAISER'S CERTIFICATION: The Supervisory Appraiser certifies and agrees that:

1. I directly supervised the appraiser for this appraisal assignment, have read the appraisal report, and agree with the appraiser's analysis, opinions, statements, conclusions, and the appraiser's certification.

2. I accept full responsibility for the contents of this appraisal report including, but not limited to, the appraiser's analysis, opinions, statements, conclusions, and the appraiser's certification.

3. The appraiser identified in this appraisal report is either a sub-contractor or an employee of the supervisory appraiser (or the appraisal firm), is qualified to perform this appraisal, and is acceptable to perform this appraisal under the applicable state law.

4. This appraisal report complies with the Uniform Standards of Professional Appraisal Practice that were adopted and promulgated by the Appraisal Standards Board of The Appraisal Foundation and that were in place at the time this appraisal

report was prepared

5. If this appraisal report was transmitted as an "electronic record" containing my "electronic signature," as those terms are defined in applicable federal and/or state laws (excluding audio and video recordings), or a facsimile transmission of this appraisal report containing a copy or representation of my signature, the appraisal report shall be as effective, enforceable and valid as if a paper version of this appraisal report were delivered containing my original hand written signature.

APPRAISER

Signature_____
Name _____
Company Name _____
Company Address_____

_____
Telephone Number _____
Email Address_____
Date of Signature and Report_____
Effective Date of Appraisal _____
State Certification #_____
or State License #_____
or Other (describe) _____ State # _____
State _____
Expiration Date of Certification or License _____

ADDRESS OF PROPERTY APPRAISED

_____
APPRAISED VALUE OF SUBJECT PROPERTY $ _____
LENDER/CLIENT
Name _____
Company Name _____
Company Address_____

Email Address_____

SUPERVISORY APPRAISER (ONLY IF REQUIRED)

Signature_____
Name _____
Company Name _____
Company Address_____

_____
Telephone Number _____
Email Address_____
Date of Signature _____
State Certification #_____
or State License #_____
State _____
Expiration Date of Certification or License _____

SUBJECT PROPERTY

☐ Did not inspect subject property
☐ Did inspect exterior of subject property from street
   Date of Inspection _____
☐ Did inspect interior and exterior of subject property
   Date of Inspection _____

COMPARABLE SALES

☐ Did not inspect exterior of comparable sales from street
☐ Did inspect exterior of comparable sales from street
   Date of Inspection _____

PURCHASE OFFER AND SALE AGREEMENT

https://www.cmich.edu/fas/fsr/cps/PropertyAcquisition/Documents/Sample-AgreementToPurchaseRealEstate.pdf

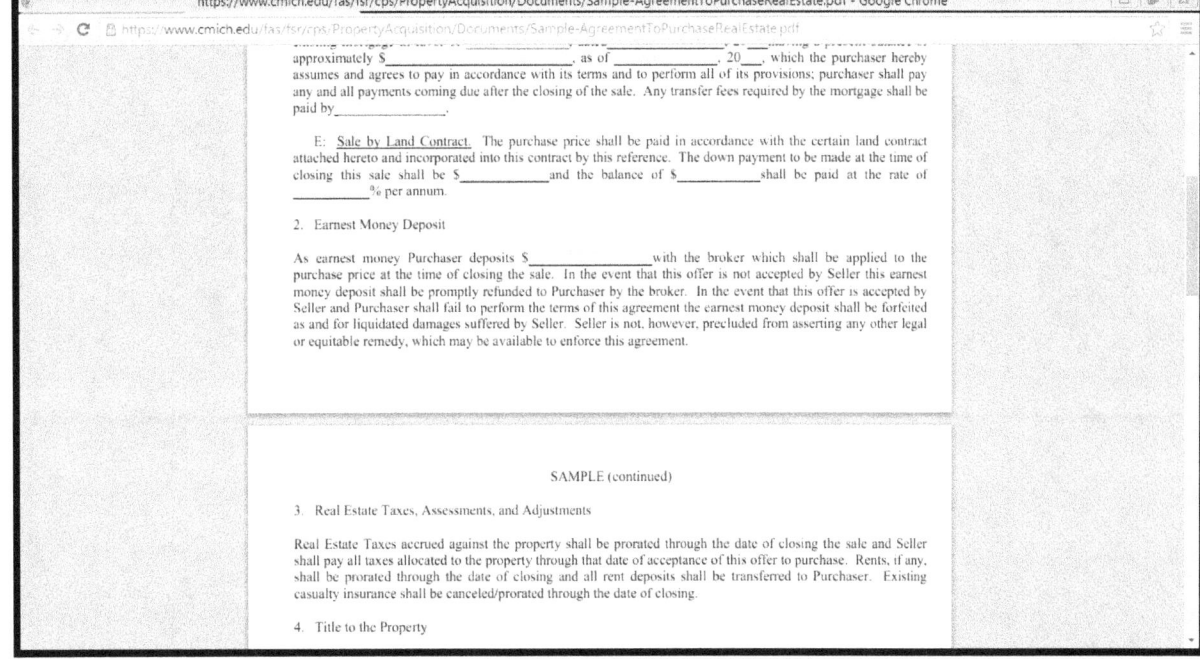

4. Title to the Property

Seller shall provide purchaser prior to the closing and promptly after the acceptance of this offer, at Seller's expense and at Seller's option an abstract of title to the property brought down to date or an owner's policy of title insurance in an amount equal to the purchase price, said abstract of policy to show marketable or insurable title to the real estate in the name of Seller subject only to easements, zoning and restrictions of record and free and clear of all other liens and encumbrances except as stated in this offer. If the abstract or title policy fails to show marketable or insurable title in Seller a reasonable time shall be permitted to cure or correct defects. Seller shall convey title to Purchaser at the time of closing by a good and sufficient general warranty deed free and clear of all liens and encumbrances except as otherwise provided in this offer and subject to easements, zoning and restrictions of record.

5. Possession of the Property

Purchaser shall be given possession of the property on _____, 20____. A failure on the part of Seller to transfer possession as specified will not make Seller a tenant of Purchaser, but in such event Seller shall pay to Purchaser $_____ per day as damages for breach of contract and not as rent. All other remedies, which Purchaser may have under law, are reserved to Purchaser.

6. Risk of Loss

The risk of loss by destruction or damage to the property by fire or otherwise prior to the closing of the sale is that of Seller. If all or a substantial portion of the improvements on the property are destroyed or damaged prior to the closing and transfer of title this agreement shall be void able at Purchaser's option and in the event Purchaser elects to avoid this agreement the earnest money deposited shall be promptly refunded.

7. Improvements and Fixtures Included

This offer to purchase includes all improvements, buildings and fixtures presently on the real estate including but not limited to electrical, gas, heating, air conditioning, plumbing equipment, built-in appliances, hot water heaters, screens, storm windows, doors, Venetian blinds, drapery hardware, awnings, attached carpeting, radio, television antennas, trees, shrubs, flowers, fences and
_____
_____
_____

8. General Conditions

It is expressly agreed that this agreement to purchase real estate includes the entire agreement of Purchaser and Seller. This agreement shall be binding upon the heirs, personal representatives, successors and assigns of both Purchaser and Seller. This agreement shall be interpreted and enforced in accordance with the laws of the State of _____.

SAMPLE (concluded)

9. Special Conditions
_____
_____
_____

10. Time for Acceptance and Closing

This offer is void if not accepted by Seller in writing on or before _____ A.M./P.M. of the _____ day of _____, 20____.

Closing of the sale shall take place _____ days after Purchaser's receipt of an abstract showing marketable title in Seller or title insurance binder showing insurable title in Seller.

This offer is made at _____, State of _____, this _____ day of _____, 20_____.

_____
(PURCHASER)

_____
(PURCHASER)

_____
(PURCHASER)

<u>Acceptance by Seller</u>

The foregoing offer to purchase real estate is hereby accepted in accordance with the terms and conditions specified above. The undersigned hereby agrees to pay a brokerage fee of $_____ to _____, broker, in accordance with the existing listing contract.

Dated this _____ day of _____, 20_____.

_____
(SELLER)

_____
(SELLER)

HOME INSPECTION FORM

http://portal.hud.gov/hudportal/documents/huddoc?id=52580.pdf

portal.hud.gov/hudportal/documents/huddoc?id=52580.pdf - Google Chrome

C portal.hud.gov/hudportal/documents/huddoc?id=52580.pdf

Inspection Checklist

Housing Choice Voucher Program

U.S. Department of Housing and Urban Development
Office of Public and Indian Housing

OMB Approval No. 2577-0169
(Exp. 04/30/2014)

Public reporting burden for this collection of information is estimated to average 0.50 hours per response, including the time for reviewing instructions, searching existing data sources, gathering and maintaining the data needed, and completing and reviewing the collection of information. This agency may not conduct or sponsor, and a person is not required to respond to, a collection of information unless that collection displays a valid OMB control number.

Assurances of confidentiality are not provided under this collection.

This collection of information is authorized under Section 8 of the U.S. Housing Act of 1937 (42 U.S.C. 1437f). The information is used to determine if a unit meets the housing quality standards of the section 8 rental assistance program.

Privacy Act Statement. The Department of Housing and Urban Development (HUD) is authorized to collect the information required on this form by Section 8 of the U.S. Housing Act of 1937 (42 U.S.C. 1437f). Collection of the name and address of both family and the owner is mandatory. The information is used to determine if a unit meets the housing quality standards of the Section 8 rental assistance program. HUD may disclose this information to Federal, State and local agencies when relevant to civil, criminal, or regulatory investigations and prosecutions. It will not be otherwise disclosed or released outside of HUD, except as permitted or required by law. Failure to provide any of the information may result in delay or rejection of family participation.

Name of Family	Tenant ID Number	Date of Request (mm/dd/yyyy)
Inspector	Neighborhood/Census Tract	Date of Inspection (mm/dd/yyyy)

Type of Inspection
Initial ☐   Special ☐   Reinspection ☐

Date of Last Inspection (mm/dd/yyyy)   PHA

A. General Information

Inspected Unit	Year Constructed (yyyy)	Housing Type (check as appropriate)
Full Address (including Street, City, County, State, Zip)		☐ Single Family Detached
		☐ Duplex or Two Family
		☐ Row House or Town House
		☐ Low Rise: 3, 4 Stories, Including Garden Apartment
Number of Children in Family Under 6		☐ High Rise: 5 or More Stories
		☐ Manufactured Home
Owner		☐ Congregate
Name of Owner or Agent Authorized to Lease Unit Inspected	Phone Number	☐ Cooperative
		☐ Independent Group Residence

portal.hud.gov/hudportal/documents/huddoc?id=52580.pdf - Google Chrome

C portal.hud.gov/hudportal/documents/huddoc?id=52580.pdf

Address of Owner or Agent	☐ Single Room Occupancy
	☐ Shared Housing
	☐ Other

B. Summary Decision On Unit (To be completed after form has been filled out)

☐ Pass ☐ Fail ☐ Inconclusive	Number of Bedrooms for Purposes of the FMR or Payment Standard	Number of Sleeping Rooms

Inspection Checklist

Item No. 1. Living Room	Yes Pass	No Fail	In-Conc.	Comment	Final Approval Date (mm/dd/yyyy)
1.1 Living Room Present					
1.2 Electricity					
1.3 Electrical Hazards					
1.4 Security					
1.5 Window Condition					
1.6 Ceiling Condition					
1.7 Wall Condition					
1.8 Floor Condition					

Previous editions are obsolete   Page 1 of 8

form **HUD-52580** (3/2001)
ref Handbook 7420.8

* Room Codes. 1 = Bedroom or Any Other Room Used for Sleeping (regardless of type of room);   2 = Dining Room or Dining Area;
3 = Second Living Room, Family Room, Den, Playroom, TV Room; 4 = Entrance Halls, Corridors, Halls, Staircases; 5 = Additional Bathroom; 6 = Other

Item No. 1. Living Room (Continued)	Yes Pas	No Fail	In-Conc.	Comment	Final Approval Date (mm/dd/yyyy)
1.9 Lead-Based Paint				Not Applicable	
Are all painted surfaces free of deteriorated paint?					

paint?
If not, do deteriorated surfaces exceed two square feet per room and/or is more than 10% of a component?

2. Kitchen

Item		Yes Pass	No Fail	In-Conc.	Comment	
2.1	Kitchen Area Present					
2.2	Electricity					
2.3	Electrical Hazards					
2.4	Security					
2.5	Window Condition					
2.6	Ceiling Condition					
2.7	Wall Condition					
2.8	Floor Condition					
2.9	Lead-Based Paint Are all painted surfaces free of deteriorated paint? If not, do deteriorated surfaces exceed two square feet per room and/or is more than 10% of a component?				Not Applicable	
2.10	Stove or Range with Oven					
2.11	Refrigerator					
2.12	Sink					
2.13	Space for Storage, Preparation, and Serving of Food					

3. Bathroom

Item		Yes Pass	No Fail	In-Conc.	Comment	
3.1	Bathroom Present					
3.2	Electricity					
3.3	Electrical Hazards					
3.4	Security					
3.5	Window Condition					
3.6	Ceiling Condition					
3.7	Wall Condition					
3.8	Floor Condition					
3.9	Lead-Based Paint Are all painted surfaces free of deteriorated paint? If not, do deteriorated surfaces exceed two square feet per room and/or is more than 10% of a component?				Not Applicable	
3.10	Flush Toilet in Enclosed Room in Unit					
3.11	Fixed Wash Basin or Lavatory in Unit					
3.12	Tub or Shower in Unit					
3.13	Ventilation					

Item no. 4. Other Rooms Used For Living and Halls	Yes Pass	No Fail	In-Conc.	Comment	Final Approval Date (mm/dd/yyyy)
4.1 Room Code* and Room Location	(Circle One) Right/Center/Left			(Circle One) Front/Center/Rear ____ Floor Level	
4.2 Electricity/Illumination					
4.3 Electrical Hazards					
4.4 Security					
4.5 Window Condition					
4.6 Ceiling Condition					
4.7 Wall Condition					
4.8 Floor Condition					
4.9 Lead-Based Paint Are all painted surfaces free of deteriorated paint? If not, do deteriorated surfaces exceed two square feet per room and/or is more than 10% of a component?				☐ Not Applicable	

10% of a component?

4.10 Smoke Detectors

| 4.1 | Room Code* and Room Location | | (Circle One) Right/Center/Left | (Circle One) Front/Center/Rear | _____ Floor Level |

4.2   Electricity/Illumination

4.3 Electrical Hazards

4.4 Security

4.5 Window Condition

4.6 Ceiling Condition

4.7 Wall Condition

4.8 Floor Condition

4.9 Lead-Based Paint   ☐ Not Applicable

Are all painted surfaces free of deteriorated paint?

If not, do deteriorated surfaces exceed two square feet per room and/or is more than 10% of a component?

4.10 Smoke Detectors

| 4.1 | Room Code* and Room Location | | (Circle One) Right/Center/Left | (Circle One) Front/Center/Rear | _____ Floor Level |

4.2   Electricity/Illumination

4.3 Electrical Hazards

4.4 Security

4.5 Window Condition

4.6 Ceiling Condition

4.7 Wall Condition

4.8 Floor Condition

4.9 Lead-Based Paint   ☐ Not Applicable

Are all painted surfaces free of deteriorated paint?

If not, do deteriorated surfaces exceed two square feet per room and/or is more than 10% of a component?

Item No.	4. Other Rooms Used For Living and Halls	Yes Pass	No Fail	In- Conc.	Comment	Final Approval Date (mm/dd/yyyy)
4.1	Room Code * and Room Location				(Circle One) Right/Center/Left (Circle One) Front/Center/Rear Floor Level	
4.2	Electricity/Illumination					
4.3	Electrical Hazards					
4.4	Security					
4.5	Window Condition					
4.6	Ceiling Condition					
4.7	Wall Condition					
4.8	Floor Condition					
4.9	Lead-Based Paint				Not Applicable	
	Are all painted surfaces free of deteriorated paint?					
	If not, do deteriorated surfaces exceed two square feet per room and/or is more than 10% of a component?					
4.10	Smoke Detectors					
4.1	Room Code* and Room Location				(Circle One) Right/Center/Left (Circle One) Front/Center/Rear Floor Level	
4.2	Electricity/Illumination					
4.3	Electrical Hazards					
4.4	Security					
4.5	Window Condition					
4.6	Ceiling Condition					
4.7	Wall Condition					
4.8	Floor Condition					
4.9	Lead-Based Paint				Not Applicable	
	Are all painted surfaces free of deteriorated paint?					
	If not, do deteriorated surfaces exceed two square feet per room and/or is more than 10% of a component?					
4.10	Smoke Detectors					
	5. All Secondary Rooms					

5.1	None Go to Part 6				
5.2	Security				
5.3	Electrical Hazards				
5.4	Other Potentially Hazardous Features in these Rooms				

Item No.	6. Building Exterior	Yes Pass	No Fail	In-Conc.	Comment	Final Approval Date (mm/dd/yyyy)
6.1	Condition of Foundation					
6.2	Condition of Stairs, Rails, and Porches					
6.3	Condition of Roof/Gutters					
6.4	Condition of Exterior Surfaces					
6.5	Condition of Chimney					

Item No.					Comment	
6.6	Lead Paint: Exterior Surfaces				Not Applicable	
	Are all painted surfaces free of deteriorated paint?					
	If not, do deteriorated surfaces exceed 20 square feet of total exterior surface area?					
6.7	Manufactured Home: Tie Downs					
	7. Heating and Plumbing					
7.1	Adequacy of Heating Equipment					
7.2	Safety of Heating Equipment					
7.3	Ventilation/Cooling					
7.4	Water Heater					
7.5	Approvable Water Supply					
7.6	Plumbing					
7.7	Sewer Connection					
	8. General Health and Safety					
8.1	Access to Unit					
8.2	Fire Exits					
8.3	Evidence of Infestation					
8.4	Garbage and Debris					
8.5	Refuse Disposal					
8.6	Interior Stairs and Common Halls					
8.7	Other Interior Hazards					
8.8	Elevators					
8.9	Interior Air Quality					
8.10	Site and Neighborhood Conditions					
8.11	Lead-Based Paint: Owner's Certification				Not Applicable	

If the owner is required to correct any lead-based paint hazards at the property including deteriorated paint or other hazards identified by a

If the owner is required to correct any lead-based paint hazards at the property including deteriorated paint or other hazards identified by a visual assessor, a certified lead-based paint risk assessor, or certified lead-based paint inspector, the PHA must obtain certification that the work has been done in accordance with all applicable requirements of 24 CFR Part 35. The Lead-Based Paint Owner Certification must be received by the PHA before the execution of the HAP contract or within the time period stated by the PHA in the owner HQS violation notice. Receipt of the completed and signed Lead-Based Paint Owner Certification signifies that all HQS lead-based paint requirements have been met and no re-inspection by the HQS inspector is required.

C. Special Amenities (Optional)

This Section is for optional use of the HA. It is designed to collect additional information about other positive features of the unit that may be present. Although the features listed below are not included in the Housing Quality Standards, the tenant and HA may wish to take them into consideration in decisions about renting the unit and the reasonableness of the rent.
Checklist any positive features found in relation to the unit.

D. Questions to ask the Tenant (Optional)

1. Living Room
- High quality floors or wall coverings
- Working fireplace or stove Balcony, patio, deck, porch Special windows or doors
- Exceptional size relative to needs of family
- Other: (Specify)

2. Kitchen
- Dishwasher
- Separate freezer
- Garbage disposal
- Eating counter/breakfast nook
- Pantry or abundant shelving or cabinets
- Double oven/self cleaning oven, microwave

4. Bath
- Special feature shower head
- Built-in heat lamp
- Large mirrors
- Glass door on shower/tub
- Separate dressing room
- Double sink or special lavatory
- Exceptional size relative to needs of family
- Other: (Specify)

5. Overall Characteristics

- Pantry or abundant shelving or cabinets
- Double oven/self cleaning oven, microwave
- Double sink
- High quality cabinets
- Abundant counter-top space
- Modern appliance(s)
- Exceptional size relative to needs of family
- Other: (Specify)

5. Overall Characteristics
- Storm windows and doors
- Other forms of weatherization (e.g., insulation, weather stripping) Screen doors or windows
- Good upkeep of grounds (i.e., site cleanliness, landscaping, condition of lawn)
- Garage or parking facilities
- Driveway
- Large yard
- Good maintenance of building exterior
- Other: (Specify)

3. Other Rooms Used for Living
- High quality floors or wall coverings
- Working fireplace or stove Balcony, patio, deck, porch Special windows or doors
- Exceptional size relative to needs of family
- Other: (Specify)

6. Disabled Accessibility
Unit is accessible to a particular disability. ☐ Yes ☐ No
Disability

1. Does the owner make repairs when asked? Yes ☐ No ☐
2. How many people live there? ☐
3. How much money do you pay to the owner/agent for rent? $ _____
4. Do you pay for anything else? (specify)_____
5. Who owns the range and refrigerator? (insert O = Owner or T = Tenant) Range _____ Refrigerator _____ Microwave ☐
6. Is there anything else you want to tell us? (specify) Yes ☐ No ☐

E. Inspection Summary/Comments (Optional)
Provide a summary description of each item which resulted in a rating of "Fail" or "Pass with Comments."

Tenant ID Number	Inspector		Date of Inspection (mm/dd/yyyy)	Address of Inspected Unit
Type of Inspection	Initial	Special	Reinspection	

Item Number	Reason for "Fail" or "Pass with Comments" Rating

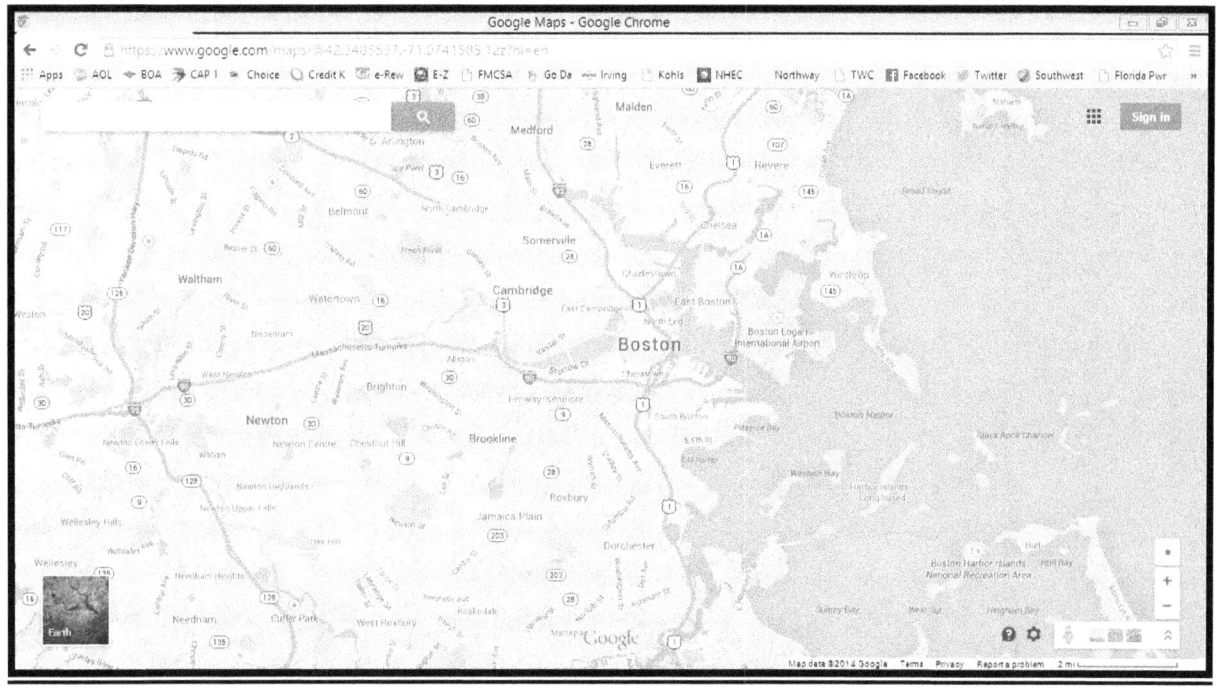

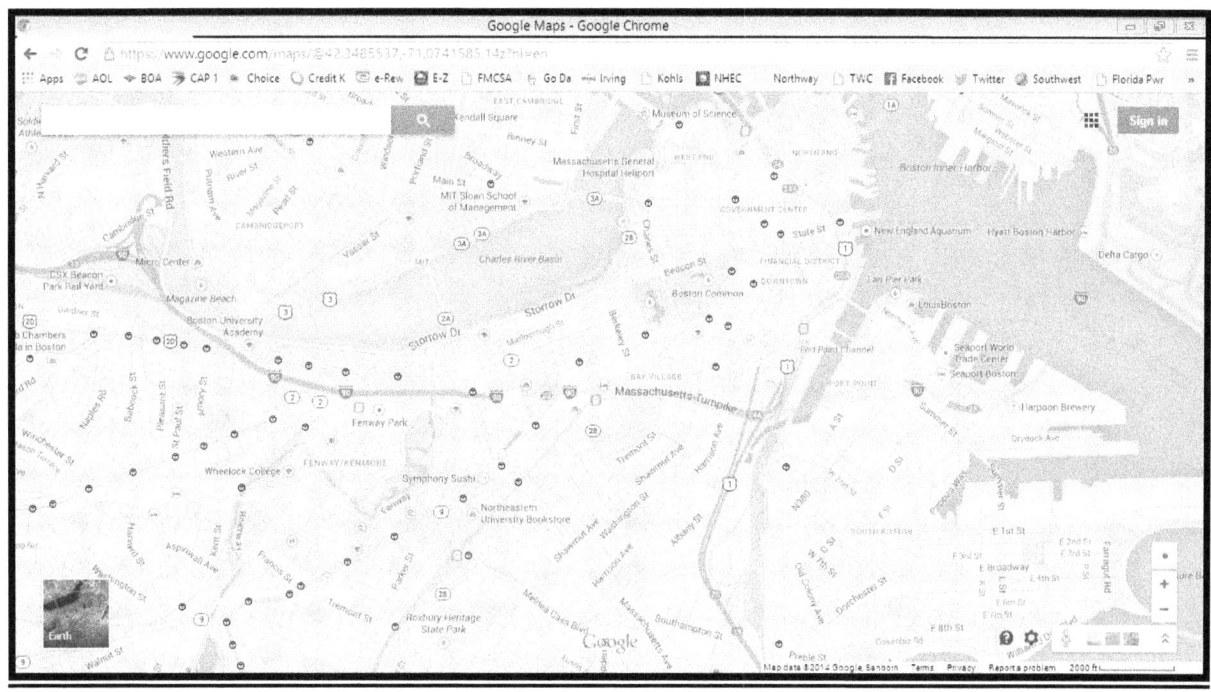

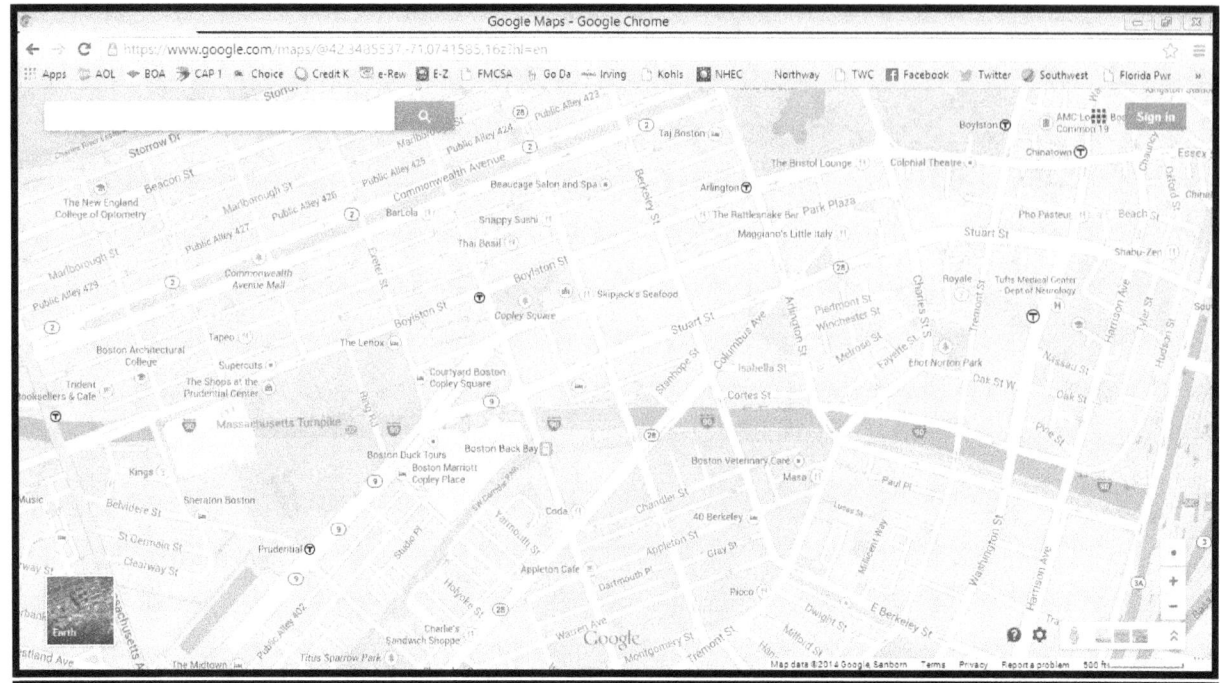

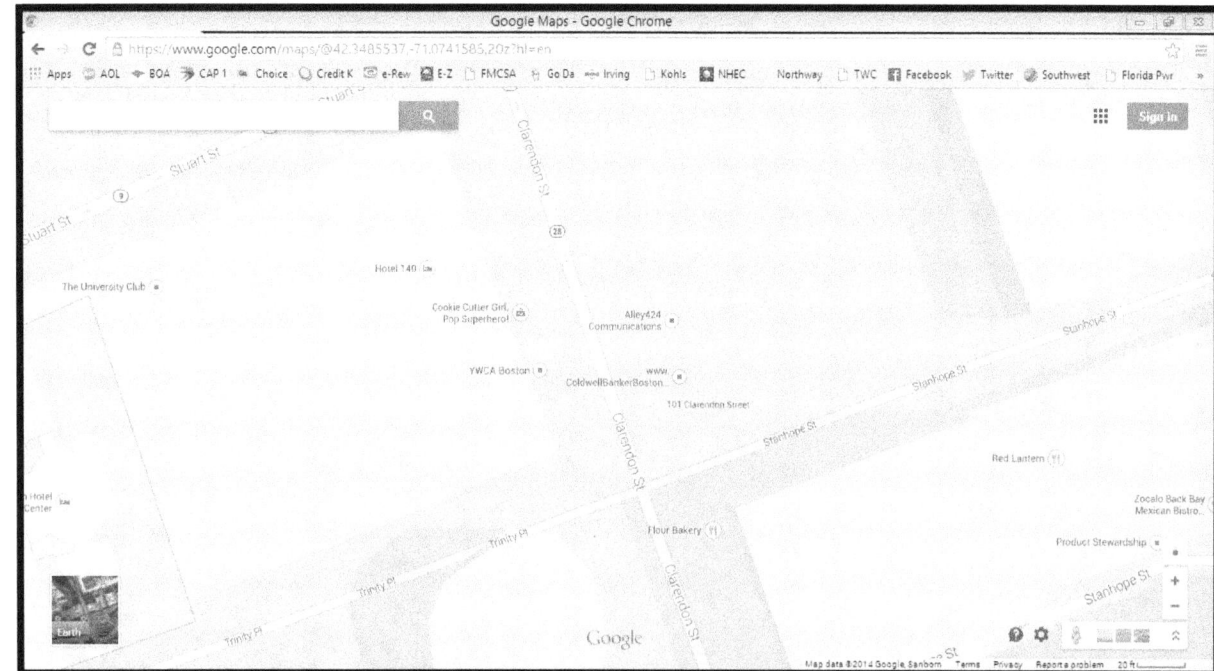

https://www.google.com/maps/@43.7442775,-71.7214984,12z

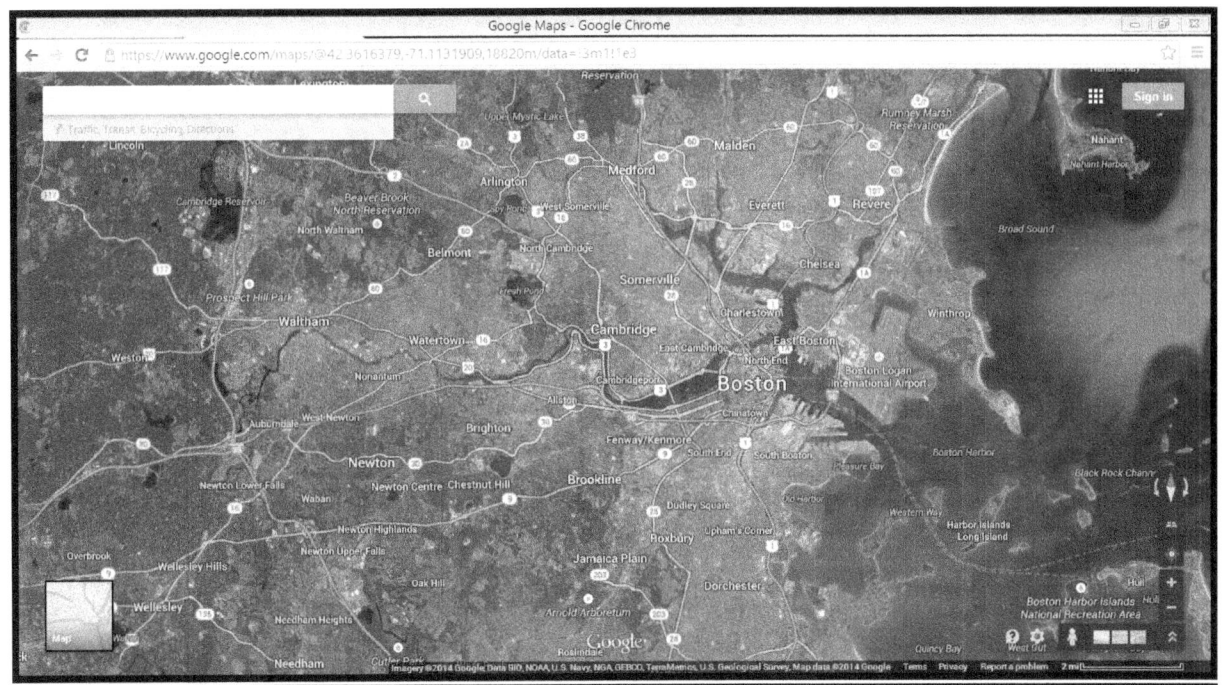

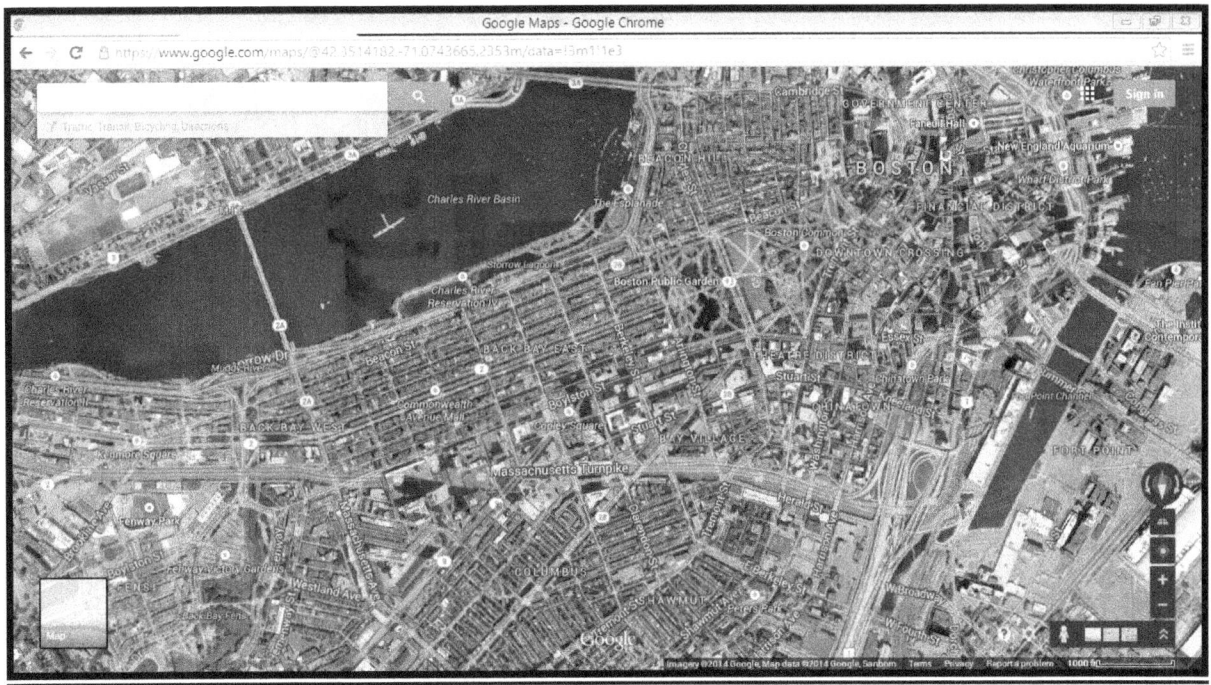

SPECIFICATIONS AND ESTIMATE

http://www.nyshcr.org/Topics/Lenders/Lenders/HomeImprovementContractNYC.pdf

HOME IMPROVEMENT CONTRACT

YOU ARE ENTITLED TO A COMPLETELY FILLED-IN COPY OF
THIS CONTRACT, SIGNED BY BOTH YOU AND THE CONTRACTOR
BEFORE ANY WORK MAY BE STARTED.

CONTRACTOR'S NAME (as on record with DCA):
_____

ADDRESS (as on record with DCA):
_____
_____

PHONE (as on record with DCA):_____

FAX:_____

CELL PHONE:_____

E-MAIL (as on record with DCA):_____

DCA HIC LICENSE #:_____

HOME IMPROVEMENT SALESPERSON'S NAME
(as on record with DCA):_____

ADDRESS (as on record with DCA):
_____

PHONE (as on record with DCA):_____

FAX:_____

CELL PHONE:_____

E-MAIL (as on record with DCA):_____

DCA HIS LICENSE #:_____

DATE: _____

BUYER'S NAME: _____
ADDRESS: _____
BUYER'S DAY PHONE: _____
BUYER'S EVENING PHONE: _____
BUYER'S CELL PHONE: _____
BUYER'S E-MAIL ADDRESS: _____
PROJECT ADDRESS: _____

_____   _____   _____
Contractor   Buyer   Buyer
Page __ of __

I. PARTIES

This Contract is entered into on this _____ day of _____,
20____ by and between _____ ("Buyer") and
_____ ("Contractor"). Buyer and
Contractor agree to the following:

II. GENERAL SCOPE OF WORK DESCRIPTION

The Contractor shall perform all work and provide all labor, supervision, materials, and equipment described below to complete in a good and workmanlike manner the following:

_____
_____
_____
_____
_____
_____

___Yes ___No: All work to be completed by the Contractor (and subcontractors, if any) is described in the attached plans and specifications dated _____ that have been signed and acknowledged by the Buyer and the Contractor.

III. DESCRIPTION OF MATERIALS AND EQUIPMENT

(Include quantity, quality, brand, model number, identifying features, and price of materials and equipment.)

Materials/Equipment   Price

_____
_____
_____
_____
_____
_____

_____ _____ _____
Contractor   Buyer   Buyer
Page __ of __

___Yes: All / some **(circle one)** materials/equipment are to be supplied by the Contractor according to the attached plans and specifications dated _____ that have been signed and acknowledged by the Buyer and the Contractor.

___No: The Buyer will supply the materials/equipment according to the attached plans and specifications dated _____ that have been signed and acknowledged by the Buyer and the Contractor.

IV. SUBCONTRACTORS
(List all subcontractors, plumbers, electricians, etc. with names, addresses, phone numbers, license numbers, and work to be provided.)

_____
_____
_____
_____

V. CONTRACT PRICE

V. CONTRACT PRICE $_____
                                          (total amount)

The Buyer shall pay the Contractor the fixed sum of $_____
(in dollars and cents) for the work to be performed under this
Contract.

VI. PROGRESS PAYMENTS AND SCHEDULE

Deposit: When the Contract is signed by both parties and returned to
the Contractor, the Buyer shall pay to the Contractor a deposit of:

$_____

Progress Payments: All payments are subject to a site inspection and
approval of work by the Buyer.

_____	_____	_____
Contractor	Buyer	Buyer

Page __ of __

Work or service performed and materials to be supplied	Amount due on completion
_____	$_____
_____	$_____
_____	$_____
_____	$_____
_____	$_____
_____	$_____
_____	$_____
_____	$_____

Final Payment: When all work is complete, the Buyer will pay the
Contractor:

$_____

The Buyer may withhold final payment if the Contractor does not
submit satisfactory evidence to the Buyer that all expenses related to
this work have been paid and no lien exists on the property as
described in the section "Additional Terms and Conditions."

VII. RIGHT TO CANCEL CONTRACT WITHIN THREE DAYS

YOU, THE BUYER, MAY CANCEL THIS CONTRACT AT ANY TIME PRIOR TO MIDNIGHT OF THE THIRD BUSINESS DAY AFTER THE DATE OF THIS TRANSACTION. SEE THE ATTACHED NOTICE OF CANCELLATION FORM FOR EXPLANATION OF THIS RIGHT.

‾‾‾‾‾‾ ‾‾‾‾‾‾ ‾‾‾‾‾‾
Contractor   Buyer   Buyer
Page __ of __

VIII. COMMENCEMENT AND COMPLETION SCHEDULE

Work will commence on: _____ **(date)**. The Buyer may cancel the Contract if work is not begun within _____ days of this stated commencement date.

Construction time through completion date is approximately _____ to _____ weeks/months **(circle one)**.

Work will be completed by: _____ **(date)**. Time is of the essence regarding this Contract unless the Buyer has appended a

the essence regarding this Contract unless the Buyer has appended a handwritten statement that extends the work timeframe.

___Yes ____No: A handwritten statement by the Buyer is appended and time is not of the essence.

No extension of time will be valid without the Buyer's written consent. The following events or contingencies may impact the Contractor's ability to perform:

‾‾‾
‾‾‾
‾‾‾

IX. CHANGE ORDERS/ADDITIONAL WORK

Written Change Orders signed by both parties are required for any changes or additional work. The Change Order shall state:
- whether the change will increase or decrease the original Contract amount
- the cost of the additional work
- the new total amount of the Contract

The Contractor shall provide the Buyer with a copy of the signed Change Order form before commencing the additional or changed work. Except for those items specifically described in the Change Order, all other Contract terms shall remain unchanged. Payment for additional or changed work is due upon completion of all of the additional or changed work and submittal of an invoice by the Contractor.

Contractor   Buyer   Buyer
Page __ of __

X. ADDITIONAL TERMS AND CONDITIONS

See page(s) attached: _____Yes _____No

ACCEPTANCE OF CONTRACT

The condition specifications and prices stated in this Contract and any referenced attachment herein are satisfactory and are hereby accepted. The Contractor is authorized to do the work as specified. Payment will be made as outlined in the Section "Progress Payments and Schedule." The Contractor will provide the Buyer with a copy of this Contract after it is signed by both parties.

_____   _____
DATE   SIGNATURE OF LICENSED SALESPERSON
               FOR THE LICENSED CONTRACTOR

               _____
               PRINT NAME

_____   _____
DATE   BUYER'S SIGNATURE

               _____
               PRINT NAME

_____   _____
DATE   BUYER'S SIGNATURE

               _____
               PRINT NAME

Contractor   Buyer   Buyer
Page __ of __

ADDITIONAL TERMS, PROVISIONS, AND CONDITIONS

1.   The Contractor or subcontractor who performs work under this

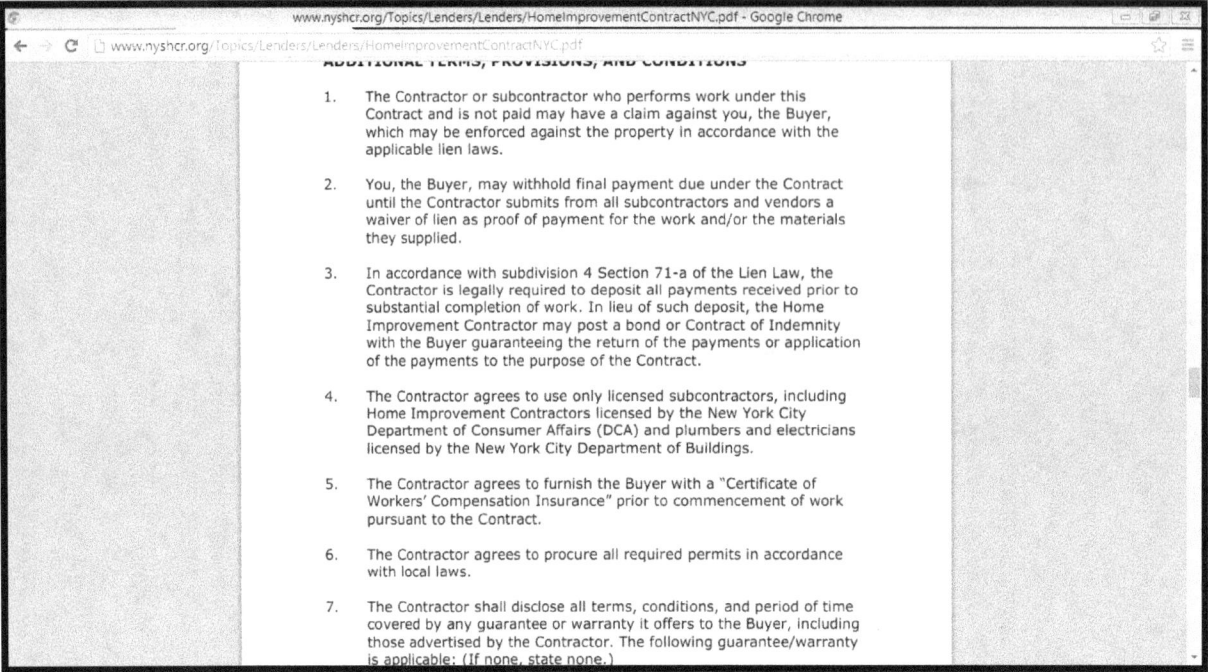

ADDITIONAL TERMS, PROVISIONS, AND CONDITIONS

1. The Contractor or subcontractor who performs work under this Contract and is not paid may have a claim against you, the Buyer, which may be enforced against the property in accordance with the applicable lien laws.

2. You, the Buyer, may withhold final payment due under the Contract until the Contractor submits from all subcontractors and vendors a waiver of lien as proof of payment for the work and/or the materials they supplied.

3. In accordance with subdivision 4 Section 71-a of the Lien Law, the Contractor is legally required to deposit all payments received prior to substantial completion of work. In lieu of such deposit, the Home Improvement Contractor may post a bond or Contract of Indemnity with the Buyer guaranteeing the return of the payments or application of the payments to the purpose of the Contract.

4. The Contractor agrees to use only licensed subcontractors, including Home Improvement Contractors licensed by the New York City Department of Consumer Affairs (DCA) and plumbers and electricians licensed by the New York City Department of Buildings.

5. The Contractor agrees to furnish the Buyer with a "Certificate of Workers' Compensation Insurance" prior to commencement of work pursuant to the Contract.

6. The Contractor agrees to procure all required permits in accordance with local laws.

7. The Contractor shall disclose all terms, conditions, and period of time covered by any guarantee or warranty it offers to the Buyer, including those advertised by the Contractor. The following guarantee/warranty is applicable: (If none, state none.)

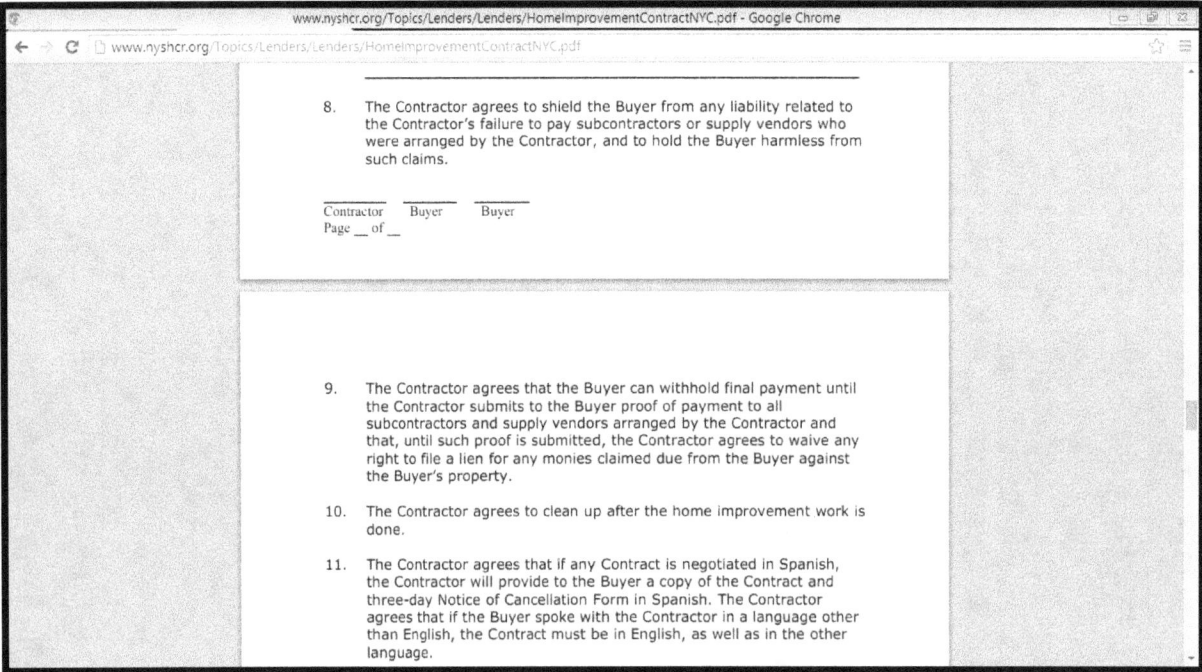

8. The Contractor agrees to shield the Buyer from any liability related to the Contractor's failure to pay subcontractors or supply vendors who were arranged by the Contractor, and to hold the Buyer harmless from such claims.

_____ _____ _____
Contractor   Buyer   Buyer
Page __ of __

9. The Contractor agrees that the Buyer can withhold final payment until the Contractor submits to the Buyer proof of payment to all subcontractors and supply vendors arranged by the Contractor and that, until such proof is submitted, the Contractor agrees to waive any right to file a lien for any monies claimed due from the Buyer against the Buyer's property.

10. The Contractor agrees to clean up after the home improvement work is done.

11. The Contractor agrees that if any Contract is negotiated in Spanish, the Contractor will provide to the Buyer a copy of the Contract and three-day Notice of Cancellation Form in Spanish. The Contractor agrees that if the Buyer spoke with the Contractor in a language other than English, the Contract must be in English, as well as in the other language.

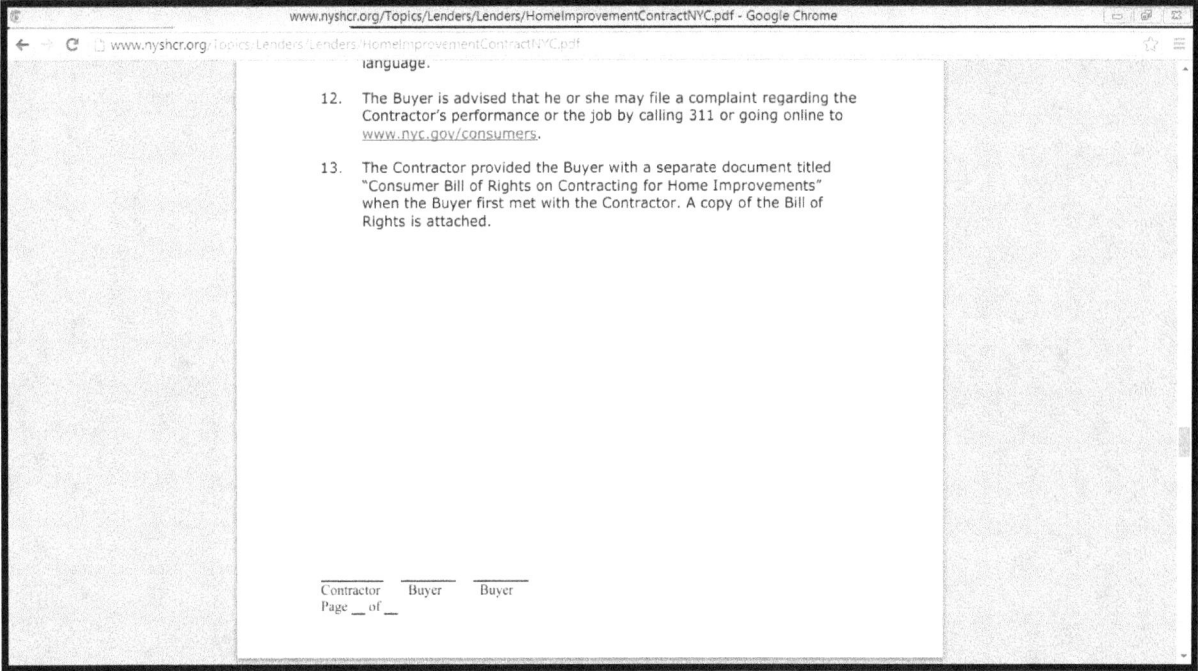

language.

12. The Buyer is advised that he or she may file a complaint regarding the Contractor's performance or the job by calling 311 or going online to www.nyc.gov/consumers.

13. The Contractor provided the Buyer with a separate document titled "Consumer Bill of Rights on Contracting for Home Improvements" when the Buyer first met with the Contractor. A copy of the Bill of Rights is attached.

_____   _____   _____
Contractor   Buyer   Buyer
Page __ of __

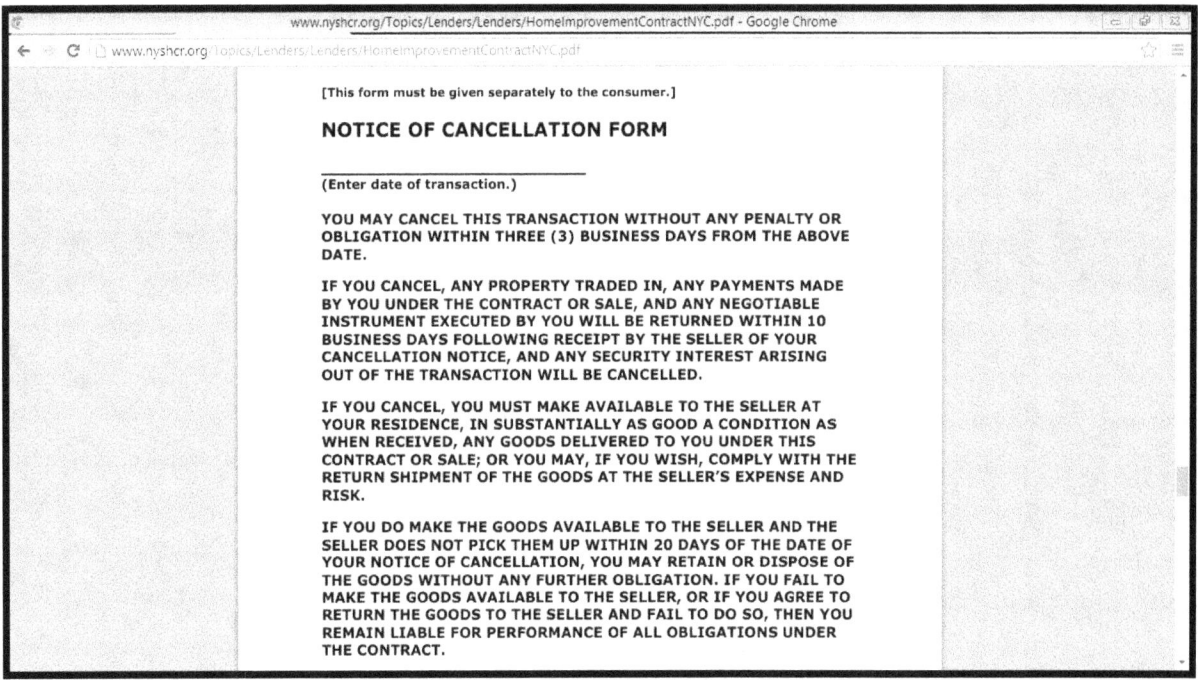

[This form must be given separately to the consumer.]

NOTICE OF CANCELLATION FORM

_____
(Enter date of transaction.)

YOU MAY CANCEL THIS TRANSACTION WITHOUT ANY PENALTY OR OBLIGATION WITHIN THREE (3) BUSINESS DAYS FROM THE ABOVE DATE.

IF YOU CANCEL, ANY PROPERTY TRADED IN, ANY PAYMENTS MADE BY YOU UNDER THE CONTRACT OR SALE, AND ANY NEGOTIABLE INSTRUMENT EXECUTED BY YOU WILL BE RETURNED WITHIN 10 BUSINESS DAYS FOLLOWING RECEIPT BY THE SELLER OF YOUR CANCELLATION NOTICE, AND ANY SECURITY INTEREST ARISING OUT OF THE TRANSACTION WILL BE CANCELLED.

IF YOU CANCEL, YOU MUST MAKE AVAILABLE TO THE SELLER AT YOUR RESIDENCE, IN SUBSTANTIALLY AS GOOD A CONDITION AS WHEN RECEIVED, ANY GOODS DELIVERED TO YOU UNDER THIS CONTRACT OR SALE; OR YOU MAY, IF YOU WISH, COMPLY WITH THE RETURN SHIPMENT OF THE GOODS AT THE SELLER'S EXPENSE AND RISK.

IF YOU DO MAKE THE GOODS AVAILABLE TO THE SELLER AND THE SELLER DOES NOT PICK THEM UP WITHIN 20 DAYS OF THE DATE OF YOUR NOTICE OF CANCELLATION, YOU MAY RETAIN OR DISPOSE OF THE GOODS WITHOUT ANY FURTHER OBLIGATION. IF YOU FAIL TO MAKE THE GOODS AVAILABLE TO THE SELLER, OR IF YOU AGREE TO RETURN THE GOODS TO THE SELLER AND FAIL TO DO SO, THEN YOU REMAIN LIABLE FOR PERFORMANCE OF ALL OBLIGATIONS UNDER THE CONTRACT.

TO CANCEL THIS TRANSACTION, MAIL OR DELIVER A SIGNED AND DATED COPY OF THIS CANCELLATION NOTICE OR ANY OTHER WRITTEN NOTICE TO [Insert Name of Seller] **AT** [Insert Address of Seller's Place of Business] **NOT LATER THAN MIDNIGHT OF**

_____.
Date

I HEREBY CANCEL THIS TRANSACTION.

_____   _____
Date   Buyer's Signature

Contractor   Buyer   Buyer
Page __ of __

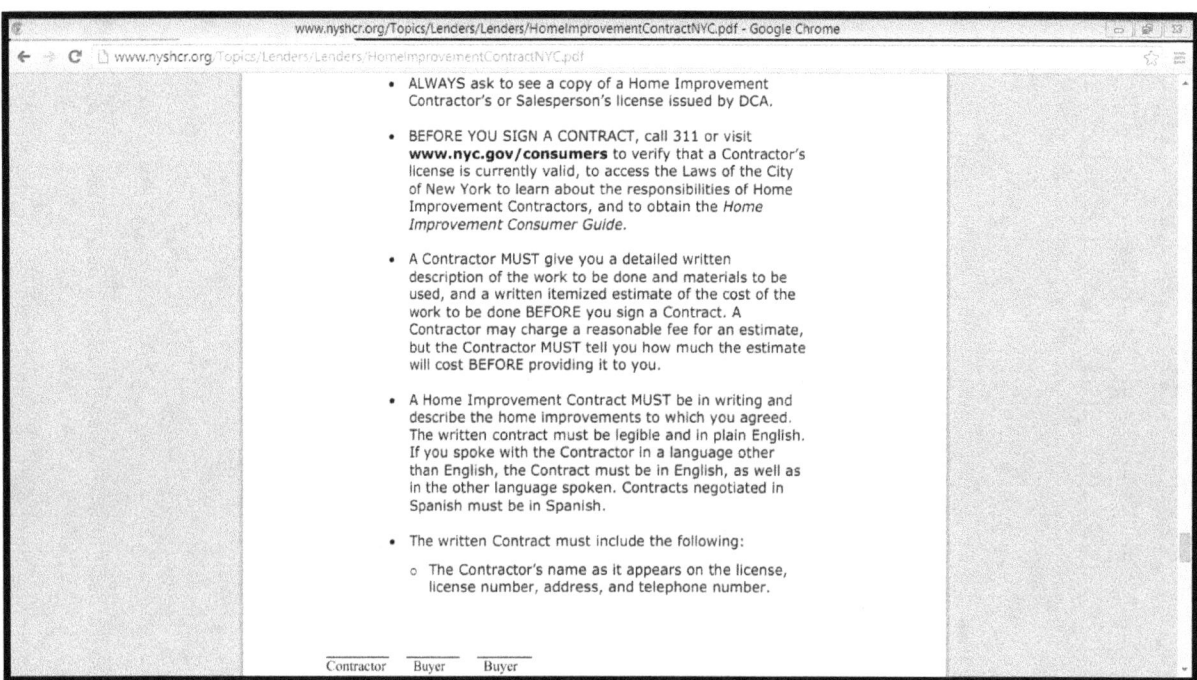

Jonathan Mintz
Commissioner

Dial 311
(212-NEW-YORK)

nyc.gov/consumers

Department of Consumer Affairs

CONSUMER BILL OF RIGHTS ON CONTRACTING FOR HOME IMPROVEMENTS

- Home Improvement Contractors are required to be licensed by the New York City Department of Consumer Affairs (DCA).

- ALWAYS ask to see a copy of a Home Improvement

- ALWAYS ask to see a copy of a Home Improvement Contractor's or Salesperson's license issued by DCA.

- BEFORE YOU SIGN A CONTRACT, call 311 or visit **www.nyc.gov/consumers** to verify that a Contractor's license is currently valid, to access the Laws of the City of New York to learn about the responsibilities of Home Improvement Contractors, and to obtain the _Home Improvement Consumer Guide._

- A Contractor MUST give you a detailed written description of the work to be done and materials to be used, and a written itemized estimate of the cost of the work to be done BEFORE you sign a Contract. A Contractor may charge a reasonable fee for an estimate, but the Contractor MUST tell you how much the estimate will cost BEFORE providing it to you.

- A Home Improvement Contract MUST be in writing and describe the home improvements to which you agreed. The written contract must be legible and in plain English. If you spoke with the Contractor in a language other than English, the Contract must be in English, as well as in the other language spoken. Contracts negotiated in Spanish must be in Spanish.

- The written Contract must include the following:
  o The Contractor's name as it appears on the license, license number, address, and telephone number.

_____   _____   _____
Contractor   Buyer   Buyer

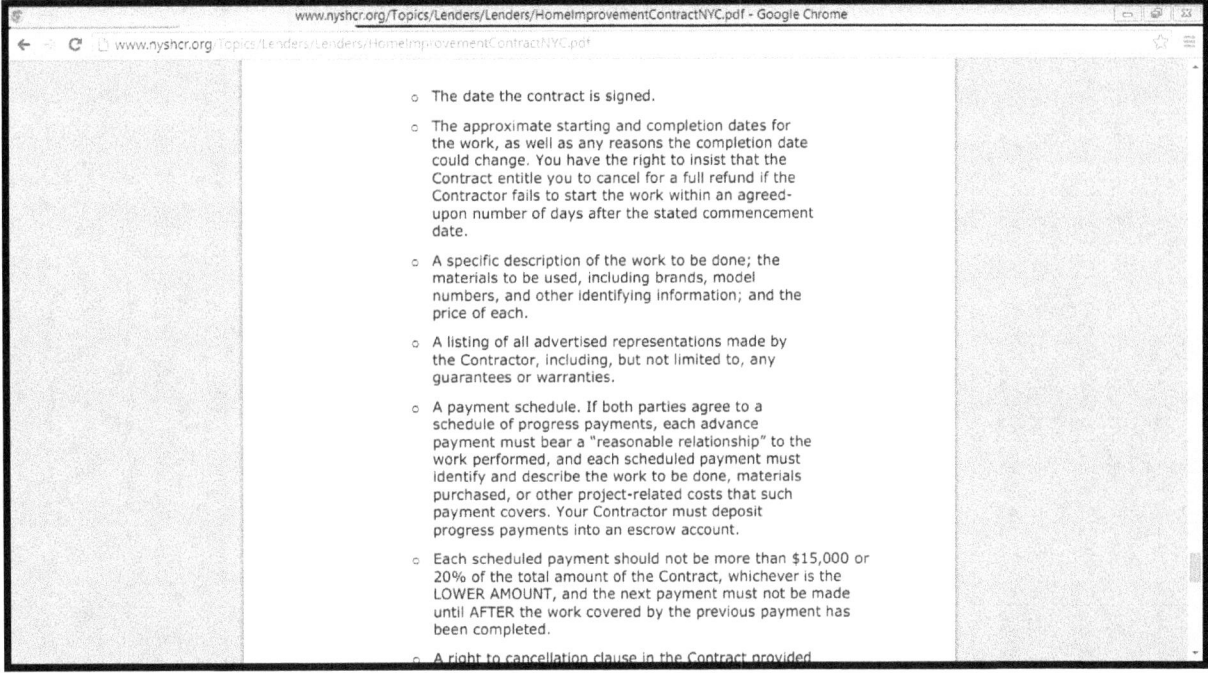

- The date the contract is signed.

- The approximate starting and completion dates for the work, as well as any reasons the completion date could change. You have the right to insist that the Contract entitle you to cancel for a full refund if the Contractor fails to start the work within an agreed-upon number of days after the stated commencement date.

- A specific description of the work to be done; the materials to be used, including brands, model numbers, and other identifying information; and the price of each.

- A listing of all advertised representations made by the Contractor, including, but not limited to, any guarantees or warranties.

- A payment schedule. If both parties agree to a schedule of progress payments, each advance payment must bear a "reasonable relationship" to the work performed, and each scheduled payment must identify and describe the work to be done, materials purchased, or other project-related costs that such payment covers. Your Contractor must deposit progress payments into an escrow account.

- Each scheduled payment should not be more than $15,000 or 20% of the total amount of the Contract, whichever is the LOWER AMOUNT, and the next payment must not be made until AFTER the work covered by the previous payment has been completed.

- A right to cancellation clause in the Contract provided

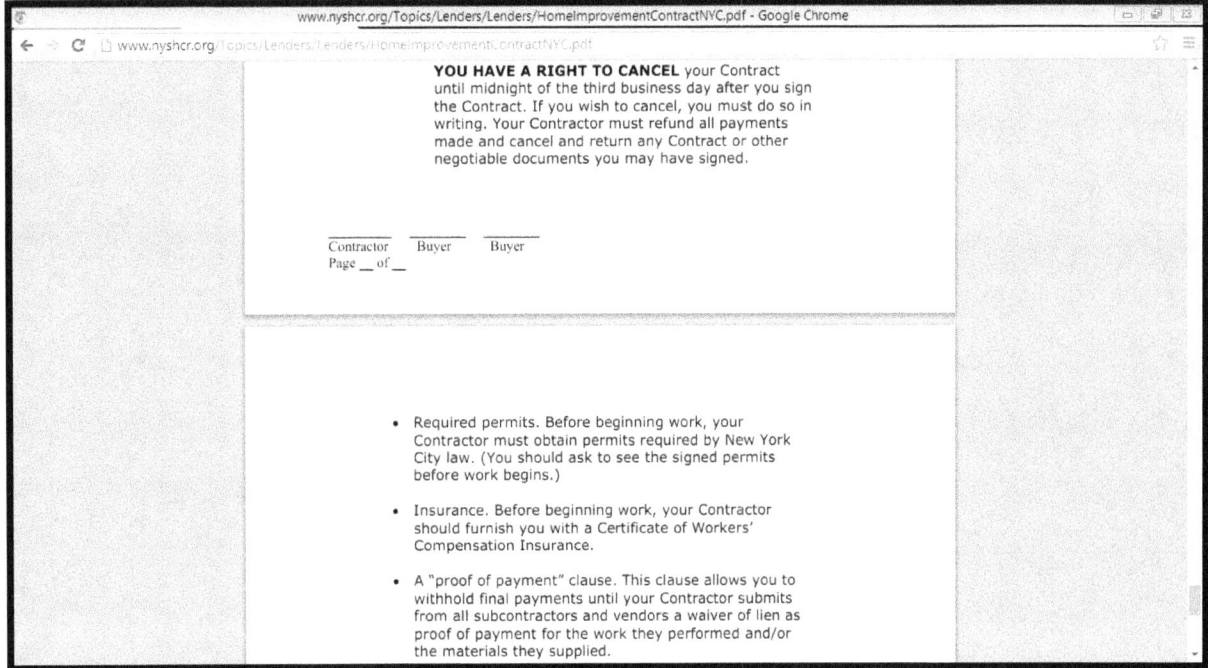

YOU HAVE A RIGHT TO CANCEL your Contract until midnight of the third business day after you sign the Contract. If you wish to cancel, you must do so in writing. Your Contractor must refund all payments made and cancel and return any Contract or other negotiable documents you may have signed.

_____ _____ _____
Contractor   Buyer   Buyer
Page __ of __

- Required permits. Before beginning work, your Contractor must obtain permits required by New York City law. (You should ask to see the signed permits before work begins.)

- Insurance. Before beginning work, your Contractor should furnish you with a Certificate of Workers' Compensation Insurance.

- A "proof of payment" clause. This clause allows you to withhold final payments until your Contractor submits from all subcontractors and vendors a waiver of lien as proof of payment for the work they performed and/or the materials they supplied.

- It is illegal for your Home Improvement Contractor to dry-scrape or sand painted surfaces in New York City. Scraping and sanding pose a danger of lead dust inhalation.

- The Contractor must clean the premises after work is completed.

- New York City law prohibits Home Improvement Contractors from acting as agents for lenders or advertising, promoting, or arranging home improvement loans.

_____   _____   _____
Contractor   Buyer   Buyer
Page ___ of ___

LISTING AGREEMENT

http://dlr.sd.gov/bdcomm/realestate/forms/listing_agreement_residential_sales.pdf

LISTING AGREEMENT
THIS IS A LEGALLY BINDING CONTRACT. IF YOU DO NOT UNDERSTAND IT, SEEK LEGAL ADVICE.

Seller:_____

Address _____

Listing Date:_____ Expiration Date:_____ (midnight)

If a purchase agreement is entered into by Seller during the term of this agreement, the termination thereof shall extend to and include the date of closing under said purchase agreement as to the purchasers only.

1. The undersigned Seller warrants that Seller is the owner of record of the property or has the written authority, attached, to execute this Agreement on behalf of the owner of record and hereby grants the undersigned Broker, for the above term, the exclusive irrevocable right and privilege to sell the following property legally described as: _____

_____

_____

Also known as:_____

For the sum of:_____ ($_____)

On the following terms: _____

_____

or with Seller's consent, for a lesser sum or on other terms, which price includes all encumbrances, taxes, and assessments.

---

2. A. Broker will represent Seller as outlined in Article I of the attached Agency Agreement Addendum. Broker will act, with Seller's consent, as outlined in Article III when showing Seller's property to buyer client(s) of Broker. Seller acknowledges and consents that Broker may represent and/or assist other sellers of similar properties. Prospective buyers will be offered the opportunity to inspect Seller's property and also any or all similar properties.

   B. Seller authorizes Broker, by initials in the appropriate space, to:

   a) cooperate with brokers who represent buyers. Yes_____/_____ No_____/_____

   b) compensate cooperating brokers. Yes_____/_____ No_____/_____

3. The term "sale" shall be deemed to include any exchange or trade to which Seller consents. In the event of an exchange or trade, Broker is permitted to represent and receive compensation from both parties.

Page 1 of 4

SDREC LISTINGAGREEMENT 2011

4. Seller represents the title of the property to be good and merchantable and hereby represents that all known encumbrances, liens or clouds on title are disclosed. In the event of a sale, exchange or trade, Seller at Seller's expense will convey good and merchantable title to said property by Warranty Deed or sufficient conveyance instrument to Buyer, thereof. In the event of an undisclosed encumbrance that results in cancellation by Buyer, discharge of Buyer from purchase price and/or assumption by Buyer who is credited on the purchase price for the undisclosed encumbrances, liens, or cloud on title, Seller shall be liable to Broker for fee outlined in Section 5 as though contract of sale was not canceled.

5. If during the period of this agreement the property is sold by Seller, Broker, a cooperating broker, or anyone else; or should any of the aforementioned produce a purchaser ready, willing, and able to purchase the property; or within _____ days after the expiration or mutual written termination of this contract, a sale is made to any person to whom the property has been shown during the listing period; Seller agrees to pay a fee for professional services of $_____ OR _____ percent of the selling price plus appropriate sales tax. Seller further agrees that Broker or Broker's authorized representative may act as escrow agent for all money, papers, and documents associated with this transaction. If this property is listed with another licensed real estate broker after expiration or mutual written termination of this listing, this contract shall be null and void in its entirety.

6. If an accepted offer and agreement to purchase does not close, both Buyer and Seller must agree in writing prior to release of earnest money in accordance with SDCL 36-21A-81. If the earnest money deposited by Buyer is forfeited, the earnest money, less expenses, will be divided between Broker and Seller with ___% to Seller and ___% to Broker. However, in no case may Broker's share exceed the commission stated herein.

7. The following personal property is included in the stated price and shall be conveyed by Seller to Buyer, free of liens and without warranty of condition, by a bill of sale at closing and in accordance with its terms:

_____

_____

_____

_____

_____

8. Seller authorizes Broker, by initials in the appropriate space, to:

A. place property with the Multiple Listing Service.   Yes_____/_____ No_____/_____
B. place a "For Sale" sign on property.   Yes_____/_____ No_____/_____
C. install a lockbox on the property.   Yes_____/_____ No_____/_____
D. request mortgage to release information to Broker.   Yes_____/_____ No_____/_____
E. request utility companies to release information to Broker. Yes_____/_____ No_____/_____
F. advertise by computerized or other media.   Yes_____/_____ No_____/_____
G. disclose to buyers or buyers' agents that Seller has
   received other offers   Yes_____/_____ No_____/_____

---

9. This property is offered for sale regardless of race, color, creed, religion, sex, disability, familial status, country of national origin or any other category protected under federal, state or local law.

10. Seller(s) shall complete and submit a property condition disclosure statement as required by SDCL 43-4-38, unless exempt pursuant to SDCL 43-4-43, with this listing agreement.

11. Seller(s) shall complete and submit a lead-based paint disclosure if property is residential and was built prior to 1978 as required by federal regulation.

12. Seller agrees to indemnify and hold harmless Broker and Broker's agents from any claim(s) arising out of misrepresented or incomplete disclosure statements made by Seller.

13. Seller acknowledges that there may be tax consequences arising out of the sale of this property and is advised to seek competent tax advice.

14. Unless otherwise agreed in writing, Seller acknowledges that Broker and Broker's agents owe no duty to conduct an independent inspection of the property or to conduct an independent investigation of Seller's financial condition, and owe no duty to independently verify the accuracy or completeness of any statement made by either party or by any source reasonably believed by Broker and Broker's agents to be reliable.

15. This Agreement shall be binding upon and inure to the benefit of Seller's heirs, executors, administrators and assigns of the respective parties to this Agreement.

16. Special instructions: _____

_____

_____

Receipt of a copy of this contract by the seller has been acknowledged.

Seller _____ Date _____

Seller _____ Date _____

Broker/Firm_____

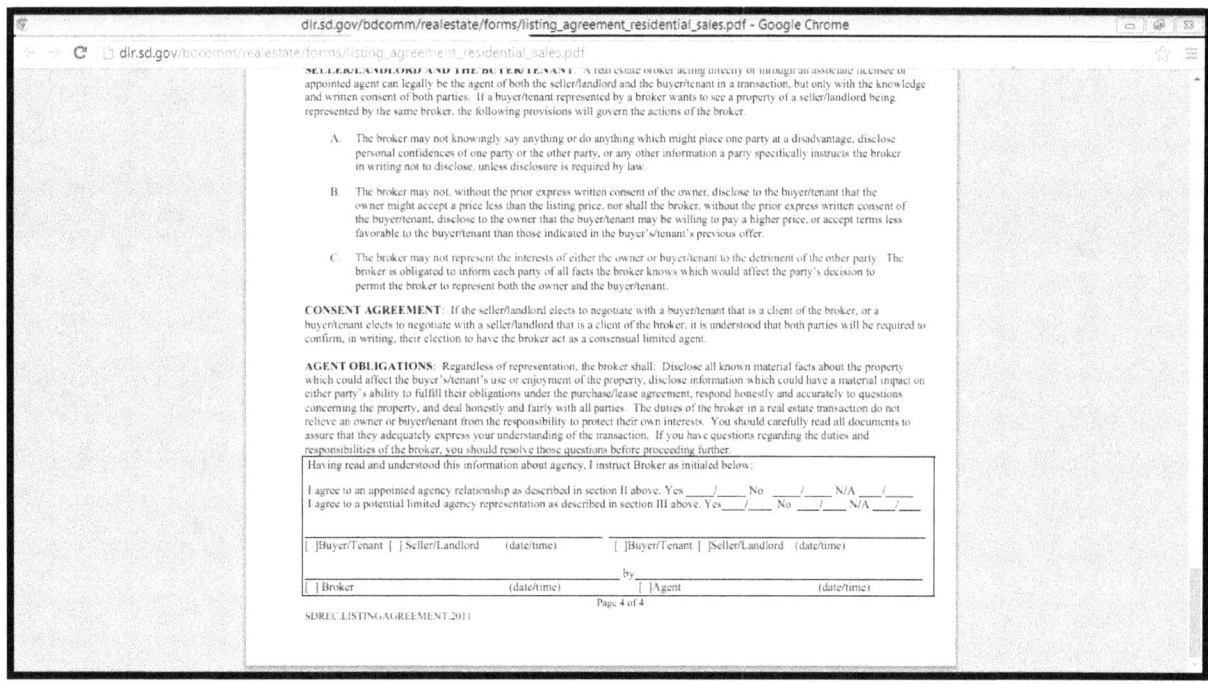

AGENCY AGREEMENT ADDENDUM

This addendum is attached to and made a part of the ___ listing agreement ___ buyer agency agreement dated _____,

between _____ (Brokerage Firm) and

_____ (Client)

I. IF THE BROKER REPRESENTS THE ___SELLER/LANDLORD or ___ BUYER/TENANT: If a broker enters into an agreement to represent a seller/landlord or buyer/tenant as a client, the broker and all licensees associated with that broker represent the client. An agent/subagent owes the client the duties of loyalty, obedience, disclosure, confidentiality, reasonable care and diligence, and full accounting.

II. IF THE BROKER APPOINTS AN ASSOCIATE LICENSEE TO REPRESENT THE ___SELLER/LANDLORD or ___BUYER/TENANT: If a broker enters into an agreement to represent a seller/landlord or buyer/tenant as a client, the broker appoints _____ as the client's appointed agent. For the purposes of this addendum, the client shall have an agency relationship with ONLY the appointed agent, the responsible broker _____ and, if applicable, responsible broker's designated broker

The responsible broker may appoint other affiliated licensees during the term of the brokerage agreement should the appointed agent not be able to fulfill the terms of the brokerage agreement or as by agreement between the responsible broker and the client. An appointment of another affiliated licensee or an additional affiliated licensee does not relieve the first appointed agent of any duties owed to the client. In an appointed agency relationship, the responsible broker and, if applicable, the responsible broker's designated broker will act in a limited agency capacity.

III. IF THE BROKER, ASSOCIATE LICENSEE OR APPOINTED AGENT REPRESENTS BOTH THE SELLER/LANDLORD AND THE BUYER/TENANT: A real estate broker acting directly or through an associate licensee or appointed agent can legally be the agent of both the seller/landlord and the buyer/tenant in a transaction, but only with the knowledge and written consent of both parties. If a buyer/tenant represented by a broker wants to see a property of a seller/landlord being represented by the same broker, the following provisions will govern the actions of the broker.

    A. The broker may not knowingly say anything or do anything which might place one party at a disadvantage, disclose personal confidences of one party or the other party, or any other information a party specifically instructs the broker in writing not to disclose, unless disclosure is required by law.

    B. The broker may not, without the prior express written consent of the owner, disclose to the buyer/tenant that the owner might accept a price less than the listing price, nor shall the broker, without the prior express written consent of the buyer/tenant, disclose to the owner that the buyer/tenant may be willing to pay a higher price, or accept terms less favorable to the buyer/tenant than those indicated in the buyer's/tenant's previous offer.

    C. The broker may not represent the interests of either the owner or buyer/tenant to the detriment of the other party. The broker is obligated to inform each party of all facts the broker knows which would affect the party's decision to permit the broker to represent both the owner and the buyer/tenant.

CONSENT AGREEMENT: If the seller/landlord elects to negotiate with a buyer/tenant that is a client of the broker, or a buyer/tenant elects to negotiate with a seller/landlord that is a client of the broker, it is understood that both parties will be required to confirm, in writing, their election to have the broker act as a consensual limited agent.

SELLER/LANDLORD AND THE BUYER/TENANT: A real estate broker acting directly or through an associate licensee or appointed agent can legally be the agent of both the seller/landlord and the buyer/tenant in a transaction, but only with the knowledge and written consent of both parties. If a buyer/tenant represented by a broker wants to see a property of a seller/landlord being represented by the same broker, the following provisions will govern the actions of the broker.

    A. The broker may not knowingly say anything or do anything which might place one party at a disadvantage, disclose personal confidences of one party or the other party, or any other information a party specifically instructs the broker in writing not to disclose, unless disclosure is required by law.

    B. The broker may not, without the prior express written consent of the owner, disclose to the buyer/tenant that the owner might accept a price less than the listing price, nor shall the broker, without the prior express written consent of the buyer/tenant, disclose to the owner that the buyer/tenant may be willing to pay a higher price, or accept terms less favorable to the buyer/tenant than those indicated in the buyer's/tenant's previous offer.

    C. The broker may not represent the interests of either the owner or buyer/tenant to the detriment of the other party. The broker is obligated to inform each party of all facts the broker knows which would affect the party's decision to permit the broker to represent both the owner and the buyer/tenant.

CONSENT AGREEMENT: If the seller/landlord elects to negotiate with a buyer/tenant that is a client of the broker, or a buyer/tenant elects to negotiate with a seller/landlord that is a client of the broker, it is understood that both parties will be required to confirm, in writing, their election to have the broker act as a consensual limited agent.

AGENT OBLIGATIONS: Regardless of representation, the broker shall: Disclose all known material facts about the property which could affect the buyer's/tenant's use or enjoyment of the property, disclose information which could have a material impact on either party's ability to fulfill their obligations under the purchase/lease agreement, respond honestly and accurately to questions concerning the property, and deal honestly and fairly with all parties. The duties of the broker in a real estate transaction do not relieve an owner or buyer/tenant from the responsibility to protect their own interests. You should carefully read all documents to assure that they adequately express your understanding of the transaction. If you have questions regarding the duties and responsibilities of the broker, you should resolve those questions before proceeding further.

Having read and understood this information about agency, I instruct Broker as initialed below:

I agree to an appointed agency relationship as described in section II above. Yes ____/____ No ____/____ N/A ____/____

I agree to a potential limited agency representation as described in section III above. Yes ____/____ No ____/____ N/A ____/____

_____   _____

[ ]Buyer/Tenant [ ] Seller/Landlord   (date/time)   [ ]Buyer/Tenant [ ]Seller/Landlord (date/time)

                       by _____

[ ] Broker   (date/time)   [ ]Agent   (date/time)

SDREC LISTING AGREEMENT 2011

SCHEDULE C

http://www.irs.gov/pub/irs-pdf/f1040sc.pdf

www.irs.gov/pub/irs-pdf/f1040sc.pdf - Google Chrome

SCHEDULE C
(Form 1040)

Department of the Treasury
Internal Revenue Service (99)

Profit or Loss From Business
(Sole Proprietorship)

▶ For information on Schedule C and its instructions, go to *www.irs.gov/schedulec.*
▶ Attach to Form 1040, 1040NR, or 1041; partnerships generally must file Form 1065.

OMB No. 1545-0074

2013

Attachment
Sequence No. **09**

Name of proprietor

Social security number (SSN)

A Principal business or profession, including product or service (see instructions)

B Enter code from instructions
▶

C Business name. If no separate business name, leave blank.

D Employer ID number (EIN), (see instr.)

E Business address (including suite or room no.) ▶
   City, town or post office, state, and ZIP code

F Accounting method: (1) ☐ Cash (2) ☐ Accrual (3) ☐ Other (specify) ▶

G Did you "materially participate" in the operation of this business during 2013? If "No," see instructions for limit on losses ☐ Yes ☐ No

H If you started or acquired this business during 2013, check here . . . . ▶ ☐

I Did you make any payments in 2013 that would require you to file Form(s) 1099? (see instructions) . . . ☐ Yes ☐ No

J If "Yes," did you or will you file required Forms 1099? . . . . ☐ Yes ☐ No

Part I Income

1	Gross receipts or sales. See instructions for line 1 and check the box if this income was reported to you on Form W-2 and the "Statutory employee" box on that form was checked . . . . . . ▶ ☐	1	
2	Returns and allowances	2	
3	Subtract line 2 from line 1	3	
4	Cost of goods sold (from line 42)	4	
5	**Gross profit.** Subtract line 4 from line 3	5	
6	Other income, including federal and state gasoline or fuel tax credit or refund (see instructions) . . .	6	
7	**Gross income.** Add lines 5 and 6 . . . . ▶	7	

Part II Expenses Enter expenses for business use of your home only on line 30.

8	Advertising	8		18	Office expense (see instructions)	18
9	Car and truck expenses (see instructions) . .	9		19	Pension and profit-sharing plans	19
				20	Rent or lease (see instructions):	
10	Commissions and fees .	10		a	Vehicles, machinery, and equipment	20a
11	Contract labor (see instructions)	11		b	Other business property . . .	20b
12	Depletion	12		21	Repairs and maintenance . . .	21
13	Depreciation and section 179 expense deduction (not included in Part III) (see instructions) .	13		22	Supplies (not included in Part III)	22
				23	Taxes and licenses	23
				24	Travel, meals, and entertainment:	
14	Employee benefit programs (other than on line 19) .	14		a	Travel	24a
				b	Deductible meals and	

www.irs.gov/pub/irs-pdf/f1040sc.pdf - Google Chrome

15	Insurance (other than health)	15			entertainment (see instructions) .	24b
16	Interest:			25	Utilities	25
a	Mortgage (paid to banks, etc.)	16a		26	Wages (less employment credits)	26
b	Other	16b		27a	Other expenses (from line 48) .	27a
17	Legal and professional services	17		b	Reserved for future use . .	27b

28	**Total expenses** before expenses for business use of home. Add lines 8 through 27a . . . . ▶	28	
29	Tentative profit or (loss). Subtract line 28 from line 7	29	
30	Expenses for business use of your home. Do not report these expenses elsewhere. Attach Form 8829 unless using the simplified method (see instructions). **Simplified method filers only:** enter the total square footage of: (a) your home: _____ and (b) the part of your home used for business: _____. Use the Simplified Method Worksheet in the instructions to figure the amount to enter on line 30	30	
31	**Net profit or (loss).** Subtract line 30 from line 29.		
	• If a profit, enter on both **Form 1040, line 12** (or **Form 1040NR, line 13**) and on **Schedule SE, line 2.** (If you checked the box on line 1, see instructions). Estates and trusts, enter on **Form 1041, line 3.**	31	
	• If a loss, you **must** go to line 32.		
32	If you have a loss, check the box that describes your investment in this activity (see instructions).		
	• If you checked 32a, enter the loss on both **Form 1040, line 12,** (or **Form 1040NR, line 13**) and on **Schedule SE, line 2.** (If you checked the box on line 1, see the line 31 instructions). Estates and trusts, enter on **Form 1041, line 3.**	32a ☐ All investment is at risk. 32b ☐ Some investment is not at risk.	
	• If you checked 32b, you **must** attach Form 6198. Your loss may be limited.		

For Paperwork Reduction Act Notice, see the separate instructions. Cat. No. 11334P Schedule C (Form 1040) 2013

Schedule C (Form 1040) 2013 Page **2**

Part III Cost of Goods Sold (see instructions)

33	Method(s) used to value closing inventory: a ☐ Cost b ☐ Lower of cost or market c ☐ Other (attach explanation)		
34	Was there any change in determining quantities, costs, or valuations between opening and closing inventory? If "Yes," attach explanation . . . . ☐ Yes ☐ No		
35	Inventory at beginning of year. If different from last year's closing inventory, attach explanation . . .	35	
36	Purchases less cost of items withdrawn for personal use	36	
37	Cost of labor. Do not include any amounts paid to yourself	37	

38	Materials and supplies	38	
39	Other costs	39	
40	Add lines 35 through 39	40	
41	Inventory at end of year	41	
42	**Cost of goods sold.** Subtract line 41 from line 40. Enter the result here and on line 4	42	

Part IV Information on Your Vehicle. Complete this part **only** if you are claiming car or truck expenses on line 9 and are not required to file Form 4562 for this business. See the instructions for line 13 to find out if you must file Form 4562.

43 When did you place your vehicle in service for business purposes? (month, day, year) ▶ / /

44 Of the total number of miles you drove your vehicle during 2013, enter the number of miles you used your vehicle for:

a Business _____ b Commuting (see instructions) _____ c Other _____

45 Was your vehicle available for personal use during off-duty hours? ☐ Yes ☐ No

46 Do you (or your spouse) have another vehicle available for personal use? ☐ Yes ☐ No

47a Do you have evidence to support your deduction? ☐ Yes ☐ No

b If "Yes," is the evidence written? ☐ Yes ☐ No

Part V Other Expenses. List below business expenses not included on lines 8–26 or line 30.

| 42 | **Cost of goods sold.** Subtract line 41 from line 40. Enter the result here and on line 4 | 42 | |

Part IV Information on Your Vehicle. Complete this part **only** if you are claiming car or truck expenses on line 9 and are not required to file Form 4562 for this business. See the instructions for line 13 to find out if you must file Form 4562.

43 When did you place your vehicle in service for business purposes? (month, day, year) ▶ / /

44 Of the total number of miles you drove your vehicle during 2013, enter the number of miles you used your vehicle for:

a Business _____ b Commuting (see instructions) _____ c Other _____

45 Was your vehicle available for personal use during off-duty hours? ☐ Yes ☐ No

46 Do you (or your spouse) have another vehicle available for personal use? ☐ Yes ☐ No

47a Do you have evidence to support your deduction? ☐ Yes ☐ No

b If "Yes," is the evidence written? ☐ Yes ☐ No

Part V Other Expenses. List below business expenses not included on lines 8–26 or line 30.

| 48 | Total other expenses. Enter here and on line 27a | 48 | |

Schedule C (Form 1040) 2013

SCHEDULE E

http://www.irs.gov/pub/irs-pdf/f1040se.pdf

Caution. The IRS compares amounts reported on your tax return with amounts shown on Schedule(s) K-1.

Part II Income or Loss From Partnerships and S Corporations **Note.** If you report a loss from an at-risk activity for which **any amount is not** at risk, you **must** check the box in column (e) on line 28 and attach **Form 6198**. See instructions.

27   Are you reporting any loss not allowed in a prior year due to the at-risk, excess farm loss, or basis limitations, a prior year unallowed loss from a passive activity (if that loss was not reported on Form 8582), or unreimbursed partnership expenses? If you answered "Yes," see instructions before completing this section. Yes ☐ No ☐

28	(a) Name	(b) Enter P for partnership; S for S corporation	(c) Check if foreign partnership	(d) Employer identification number	(e) Check if any amount is not at risk
A					
B					
C					
D					

	Passive Income and Loss		Nonpassive Income and Loss		
	(f) Passive loss allowed (attach Form 8582 if required)	(g) Passive income from Schedule K-1	(h) Nonpassive loss from Schedule K-1	(i) Section 179 expense deduction from Form 4562	(j) Nonpassive income from Schedule K-1
A					
B					
C					
D					

| 29a | Totals | | | | |
| b | Totals | | | | |

30	Add columns (g) and (j) of line 29a		30	
31	Add columns (f), (h), and (i) of line 29b		31	( )
32	**Total partnership and S corporation income or (loss).** Combine lines 30 and 31. Enter the result here and include in the total on line 41 below		32	

Part III Income or Loss From Estates and Trusts

33	(a) Name	(b) Employer identification number
A		
B		

	Passive Income and Loss		Nonpassive Income and Loss	
	(c) Passive deduction or loss allowed (attach Form 8582 if required)	(d) Passive income from Schedule K-1	(e) Deduction or loss from Schedule K-1	(f) Other income from Schedule K-1
A				
B				

| 34a | Totals | | | |
| b | Totals | | | |

35	Add columns (d) and (f) of line 34a		35	
36	Add columns (c) and (e) of line 34b		36	( )
37	**Total estate and trust income or (loss).** Combine lines 35 and 36. Enter the result here and include in the total on line 41 below		37	

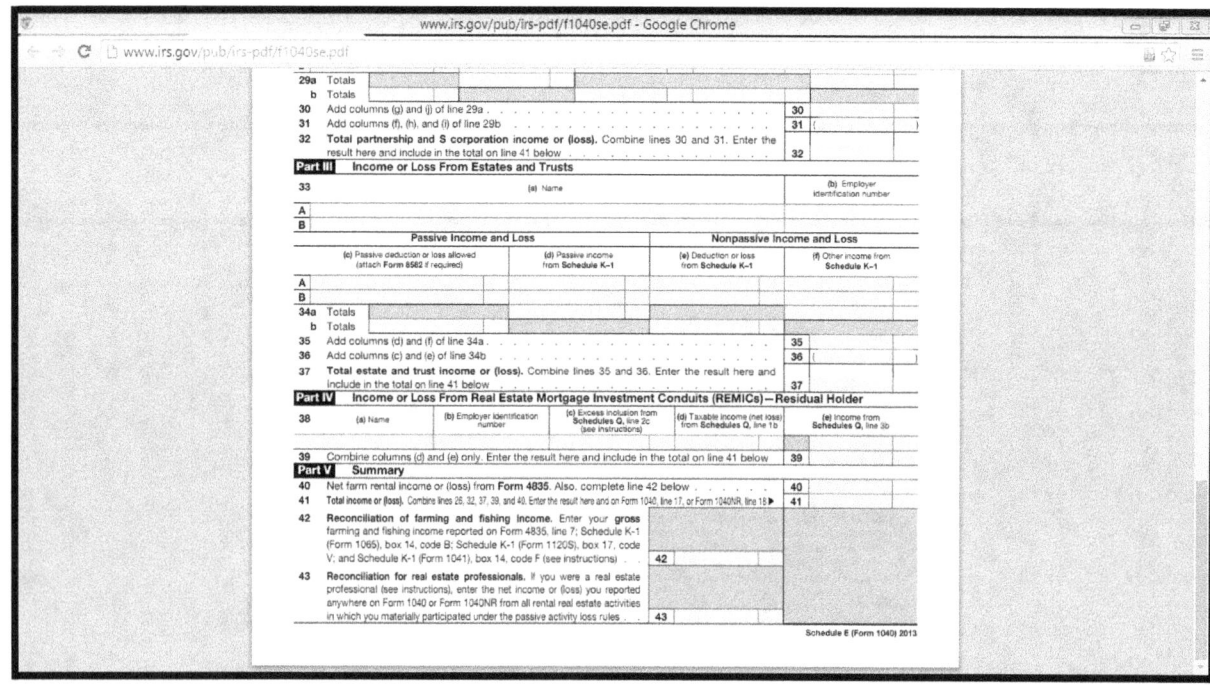

Part IV Income or Loss From Real Estate Mortgage Investment Conduits (REMICs)—Residual Holder

38	(a) Name	(b) Employer identification number	(c) Excess inclusion from Schedules Q, line 2c (see instructions)	(d) Taxable income (net loss) from Schedules Q, line 1b	(e) Income from Schedules Q, line 3b

| 39 | Combine columns (d) and (e) only. Enter the result here and include in the total on line 41 below | | 39 | |

Part V Summary

| 40 | Net farm rental income or (loss) from **Form 4835.** Also, complete line 42 below | | 40 | |
| 41 | **Total income or (loss).** Combine lines 26, 32, 37, 39, and 40. Enter the result here and on Form 1040, line 17, or Form 1040NR, line 18 ▶ | | 41 | |

42   **Reconciliation of farming and fishing income.** Enter your **gross** farming and fishing income reported on Form 4835, line 7; Schedule K-1 (Form 1065), box 14, code B; Schedule K-1 (Form 1120S), box 17, code V; and Schedule K-1 (Form 1041), box 14, code F (see instructions)   42

43   **Reconciliation for real estate professionals.** If you were a real estate professional (see instructions), enter the net income or (loss) you reported anywhere on Form 1040 or Form 1040NR from all rental real estate activities in which you materially participated under the passive activity loss rules   43

Schedule E (Form 1040) 2013

SCHEDULE D

http://www.irs.gov/pub/irs-pdf/f1040sd.pdf

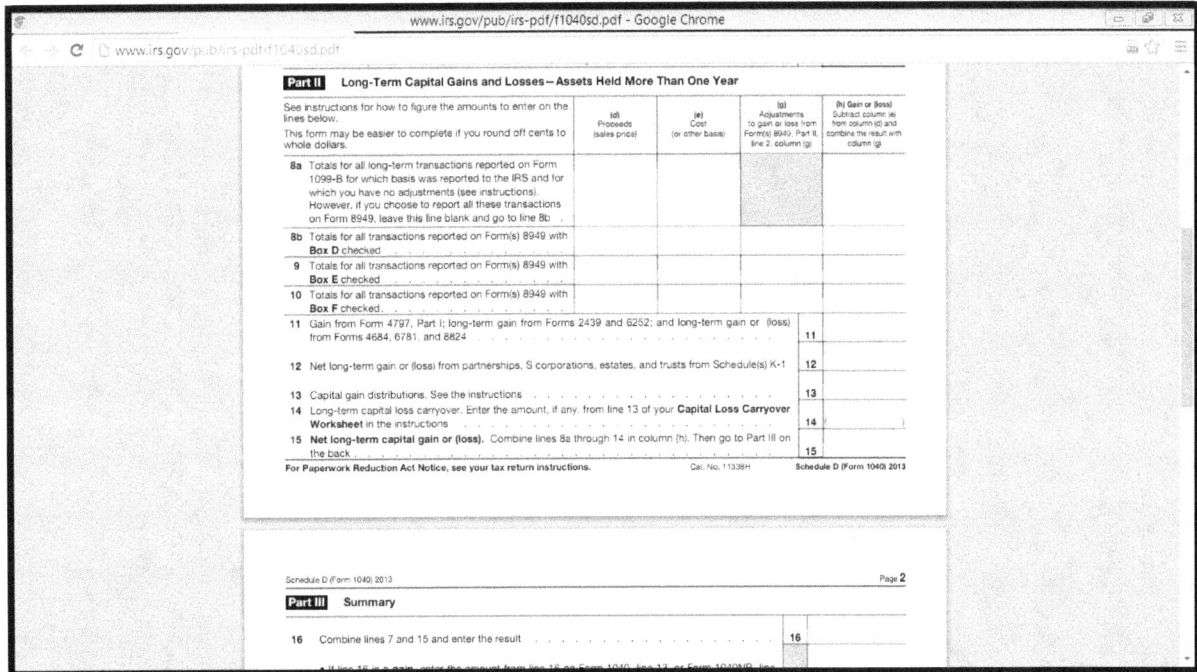

16 Combine lines 7 and 15 and enter the result . . . . | **16** |

- If line 16 is a **gain,** enter the amount from line 16 on Form 1040, line 13, or Form 1040NR, line 14. Then go to line 17 below.
- If line 16 is a **loss,** skip lines 17 through 20 below. Then go to line 21. Also be sure to complete line 22.
- If line 16 is **zero,** skip lines 17 through 21 below and enter -0- on Form 1040, line 13, or Form 1040NR, line 14. Then go to line 22.

17 Are lines 15 and 16 **both** gains?
☐ **Yes.** Go to line 18.
☐ **No.** Skip lines 18 through 21, and go to line 22.

18 Enter the amount, if any, from line 7 of the **28% Rate Gain Worksheet** in the instructions . . ▶ | **18** |

19 Enter the amount, if any, from line 18 of the **Unrecaptured Section 1250 Gain Worksheet** in the instructions . . . . ▶ | **19** |

20 Are lines 18 and 19 **both** zero or blank?
☐ **Yes.** Complete the **Qualified Dividends and Capital Gain Tax Worksheet** in the instructions for Form 1040, line 44 (or in the instructions for Form 1040NR, line 42). **Do not** complete lines 21 and 22 below.

☐ **No.** Complete the **Schedule D Tax Worksheet** in the instructions. **Do not** complete lines 21 and 22 below.

21 If line 16 is a loss, enter here and on Form 1040, line 13, or Form 1040NR, line 14, the **smaller** of:

- The loss on line 16 or
- ($3,000), or if married filing separately, ($1,500) . . . . | **21** (   ) |

Note. When figuring which amount is smaller, treat both amounts as positive numbers.

22 Do you have qualified dividends on Form 1040, line 9b, or Form 1040NR, line 10b?

☐ **Yes.** Complete the **Qualified Dividends and Capital Gain Tax Worksheet** in the instructions for Form 1040, line 44 (or in the instructions for Form 1040NR, line 42).

☐ **No.** Complete the rest of Form 1040 or Form 1040NR.

Schedule D (Form 1040) 2013

WEB SITE LINKS

CHAPTER 1

http://www.irs.gov/Forms-&-Pubs

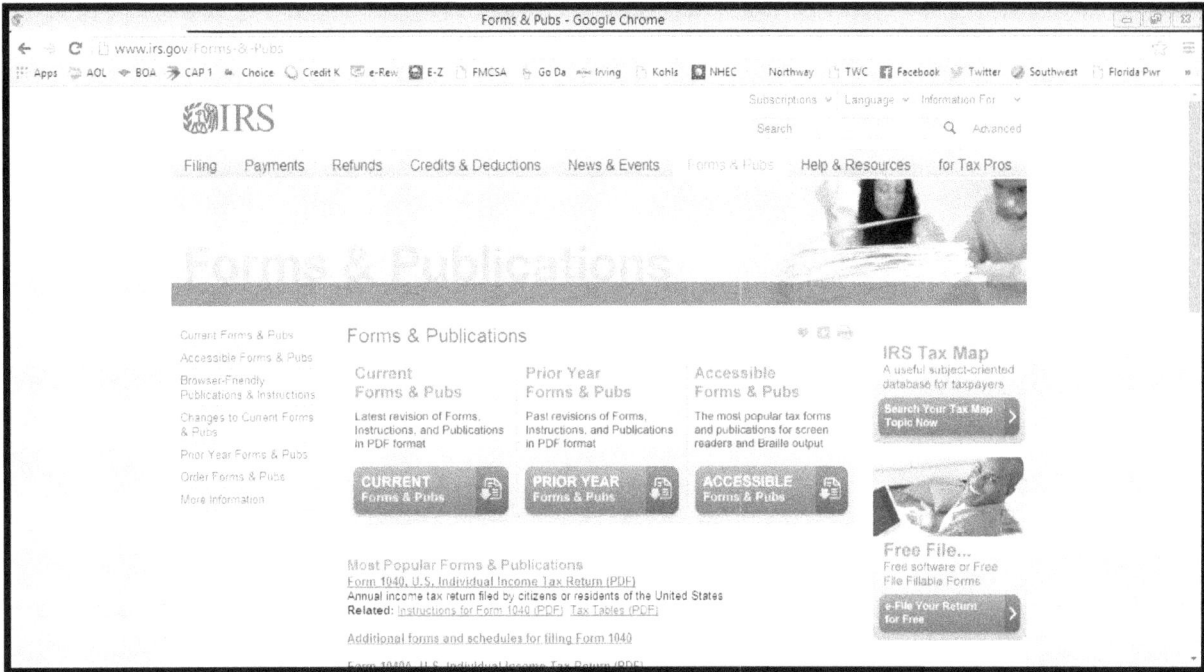

http://quickbooks.intuit.com/

https://accounts.google.com/ServiceLogin?sacu=1&scc=1&continue=https%3A%2F%2Fmail.g oogle.com%2Fmail%2Fca%2F&hl=en&service=mail

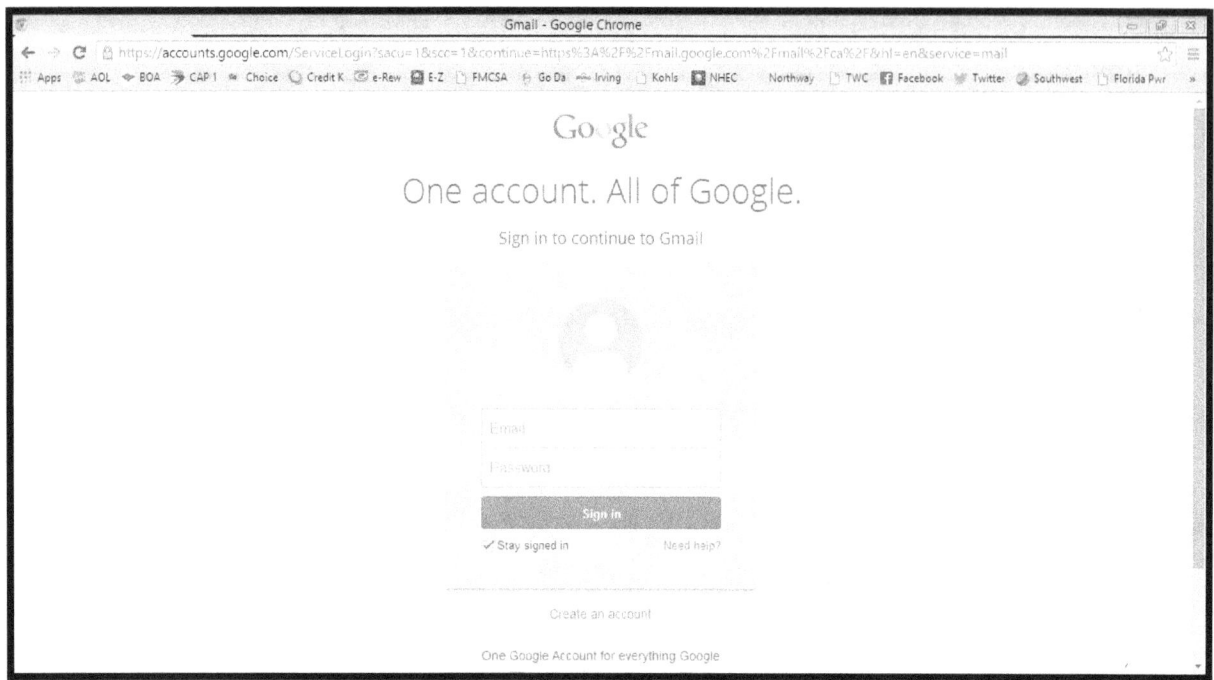

https://www.google.com/webhp?source=search_app

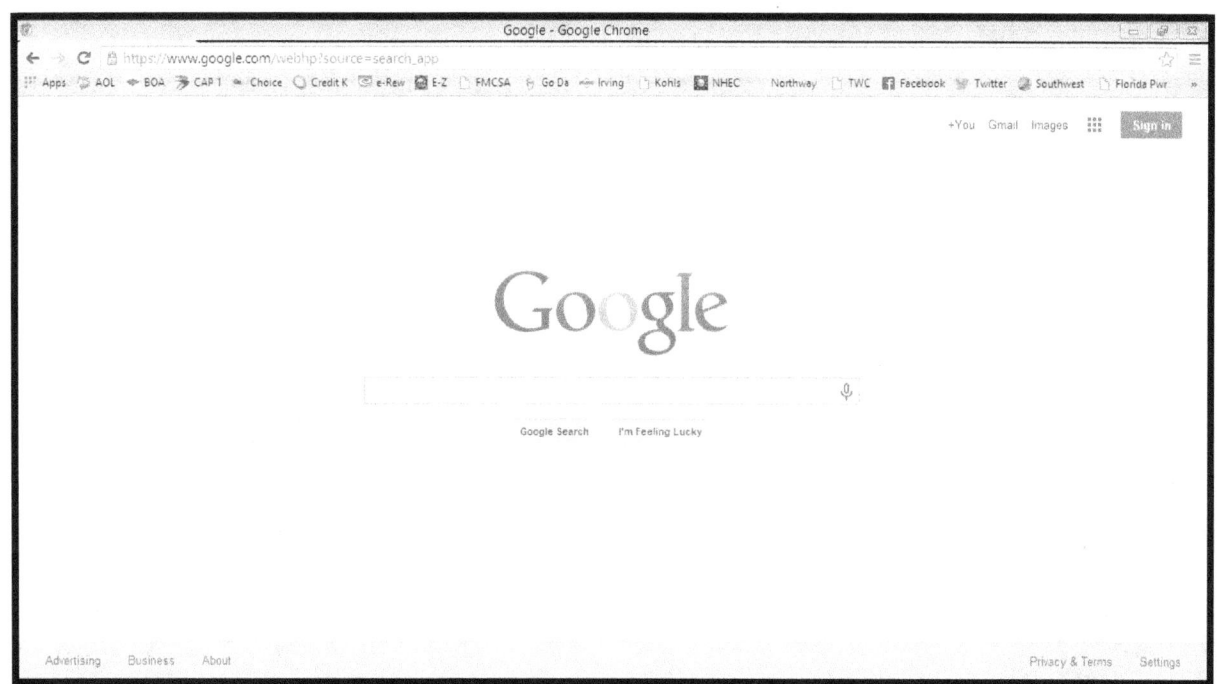

CHAPTER 2

http://www.godaddy.com/

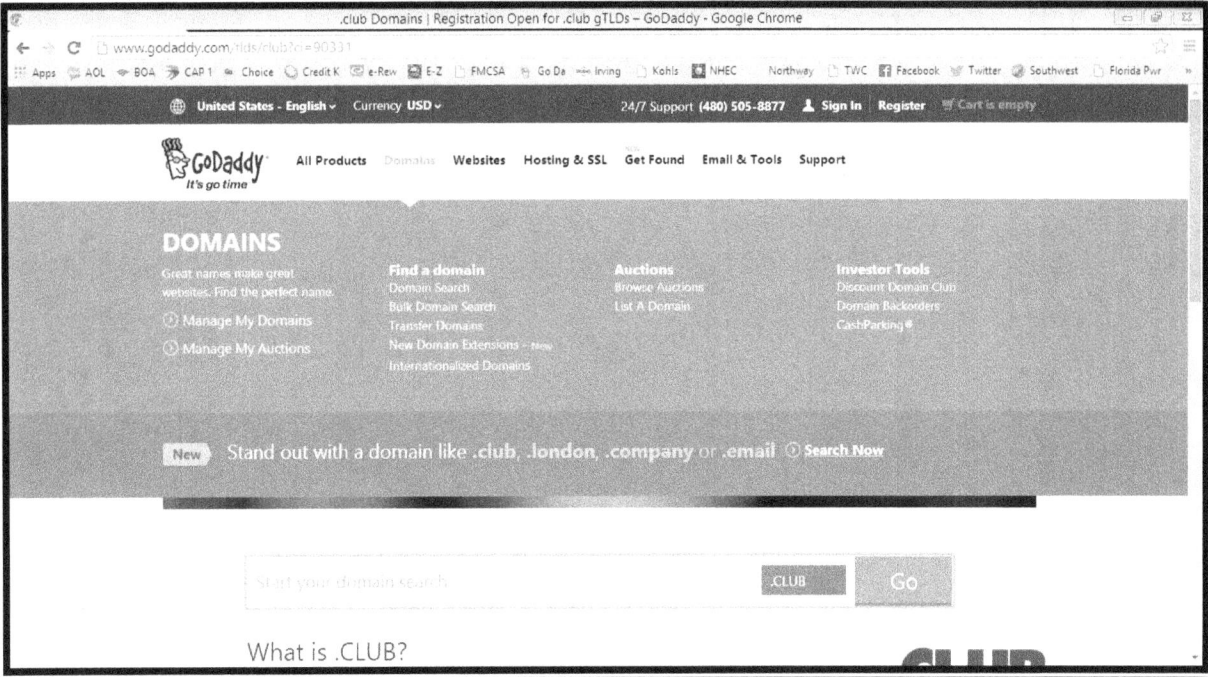

http://www.adt.com/

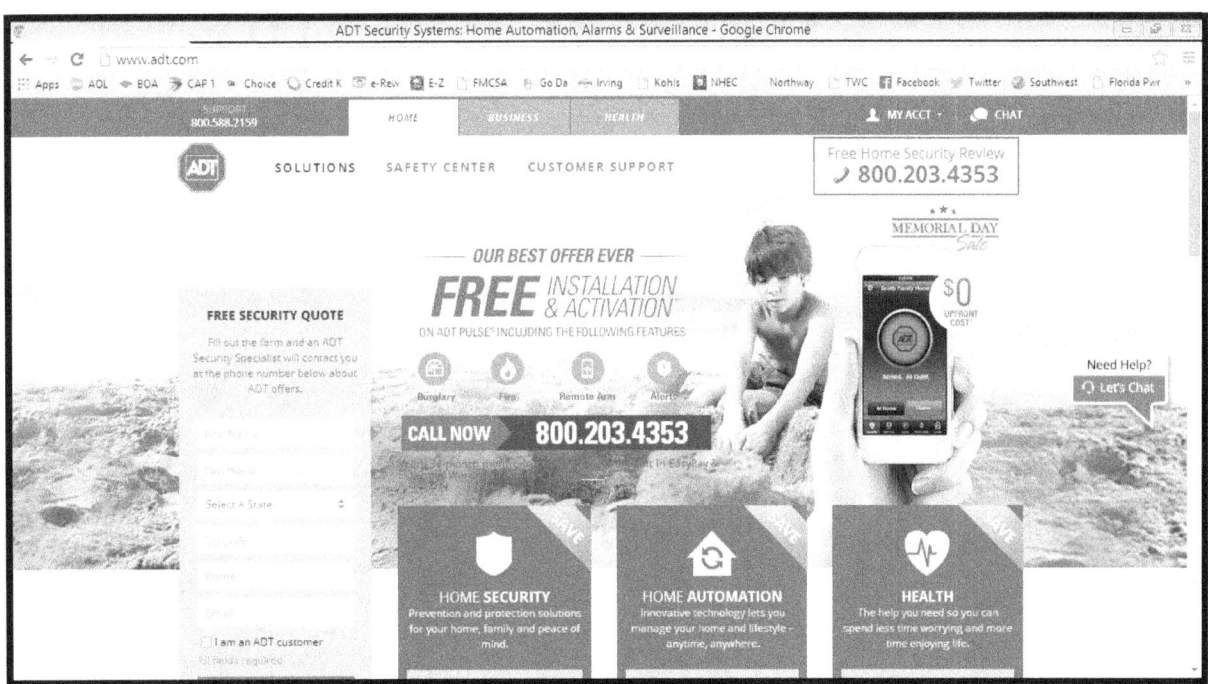

http://www.webstreet101.com/

H

CHAPTER 3

http://www.trulia.com/

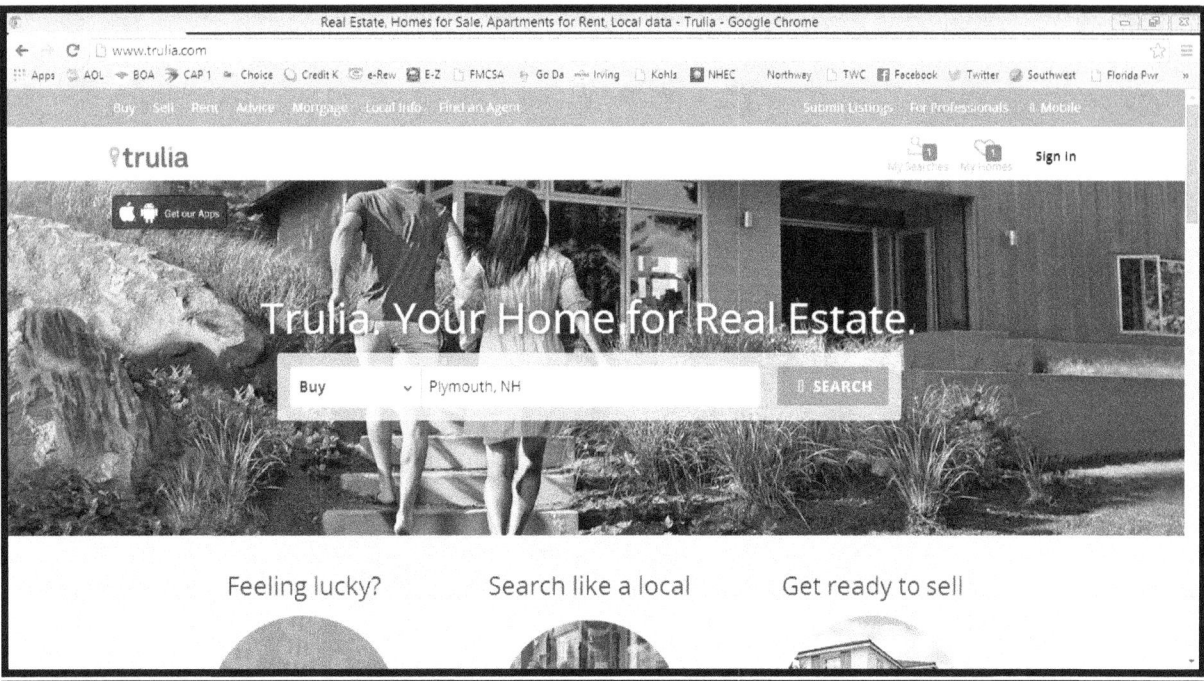

http://www.zillow.com/

http://www.realtor.com/

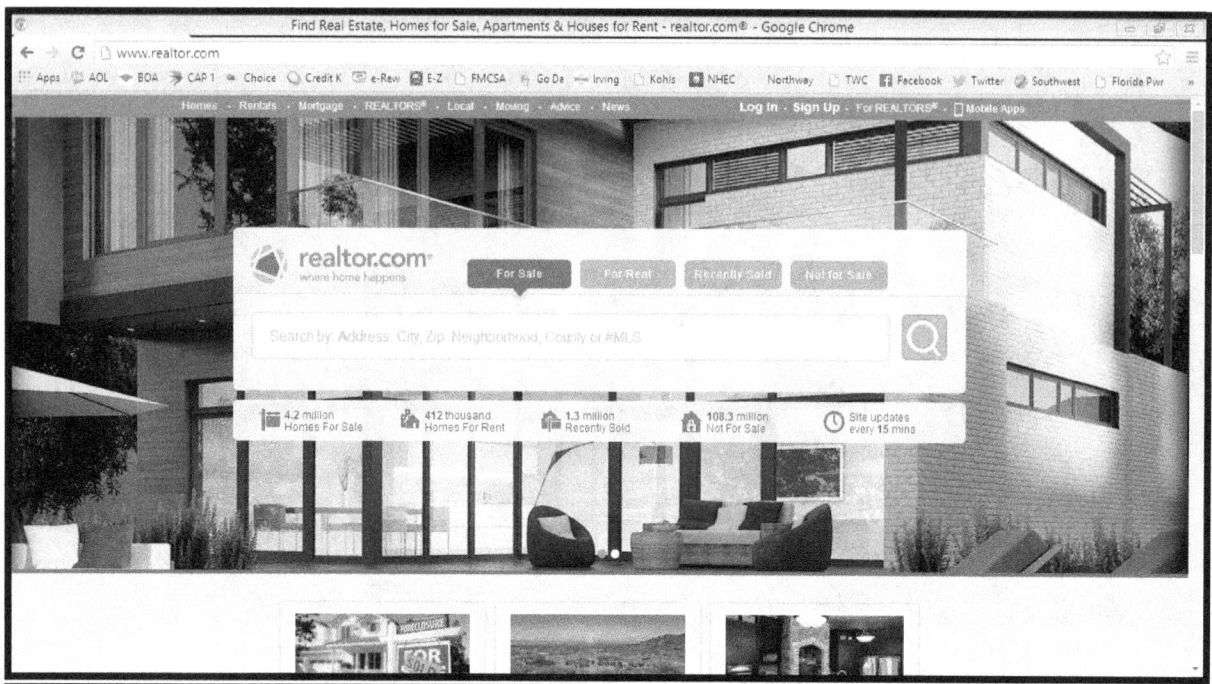

http://portal.hud.gov/hudportal/HUD?src=/topics/homes_for_sale

CHAPTER 4

http://www.appraisalinstitute.org/

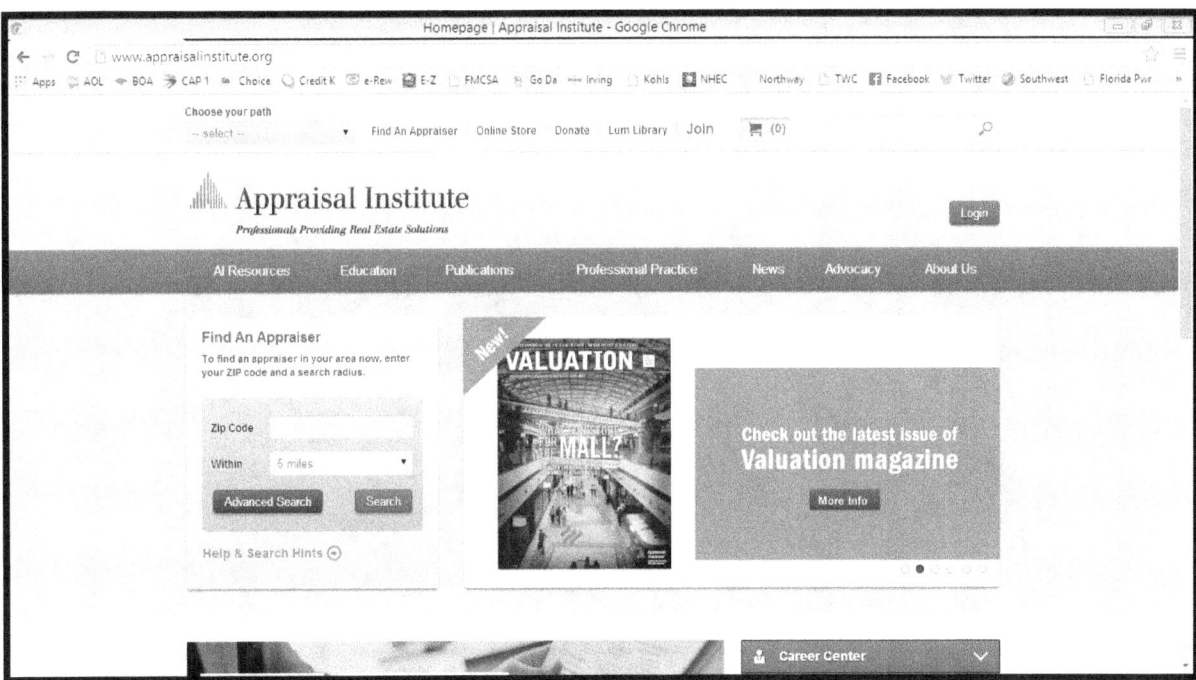

http://www.nahi.org/

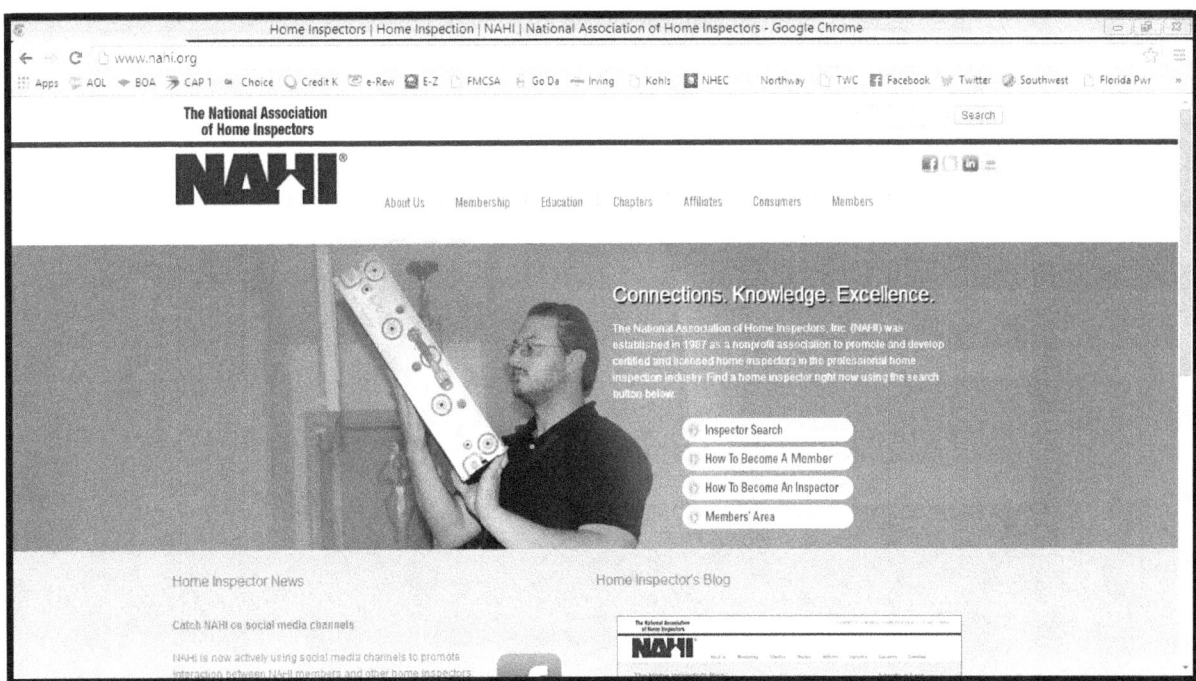

http://www.americanbar.org/aba.html

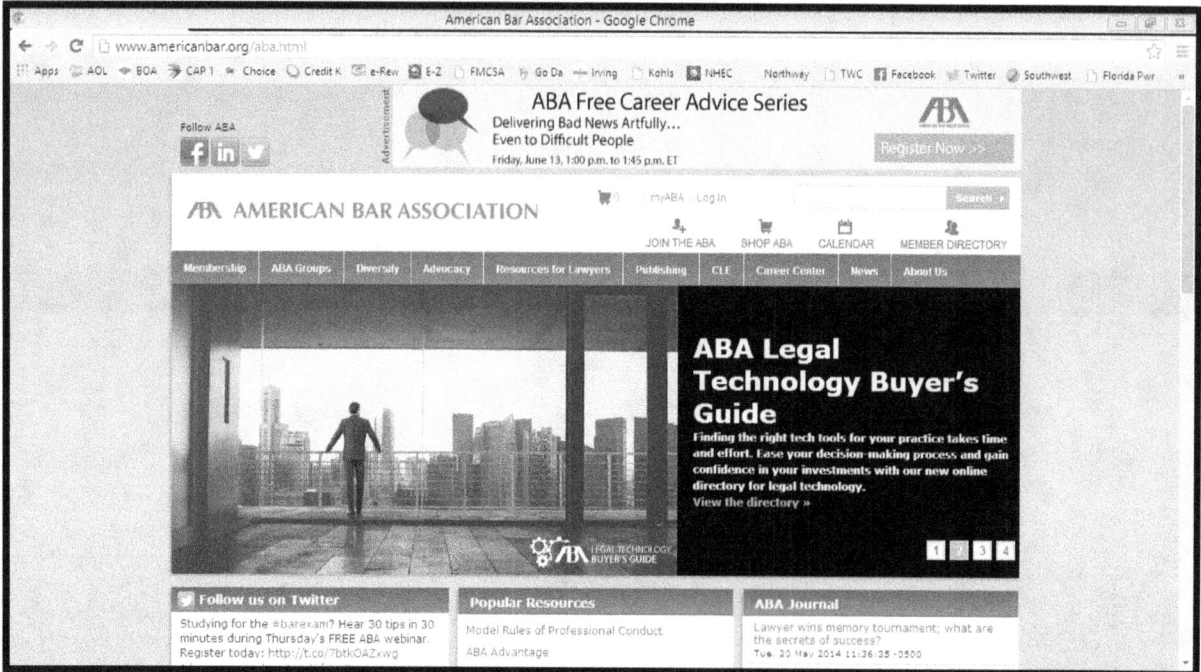

https://www.statefarm.com/insurance/home-and-property/homeowners

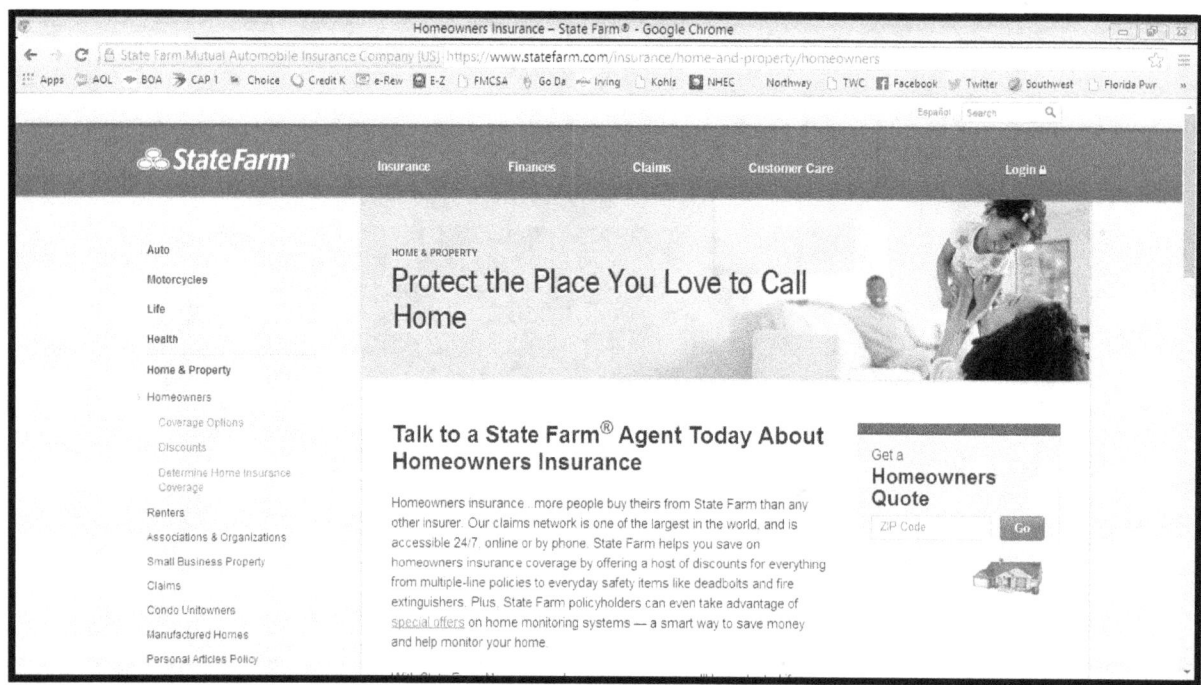

https://home.adt.com/?ecid=NewHomepage_test_03262014

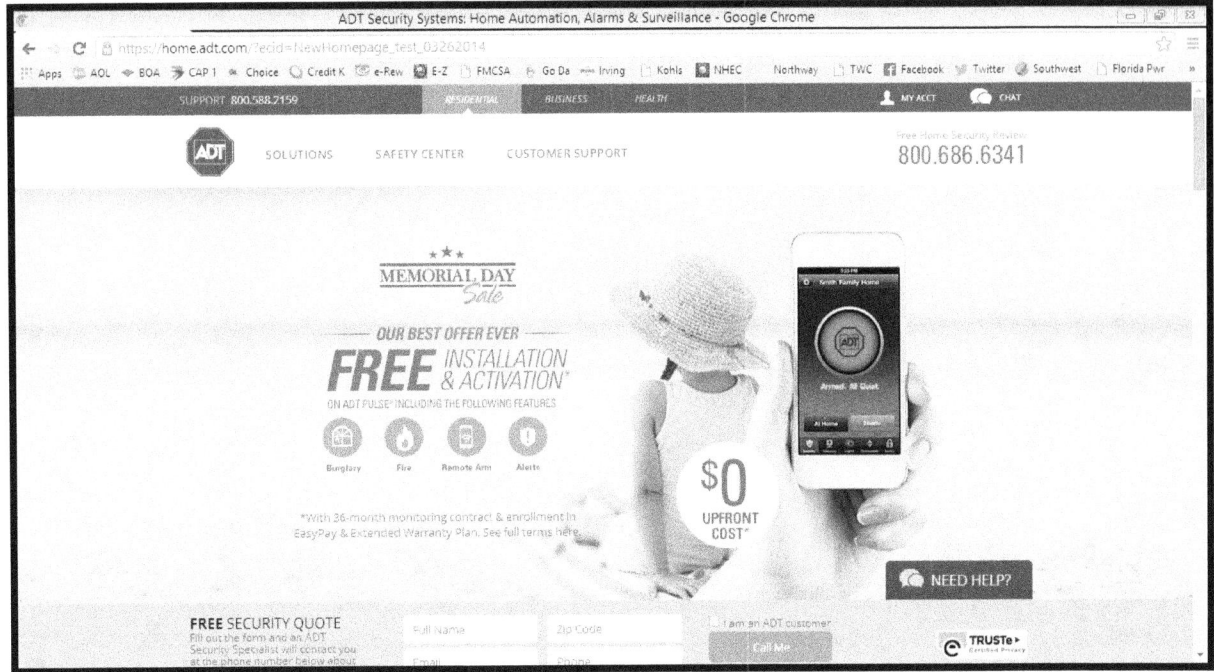

http://www.craigslist.org/about/sites

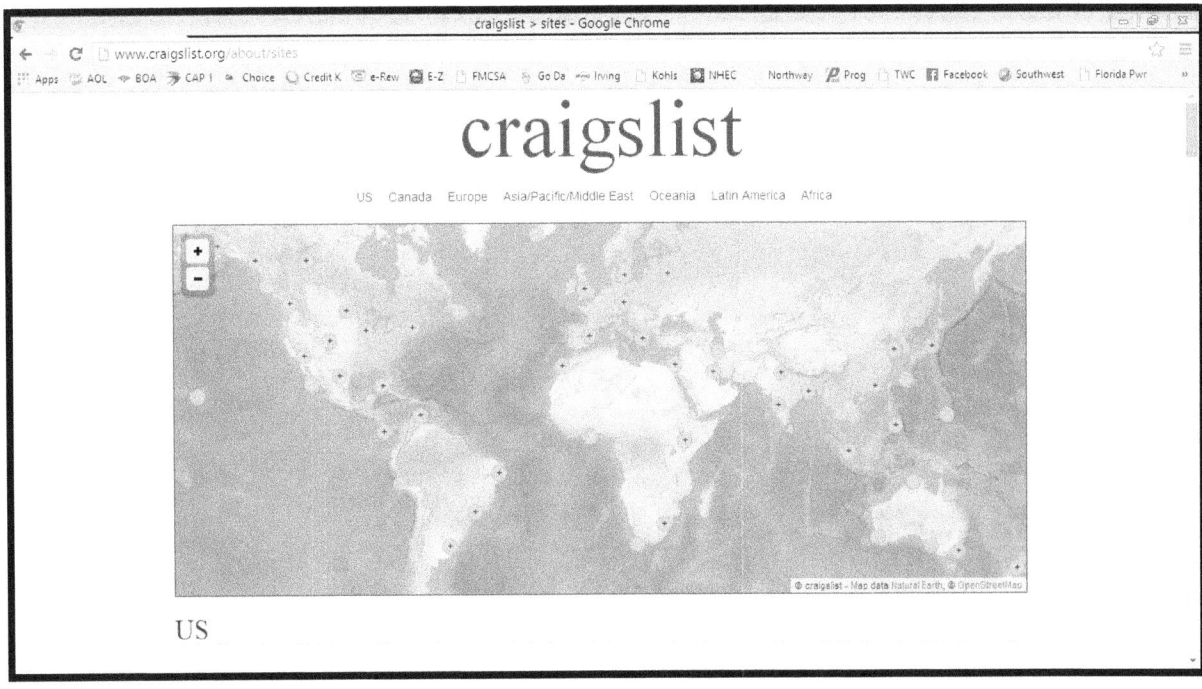

http://www.angieslist.com/

http://www.homedepot.com/

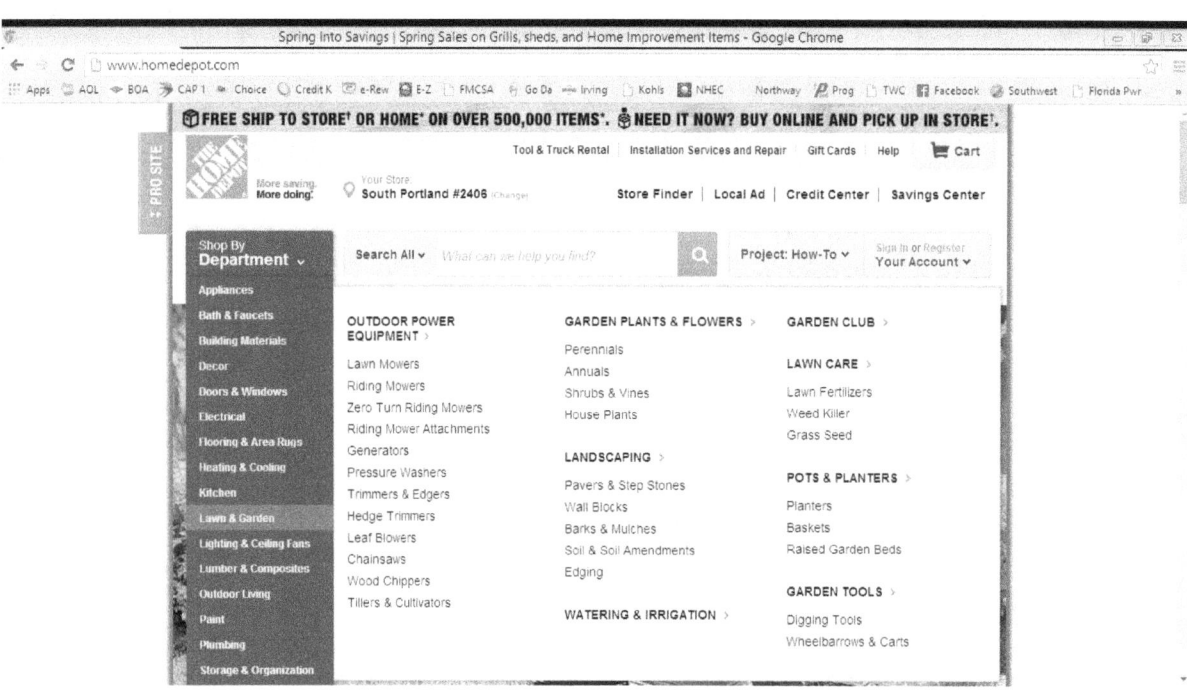

http://www.lowes.com/

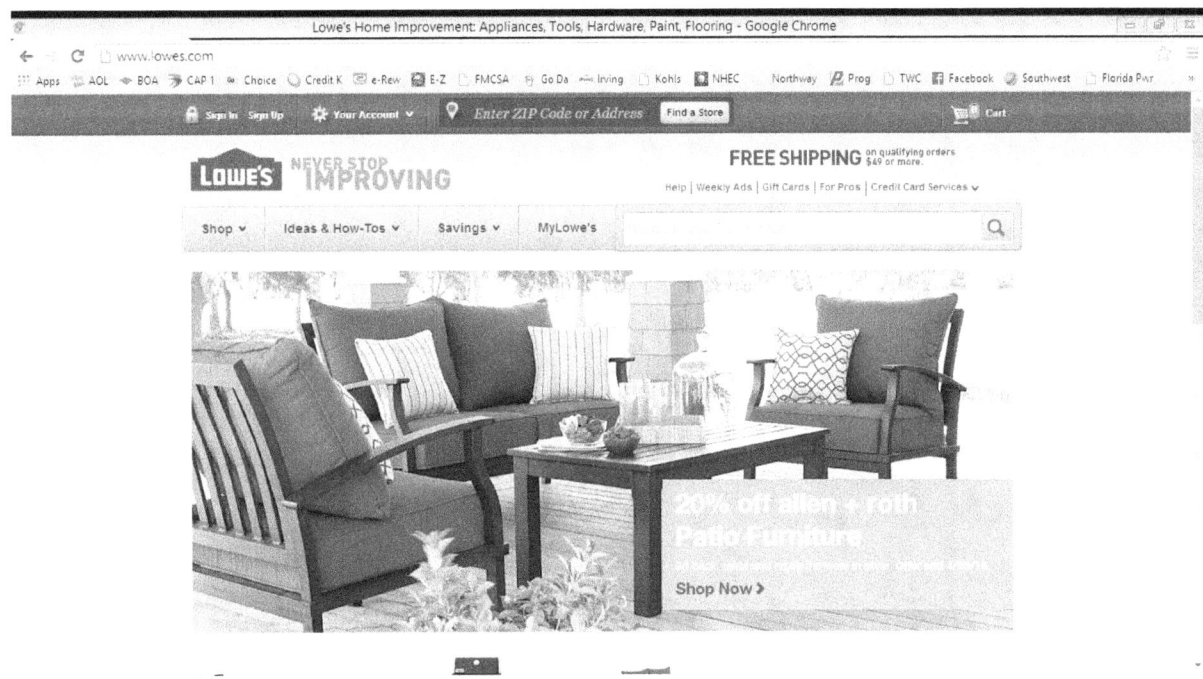

http://www.century21.com/

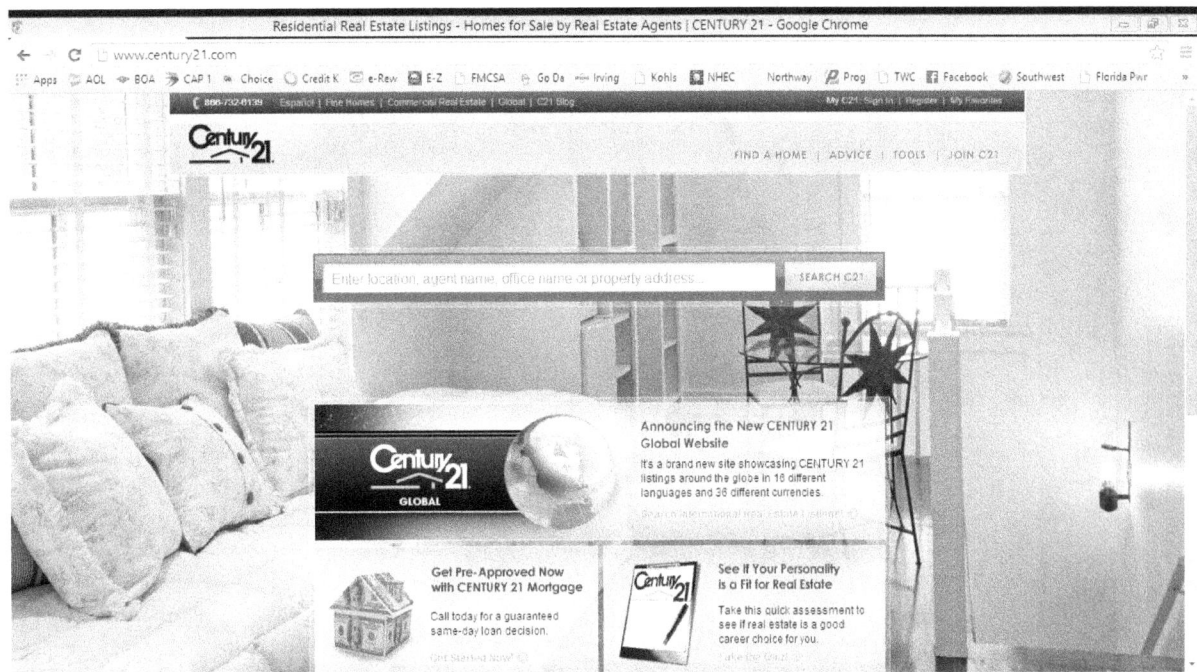

CHAPTER 5

http://www.zillow.com/homes/recently_sold/

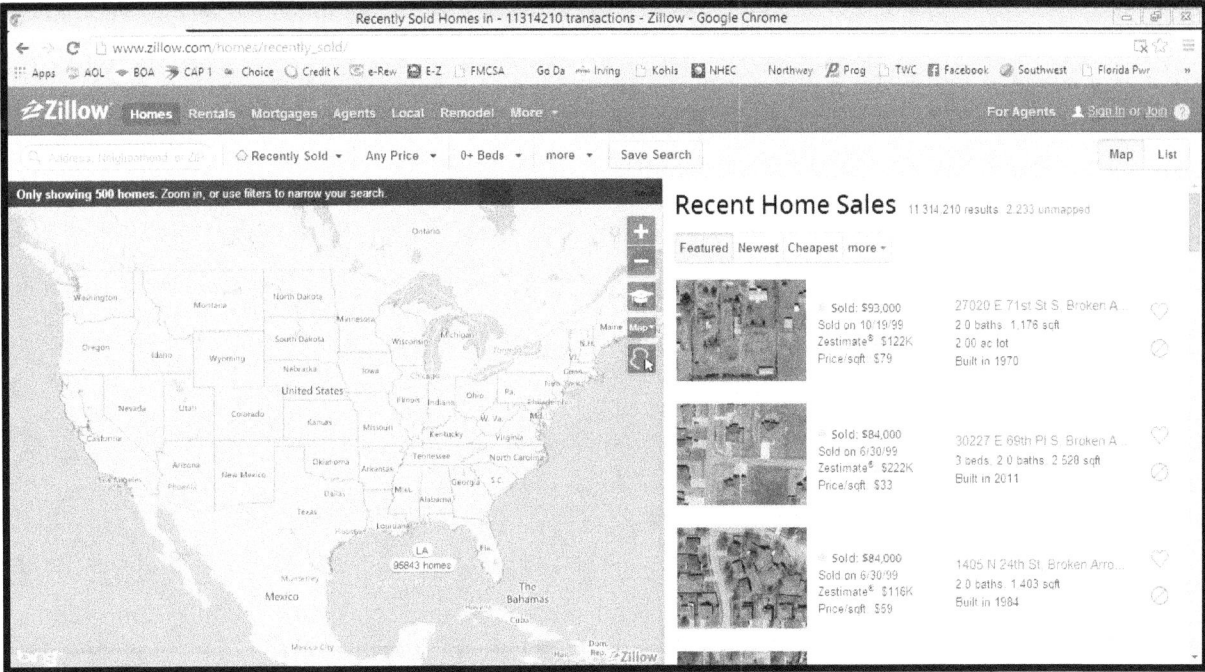

http://www.trulia.com/voices/q_Comparable+Home+Sales+In+My+Neighborhood/

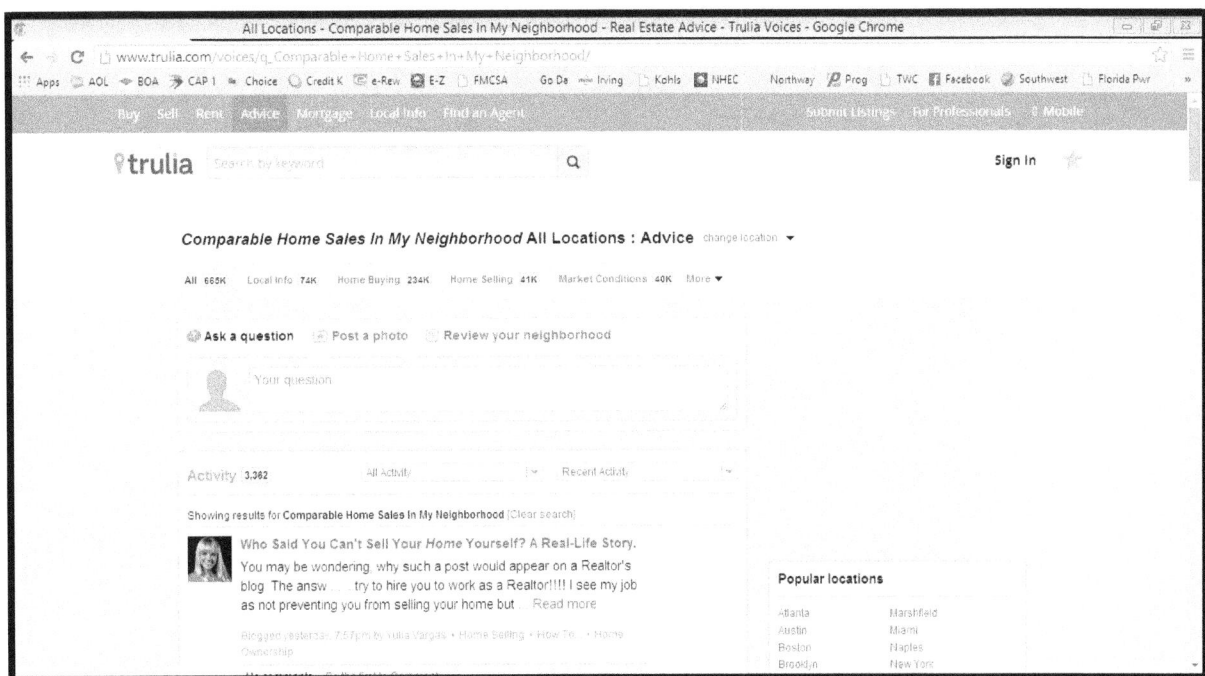

http://www.eppraisal.com/

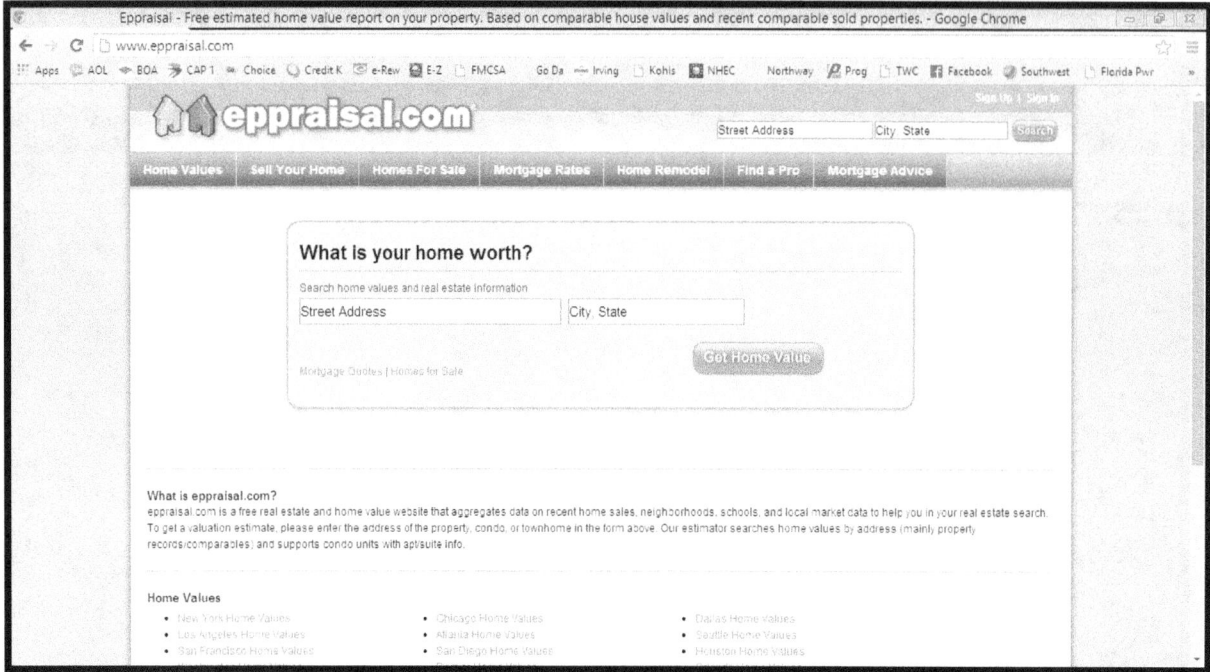

http://www.homeadvisor.com/cost/

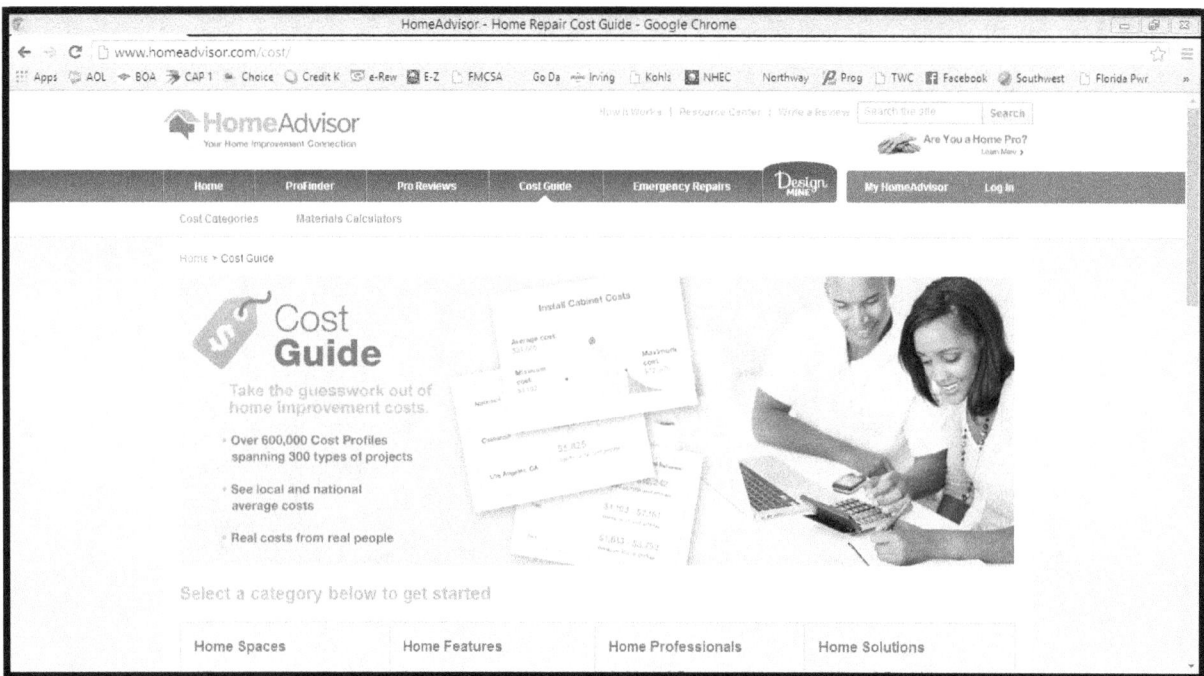

http://www.inspectionlibrary.com/costs.html

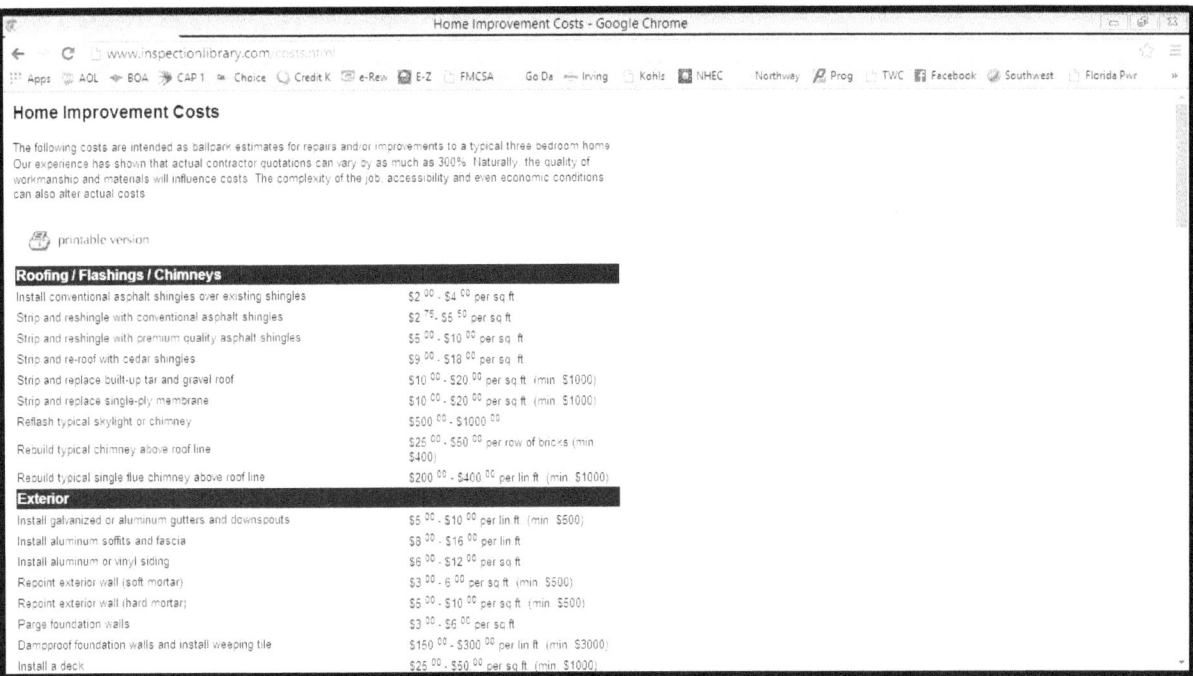

http://www.improvenet.com/r

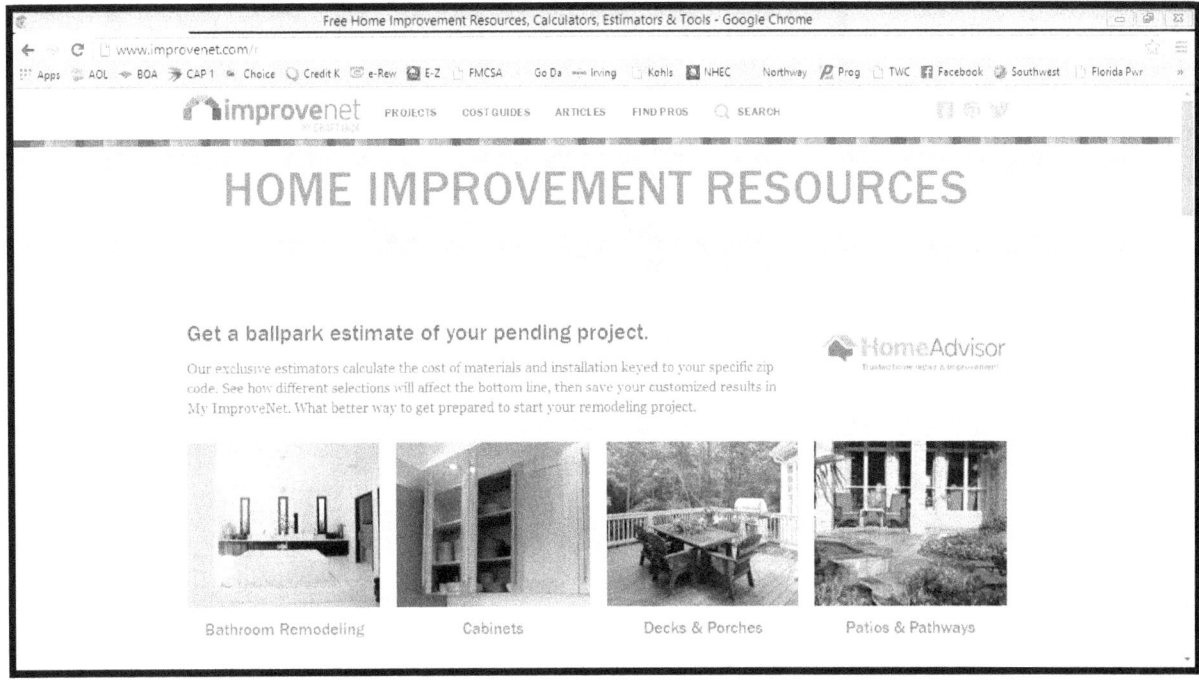

http://new.realtor.com/basics/buy/chooseoffer/makeoffer.asp

http://www.lawdepot.com/contracts/real-estate-purchase-offer/

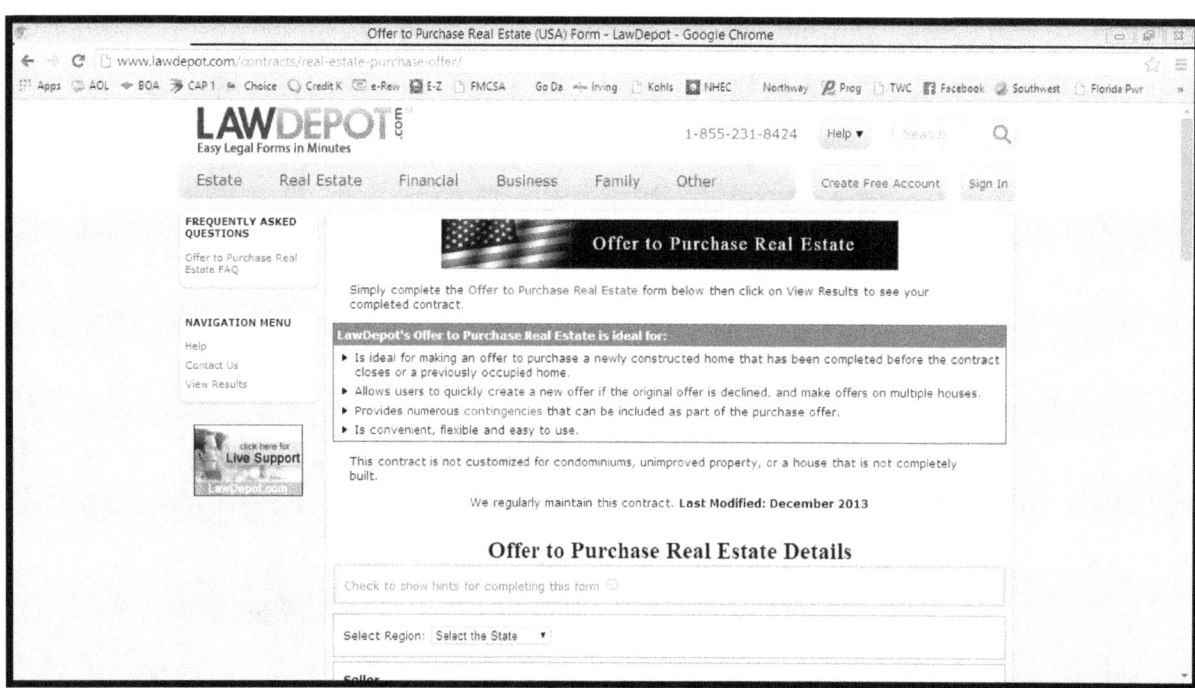

https://www.cmich.edu/fas/fsr/cps/PropertyAcquisition/Documents/Sample-AgreementToPurchaseRealEstate.pdf - Google Chrome

https://www.cmich.edu/fas/fsr/cps/PropertyAcquisition/Documents/Sample-AgreementToPurchaseRealEstate.pdf

Apps   AOL   BOA   CAP 1   Choice   Credit K   e-Rew   E-Z   FMCSA   Go Da   Irving   Kohls   NHEC   Northway   Prog   TWC   Facebook   Southwest   Florida Pwr

SAMPLE

AGREEMENT TO PURCHASE REAL ESTATE

The undersigned (herein "Purchaser") hereby offers to purchase from the owner (herein "Seller") the real estate located at _____ in the city of _____, County of _____, State of _____, the legal description of which is: _____

_____

_____

upon the following terms and conditions:

1. Purchase Price and Conditions of Payment

The purchase price shall be _____ Dollars ($_____) to be paid in accordance with subparagraph_____, below:

A: <u>Cash.</u> The purchase price shall be paid in its entirety in cash at the time of closing the sale.

B: <u>Cash Subject to New Mortgage.</u> The purchase price shall be paid in cash at the time of closing the sale subject, however, to Purchaser's ability to obtain a first mortgage loan within _____days after the acceptance of this offer by Seller in the amount of $_____, payable in not less than _____monthly installments, including interest at a rate not to exceed _____% financing. If such financing cannot be obtained within the time specified above then either Purchaser or Seller may terminate this agreement and any earnest money deposited by Purchaser will be promptly refunded.

C: <u>Cash Subject to Existing Mortgage.</u> The purchase price shall be paid in cash at the time of closing the sale after deducting from the purchase price the then outstanding balance due and owing under the existing mortgage in favor of _____, dated_____, 20___, in the original amount of $_____; of such mortgage debt is approximately $_____ as of _____, 20___.

D: <u>Cash With Assumption of Existing Mortgage.</u> The purchase price shall be paid in cash at the time of the closing of the sale after deducting from the purchase price the then outstanding balance due and owing under the

CHAPTER 6

http://www.realtor.com/Basics/Buy/InspNegot/Yes.asp

http://www.realtor.com/Basics/Buy/InspNegot/Bidding.asp

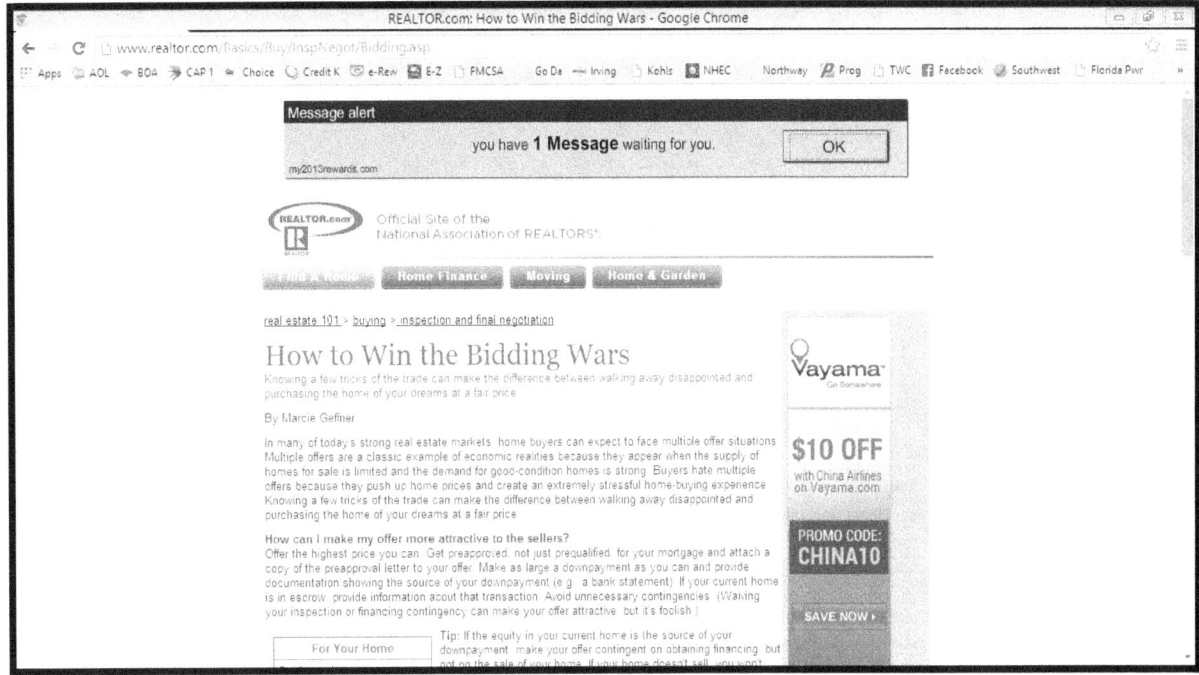

http://www.zillow.com/home-buying-guide/negotiating-home-price/

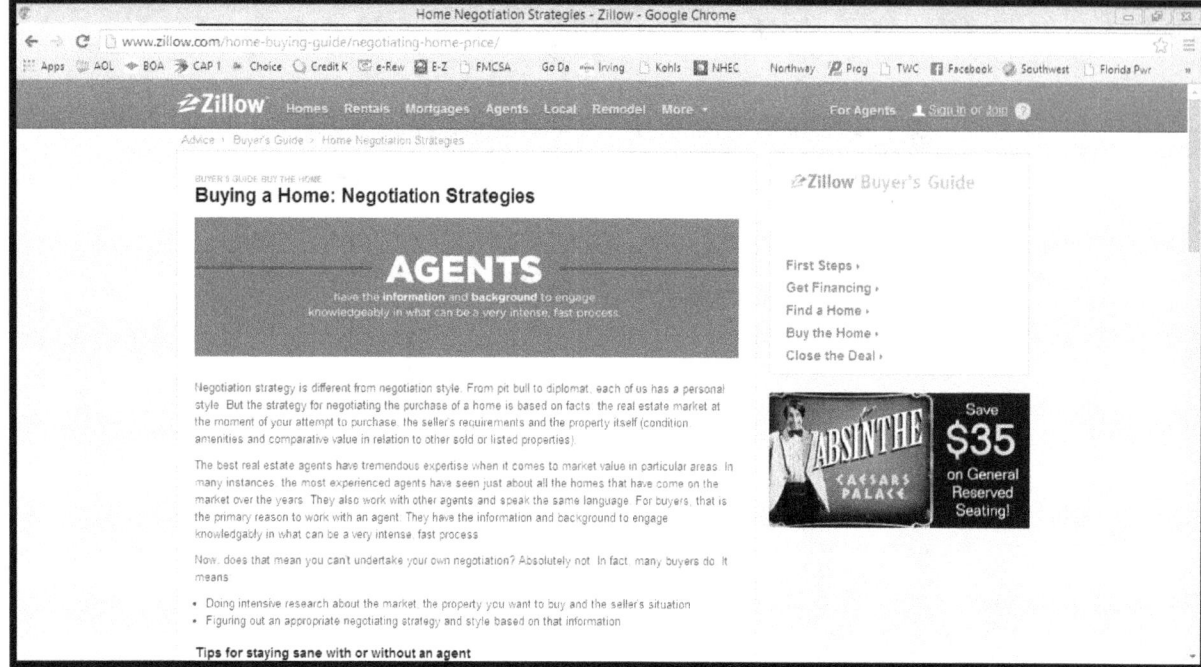

http://office.microsoft.com/en-us/templates/home-construction-project-plan-TC001018452.aspx

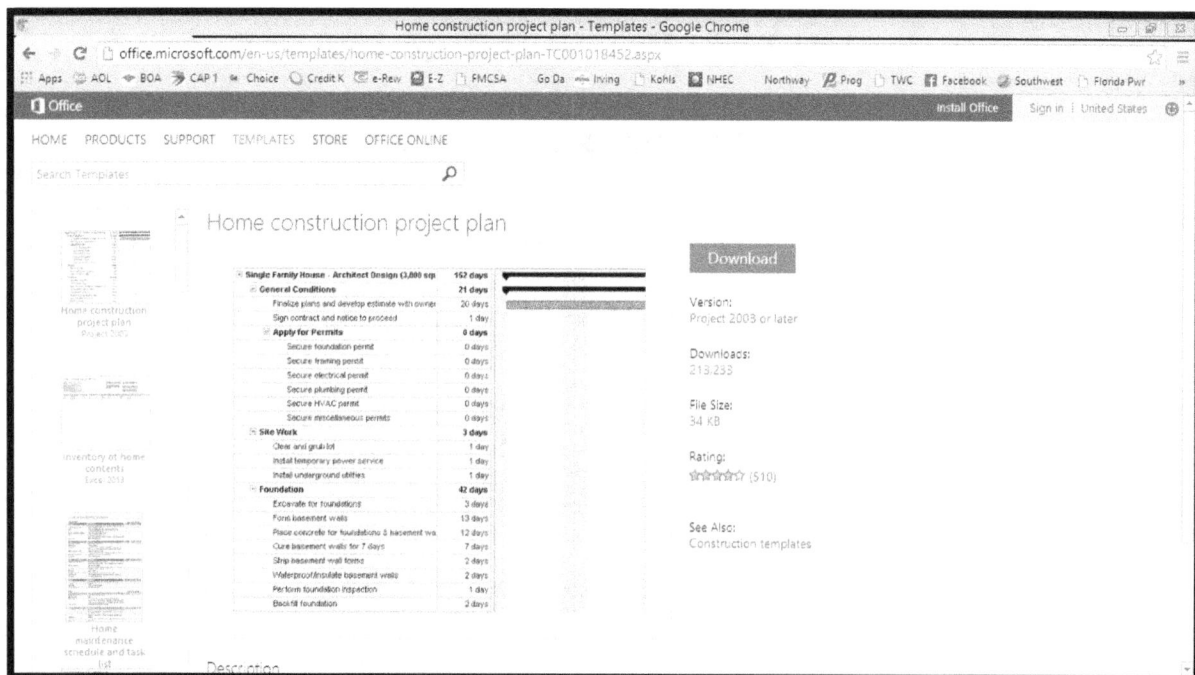

http://www.aecsoftware.com/resources/project-management-templates/construction.asp

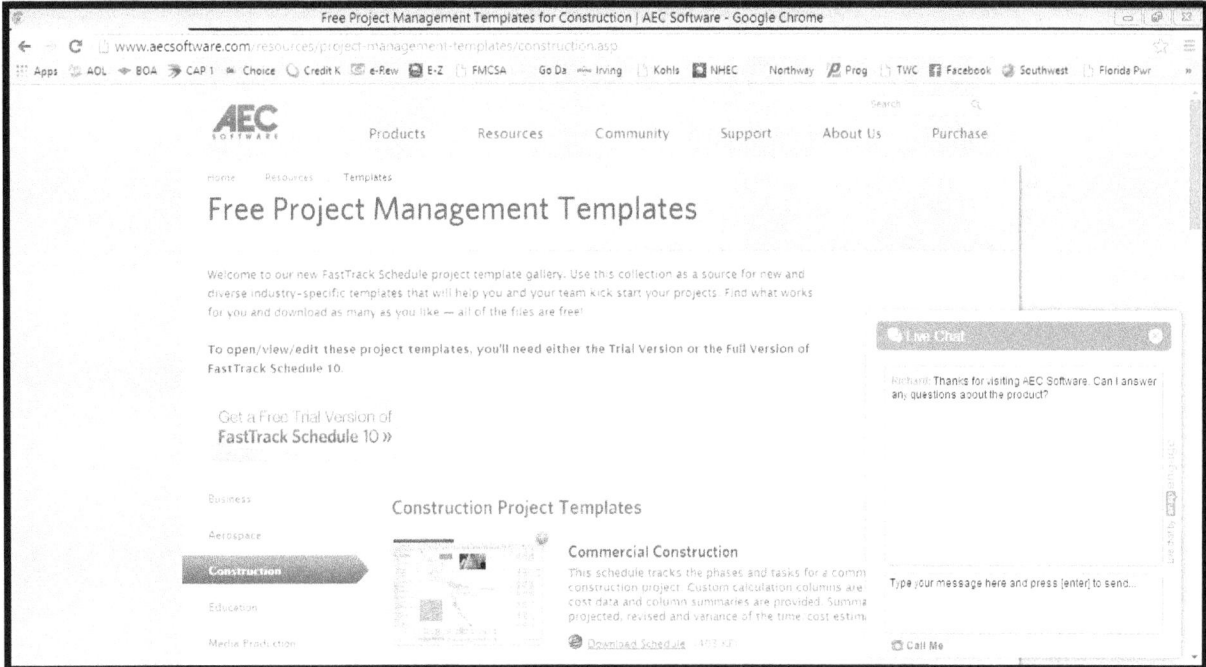

http://www.youtube.com/watch?v=kcHaiEaQj24

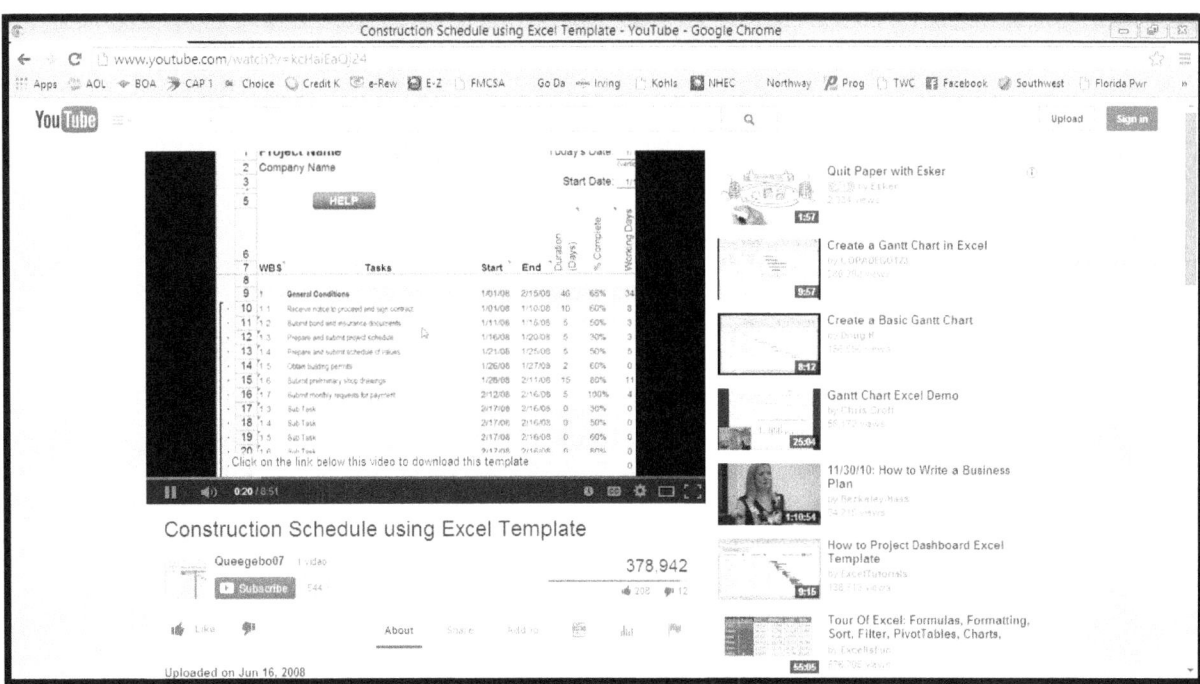

http://planningtemplate.com/

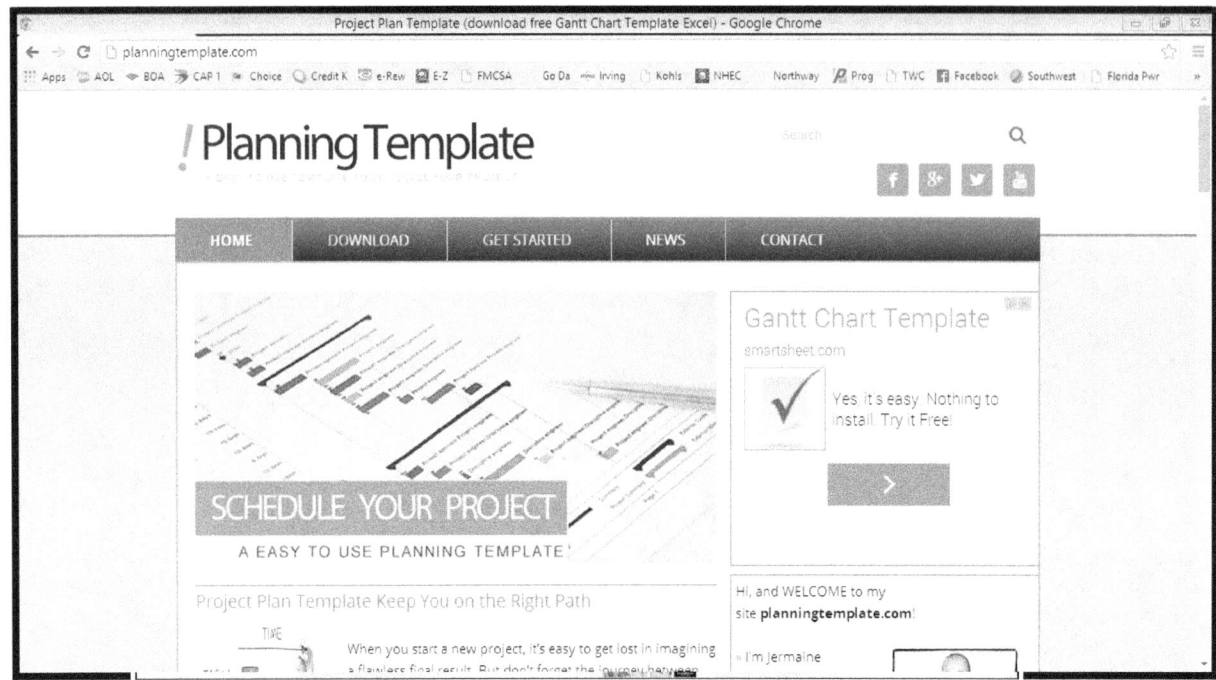

Chapter 8

http://www.wnymetrofinehomes.com/web/pgcnflD_120344/Round-Robin-Auction

http://money.cnn.com/2006/02/24/real_estate/quick_home_sales/

CHAPTER 9

http://www.buildingtrades.com/

http://en.wikipedia.org/wiki/List_of_construction_trades

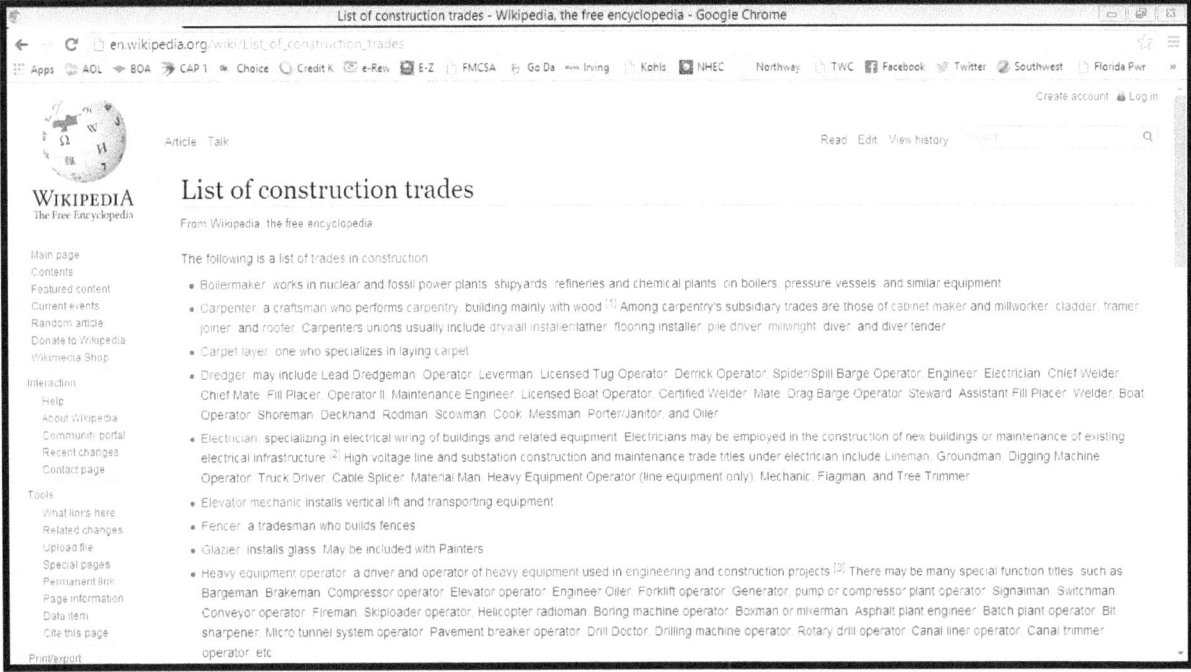

http://www.energystar.gov/?c=home_improvement.hm_improvement_index

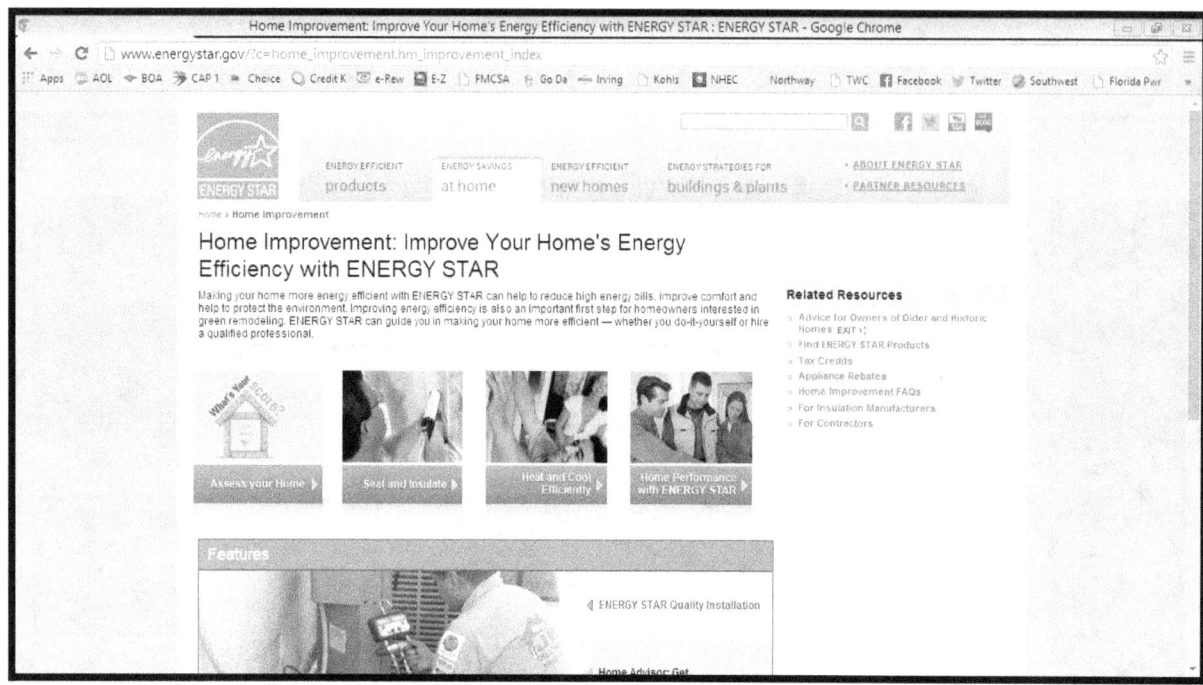

CHAPTER 10

http://www.wholesalesolar.com/solarpowersystems/large-home-4-off-grid-solar-power-system.html?gclid=CJfo7rfWuL4CFdRj7Aod5g8AnA

http://www.realestate.com/advice/10-best-home-improvements/

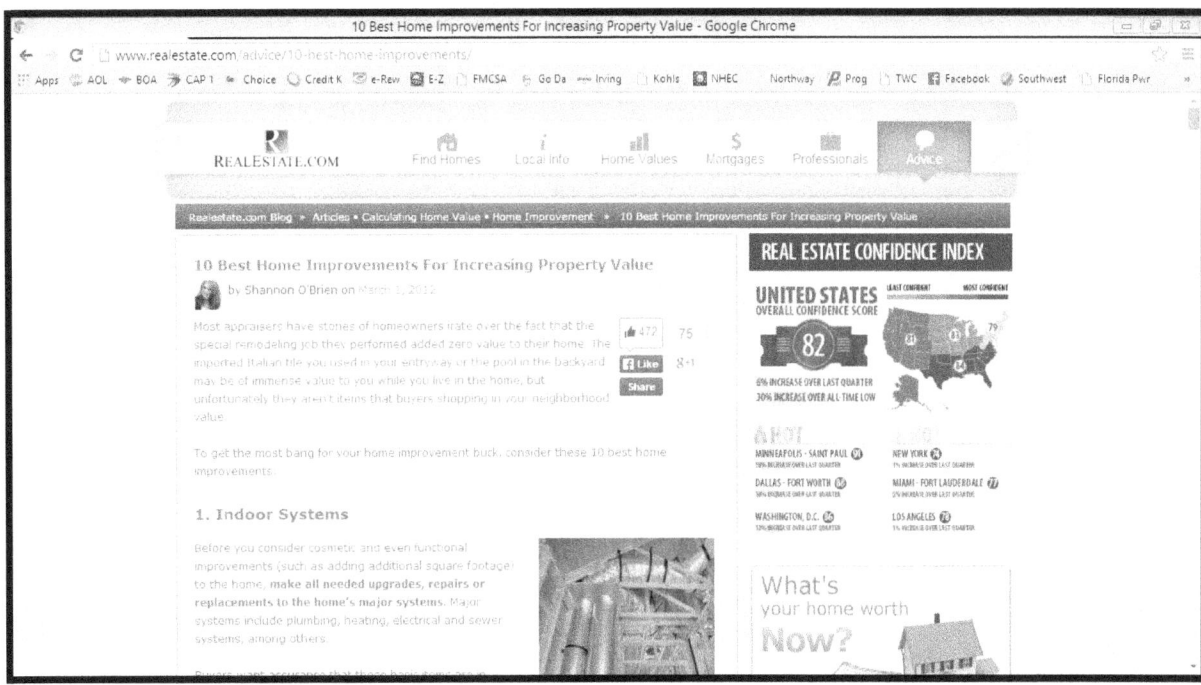

CHAPTER 11

https://www.google.com/search?hl=en&site=imghp&tbm=isch&source=hp&biw=1366&bih=643&q=components+of+a+house&oq=components+of+a+house&gs_l=img.12..0j0i5j0i24l6.2600.11545.0.14571.21.15.0.6.6.0.137.1710.0j15.15.0....0...1ac.1.43.img..0.21.1762.EaavKtBnhK0

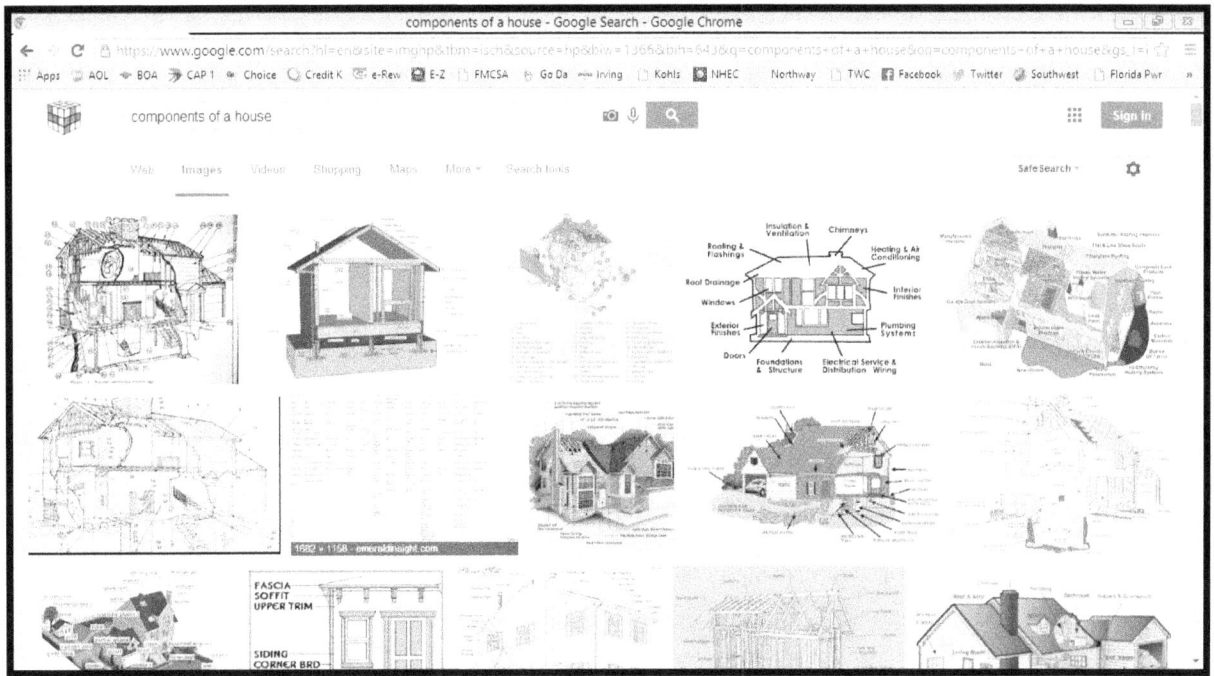

www.ingramcontent.com/pod-product-compliance
Lightning Source LLC
Chambersburg PA
CBHW080252180526
45167CB00006B/2496